Farouk of Egypt

By the same author

AMAZON JOURNEY: *seven thousand miles through Peru and Brazil*

Farouk of Egypt

A Biography

Barrie St. Clair McBride

South Brunswick and New York
A. S. Barnes and Company

Contents

Contents

Preface

In March 1965 very little space was devoted in the national press to announce the death of a man whose name is still a household word and who once dominated pages in the Sunday papers, long footage of celluloid at the cinema, and after-dinner discussions.

I had never met him, nor seen him and had only spent three weeks in his country but his reputation was sufficiently strong in my mind to make me want to investigate this enigmatic man, find out why he failed, and to put the story down in this book.

This is the life story of one of the most notorious figures of the century. It starts with the invasion and occupation of Egypt by the British in 1882 and traces the Mohamed Ali dynasty from its founder's massacre of the Mamelukes, and the excesses of successive Sultans and Khedives, to the rule of Farouk's father Fuad whose untimely death cut short the education of his son. Farouk, as a beloved, handsome prince, raised in a world of women, came to the throne too young and slowly turned from a fine young man into a disillusioned satrapic potentate famed for his girls, his gambling, his collections and pornography, his debauchery and corruption.

This is the story of that good-hearted and sad man with sybaritic palaces but no home, and his struggle against overwhelming odds of a sychophantic court, two unsuccessful marriages and numerous affairs; humiliation at the hands of a domineering British Ambassador; conflict with an ageing Prime Minister; and political problems such as rising nationalism in the clandestine Free Officers' movement led by Nasser, and the sinister Moslem Brotherhood; the Egyptian Army's abortive campaign against the Jews in Palestine; guerilla warfare against the British garrisons; the Black Saturday burning of Cairo in 1952, and finally the *coup d'état*. There followed long lonely years in exile which ended when Farouk suffered a heart attack in a Rome nightclub in 1965.

The Aga Khan once wrote of Farouk: "Each of us, it is said, is composed of many and conflicting elements; seldom in one human being has the mingling been more complex and more contradictory than in this ill-starred yet amiable and talented king." To establish the truth about a man whose life was enmeshed with mystery and intrigue I have drawn on published and hitherto unpublished material and have sought out those who knew the king well and who are prepared to talk. A chef who once peered over a wall for a What-the-Butler-Saw view of Farouk's licentious parties in Cyprus, and a retired British General, the only man left alive who was in the king's study on the night of 4th February in 1942 when the British threatened Farouk with abdication, and who re-enacted the scene with me in his club in Pall Mall, beginning by placing me in a chair and saying, "Now, you're the king . . .", are the extremes which indicate the broad area from which my informants are drawn. Included are the king's midwife, governess, tutor, wartime friends, ambassadors, a Minister of State, Intelligence men, Field Marshals and close relatives; Turks, French, English and Egyptians. This book is the result.

Esher   BARRIE ST. CLAIR MCBRIDE

Acknowledgements

I would like to mention the following persons and institutions. They have all aided me to some degree in preparing this book and are listed in the rough order in which my inquiries led me. I am grateful to them all, including some not named, particularly to those who entertained me and spent time discussing my subject, of whom most had personal experience, and who wrote notes for me or lent me their diaries or photographs. Their help has been invaluable.

Earl Mountbatten of Burma, Earl Alexander of Tunis, Viscount Chandos, Air Chief Marshal Sir John Baker, Vice Admiral Ian Campbell, Remy and Sally Ades, Sir Edward Ford, Christopher Sykes, Virginia Williams, Mrs. Ina Naylor, M. Chapman-Walker, Sir Charles Duke, Lord Kinross, Field Marshal Sir Claude Auchinleck, John Hamilton, Sir James Bowker, Roger Gued, J. C. Smuts, Commander C. R. Thompson, Sir Ronald Campbell, Sir Ralph Stevenson, General R. G. W. H. Stone, Bulent Rauf, Adel Sabet, Bambos Pais, Tom Little, Madame F. Zulficar, The Reverend C. E. Leighton Thomson, Mrs. Gladys Johnston, Lady Holmes, H. A. Barker, Charles Rees, Miss Lucy Sergeant, Sir Bernard and Lady Burrows, Patrick Domuile, David Abercrombie, Mrs. Jennifer Gough, Lieutenant-General Sir John Bagot Glubb, Lieutenant-Colonel T. W. F. Paterson, Brigadier E. B. W. Cardiff, Madame Emine Foat Tugay, P. Anthony Dove, Baron van den Bosch, Robin Fedden, Gracie Fields, Jefferson Caffery, Susan Graham, Tim Clark, Catherine Robins, Kenneth Snowman, Cyril Harmer, Albert Baldwin, Barbara Hare, John Synge, Lady Diana Cooper, T. E. Evans, Ardeshir Zahedi, Robert Simpson, General F. H. Theron, Lady Crocker, Dr. J. Gibson Graham, Major-General R. A. Stephen, Major-General R. E.

Barnsley, Sir Ralph Marnham, Ella Hughes, Mrs. Vera Buxton Knight, Ismail Sherin, P. T. Telfer Smollet of Bonhill, D. J. Waterston, Sir Michael Creswell, M. George Lee, Major A. W. Sansom, Joyce Smith, Douglas Nichols, Florence Harvey and Major Eric Titterington.

Esher Central Library (in particular Michael Wemms), Westminster Central Reference Library, British Museum Reading Room, British Museum Newspaper Library, London Library, Royal Institute of International Affairs, Imperial War Museum (in particular J. S. Lucas), German Institute, London, Institut für Zeitgeschichte, Munich, Royal Military School of Music (R. W. Sanders, Librarian), Movietone News Library, Pathé News Library, Swiss Embassy, London, Egyptian Information and Tourist Office, London.

And Mrs. M. L. Rhodes who typed this book.

B. St.C. McB.

I am grateful to the following publishers and agents for allowing me to quote from works published by them. All these extracts, together with a number of additional brief items, are acknowledged on the pages on which they occur:

Ernest Benn Ltd. (*Modern Egypt* by Tom Little); Cassell and Company Ltd. (*The Second World War* by Winston S. Churchill, and *The Eden Memoirs: Full Circle* by Lord Avon); Curtis Brown Ltd. (*Middle East Diary* by Noël Coward); Chicago Sun-Times, U.S.A. (*Count Ciano's Diaries*); Collins (*The Years of Command* by Lord Douglas); Editions du Seuil, Paris (*Egypt in Transition* by J. and S. Lacouture); Fitzwilliam Museum (*Secret History of the English Occupation of Egypt* by Wilfrid Scawen Blunt); George G. Harrap and Company Ltd. (lines by F. E. Hughes from *Poems from the Desert*); Rupert Hart-Davis Ltd. (*Trumpets from the Steep* by Diana Cooper); Hughes Massie Ltd. (*Egypt's Destiny* by Mahomed Neguib); Herbert Jenkins Ltd. (*Fuad: King of Egypt* by Ali Shah); John Murray

(*Egyptian Service 1902–46* by Russell Pasha); Odhams Books Ltd. (*My Early Life* by Winston S. Churchill); Oxford University Press (*Three Centuries* by E. F. Tugay); A. D. Peters & Company (*The Memoirs of Lord Chandos*); Laurence Pollinger Ltd. (*African Trilogy* by Alan Moorehead); Routledge and Kegan Paul Ltd. (*Koran: Sir John Lubbock's 100 Books*, ed. George Sale); Simon and Schuster, Inc., U.S.A. (*The Memoirs of the Aga Khan*); United Arab Republic Tourist and Information Centre (*The Philosophy of the Revolution* by Gamal Abdel Nasser); A. P. Watt and Son (*One Viceroy Resigns* by Rudyard Kipling); The Bond Wheelwright Company, U.S.A. (*Muhammad's People* by Eric Schroeder); Chalmers, Impey and Company for Allan Wingate (*Revolt on the Nile* by Anwar el Sadat).

Egypt served my turn.
You'll never plumb the oriental mind,
And if you did, it isn't worth the toil.

Kipling: *One Viceroy Resigns*

This book is dedicated to Egypt, more specifically to: a Greek woman with a broken arm who said "Welcome to Egypt"; a fat bus conductor who gave me a jasmine flower; the weaver of a wheat motif which hung on a door of the Kalawun mosque; the rosary seller who cries "Koran, Koran" in Khan Khalil bazaar; Mohammed Ali; Champillon; Imhotep; Cheops; Chephren; Mycerinos; the dragoman who took me up a pyramid; Nakht; Horemheb; Sennefer; Amenkhepeshf; Seti I and some others; the artist who left his chalk guide marks in a tomb; Howard Carter; the maker of Tutankhamen's ostrich feather fan; the tailor of my *galabiya*; Hatshepsut; Horus and Osiris; the teacher of English who showed me Joseph's grain store and told me the seven lean years story; Ahmed, Willcocks's head gardener, and a Nubian prince; Kitchener; Virginia and Patricia, two Armenian visitors; the High Dam workers; Rameses II and Nefertari.

Chapter 1

A Necessary Prelude
(1769—1919)

In March 1801 an English expedition of 17,000 men under Sir Ralph Abercrombie landed at Abu Kir near Alexandria and had little difficulty in defeating the French occupiers of Egypt. Napoleon had landed three years earlier near Alexandria and had defeated the Mamelukes at the Battle of the Pyramids.

> We longed for you, O General,
> O you handsome one with the hanging cloak,
> Your sword in Egypt made havoc
> of the Ghuz and the Urban
> Ya Salam!
> O Splendid republican,
> With the lock on the head
> You brought light into Egypt,
> And came in like a crystal lamp,
> Ya Salam!

Now Napoleon's short-lived occupation was over. By September the French had left Egypt.

In these three years much had been achieved: the French could claim to have discovered modern Egypt. More tangible was the discovery of the Rosetta stone by a French officer called Bouchard which the English sent to the British Museum where it waited twenty-one years before Champollion, again a Frenchman, deciphered the common inscription in hieroglyphic, demotic and Greek and so, in a sense, effected also the discovery of ancient Egypt.

In March 1803, after exactly two years, the British left Egypt and deliberations were begun on how best to restore to the

Mamelukes the power of which Napoleon had deprived them.

These Mameluke rulers of Egypt had their origin in Georgia and the Caucasus, whence they had been purchased as slaves and brought to Egypt, trained from childhood as horsemen and warriors, and with the notion that marriage would weaken their profession as soldiers firmly instilled in them, they imported more children as their heirs, so keeping the caste as pure as possible. Lane in *Modern Egyptians* described the Mamelukes as "A band of lawless adventurers, slaves in origin, butchers by choice, turbulent, bloodthirsty and too often treacherous. . . ."

Six weeks after the English had left, the Albanian soldiers in the service of the Turkish Governor, Mohamed Khosrev, surrounded the house of the finance minister and violently demanded their pay. The minister vainly asked the Governor to meet the demand but instead of pay the insurgent Albanians were met with Turkish artillery fire from the Governor's palace. The Albanian commander, Tahir, then gained entry to the citadel which holds a commanding position over Cairo and made good use of his advantage in height by lobbing balls from his cannon over the intervening roofs and into the palace. This, and an accompanying siege, was too much for Khosrev who collected his baggage, women and servants and escaped down the Nile to Damietta. Tahir became Governor but was assassinated twenty-three days later. The palace was plundered and burned. This full conflict between Turk and Albanian marks the beginning of a dynasty which ended in 1965.

> The Turk as Sovereign Lord behaves,
> And all earth's children else like slaves.

The Turks were ultimately expelled and the Albanian Mohamed Ali rose to power.

Mohamed Ali was born in 1769, the same year as Napoleon, at Cavalla, a small Macedonian port on the Aegean Sea, in what is now Greece. He came of poor parentage and was brought up as an orphan by the mayor of the town and by a kindly French tobacco merchant called Leon. No doubt with an early eye for power he married the mayor's daughter. He had three sons, Ibrahim, Toussoun and Ismail who were the beginning of his family which was to number ninety-five children by different unions.

Mohamed Ali was a volunteer, second in command of a troop of bashi-bazouks in the Turkish army which endeavoured to land in Egypt at Abu Kir in 1799, but which ended in the defeated Turks rushing for the sea. Someone pulled him out of the water and we next hear of him in Cairo where, step by careful step, his natural aptitude of gaining power in a mixed society where no particular rules of succession existed soon showed itself. There was a state of civil war between the Turks and Mamelukes and Mohamed Ali supported neither, but with a force of over 10,000 men who had chosen to follow him, maintained a police rule to control the two factions, aiding one while abetting or abating the other, all the while seeking the destruction of both parties and his own rise to power. This was confirmed by the people in 1805: the deposed Mameluke beys plotted his overthrow.

In March 1807 a British expedition of 5,000 men under General Fraser landed at Alexandria to support the Mamelukes but Mohamed Ali persuaded them to join him against the invaders and, after two defeats at Rosetta, the British left Egypt in September. Heads of the British dead decorated stakes in Cairo. Then Mohamed Ali suffered the Mamelukes six more years of uneasy peace broken by bouts of war until on 1st March 1811 all the Mameluke beys in Cairo were invited to the citadel to the investiture of Mohamed Ali's son Toussoun as commander of an expedition due to leave to fight the Wahhabis in Arabia. Having taken coffee together the Mamelukes, escorted in front and behind by Mohamed Ali's troops, descended the narrow roadway down to the gate of the citadel, which slammed shut in their faces as they arrived and simultaneously a deadly fire from above and behind opened on the beys. Pandemonium broke out in the narrow street, many fell immediately, others drew swords and dismounted in brief resistance. Four hundred and seventy Mamelukes were massacred and in a few treacherous moments their rule in Egypt effectually finished for ever.

"The Massacre of the Mamelukes", said Sir Charles Murray, the British Consul-General, "was an atrocious crime, but it was a necessary prelude to all subsequent reforms."

Modern Egypt is based on these reforms. Mohamed Ali confiscated almost all privately owned land; he built and improved factories; encouraged commerce, particularly through

Alexandria; built a canal from that port to the Nile; greatly aided Egypt's economic progress by establishing the cultivation of cotton from 1822 onwards; started the barrage across the Nile at the beginning of the Delta, conquered the Sudan; and slowly weakened the old ties between Egypt and Turkey. To Bowring, a Member of Parliament sent to Egypt by Palmerston in 1838, Mohamed Ali said, ". . . my peasantry are suffering from the disease of ignorance to their true interests, and I must act the part of the doctor. I must be severe when anything goes wrong." And later, "Your country, England, has reached its present eminence by the labours of many generations; and no country can be made suddenly great and flourishing. Now I have done something for Egypt. I have begun to improve her; and she may be compared in some respects not only with Eastern, but with European countries. I have much to learn, and so have my people; and I am now sending Edhem Bey with fifteen young men to learn what your country can teach. They must see with their own eyes. They must learn to work with their own hands, they must examine your manufactures, they must try to discover how and why you are superior to us; and when they have been among your people a sufficient time, they must come home and instruct my people."

"I love Egypt," Mohamed Ali once said, "with the ardour of a lover, and if I had ten thousand lives I would willingly sacrifice them all to possess her."

By 1848 Mohamed Ali's mental health was such that a regency council, with his eldest son, the great soldier Ibrahim, as president was formed to rule under him.

Ibrahim Pasha, commented Lord Cromer, "was a distinguished soldier and a man of great personal courage. It must be added that he was a half-lunatic savage". He suffered tuberculosis of the lungs and within four weeks was dead (having consumed two bottles of iced champagne on a hot day), to be outlived by only nine months by his eighty-year-old father who, sick and saddened by the loss of his son, died in Alexandria on 2nd August 1849. Abbas, son of Toussoun, succeeded.

Madame Tugay gives this account of Mohamed Ali's last day: "Death came to the aged fighter in his country house at Moharram Bey, near Alexandria, on the 3rd April 1849. His energy was such that the agonizing illness which caused his death could only keep him in bed for a few days. Leaning on the arm of an attendant, he would persist in walking round the room, though in terrible pain. . . . No single complaint passed his lips till the very end. When it came he could no longer recognize his son Said Pasha and two of his daughters who were standing beside his bed. Moaning softly, he murmured: 'Be merciful to me, my Lord, he comes . . . he comes . . .', and quietly yielded up his soul.''

"The ceremonial of the funeral", wrote the British Agent, "was a most meagre affair. In short, a general impression prevails that Abbas Pasha has shown a culpable lack of respect for the memory of his illustrious grandfather."

Abbas was fat, morose, taciturn; he disliked what his grandfather had admired and supported, and could not bring himself to carry on the work of reforms. He was of the old school, a traditionalist, with a hatred of foreigners and their ideas. His obstinacy reversed the progress made by his grandfather, "schools were shut, academic institutions abolished, factories abandoned with the engines and other expensive material left, to rot in a world of heat and dust". He reduced the army, once the pride of Mohamed Ali, to a mere nine thousand men; and retired to the pleasures of his palace. This reign of sullen selfishness came to a sudden end after six years when two of his own slaves, more by sordid impulse than ambition, stabbed him to death. Said, son of Mohamed Ali, uncle of Abbas, succeeded as Pasha of Egypt. The year was 1854.

Said, too, was fat as a young boy, to his father's annoyance. The family were prone to corpulence but Mohamed Ali had remained a reasonable size by exercise and an energetic rule. For young Mohamed Said he had prescribed running, mast-daubing, riding and dieting. Ferdinand de Lesseps had shown an interest in the boy's education but Mohamed Ali was not so interested in academic achievement for this son, more that he should lose weight. "I was forty before I learnt to read", he had told De Lesseps, "and even now I read very little. When Said's marks are shown to me, I only look at the last column: where his weekly weight is registered. If I find he has put on weight, I have him punished. If I find he has reduced, I have him rewarded."

Said's appetite found satisfaction in the French Consulate

where De Lesseps cooked macaroni for him. By indulging a
gluttonous schoolboy De Lesseps gained the Suez Canal.

On 25th April 1859, first ground was broken on the Suez
Canal Company's concession line of territory. The canal took
ten years to build. Of course it was not a new idea. It seems that
a canal existed between the Nile and the Red Sea in the time of
Seti I (1380 B.C.). Pharaoh Necho (609 B.C.) began another but
desisted, not because 120,000 men, according to Herodotus,
perished in the undertaking, but because, if he persisted, he
thought waters from the Red Sea might flood all Egypt. Harun
al-Rashid thought of cutting the Suez Isthmus with a canal in
the eighth century but abandoned the idea when he saw how
accessible this would make Arabia to the Byzantine navy. The
Venetians, after the Cape route to India was discovered in the
fifteenth century, suggested a canal to the Egyptians but the
Turks put a stop to the idea. Napoleon spent ten days at Suez
but did little more than prospect the canal route.

Towards the end of 1862 Said Pasha (who had found entertainment in his reign by shooting Bedouin out of cannons) grew
rapidly and radically thin. In January 1863 Said died, and was
succeeded by his nephew Ismail, a son of Ibrahim.

The 16th November 1869 was a great day for Egypt and the
world. Distinguished visitors and princes, headed by the Empress Eugénie of France, the Emperor Francis Joseph of Austria-
Hungary and the Crown Prince of Prussia were at Port Said.
At 8 a.m. the *Aigle* carrying the Empress anchored between the
Khedive Ismail's yacht, the *Mahroussa*, and the Austrian imperial yacht. De Lesseps and Ismail went on board to welcome
the Empress. In the afternoon Moslem Ulemas, Greek Orthodox, Coptic and Roman Catholic priests pronounced a benediction and then the royal procession moved to the Khedive's
pavilion for prayers in Arabic and eloquent speeches in praise of
De Lesseps and Ismail.

The next morning the Canal was formally opened at 8 a.m.
and a procession of ships, headed by the *Aigle*, proceeded slowly
through the desert to Ismailia where everyone disembarked for
further festivities, banqueting and dancing in the newly erected
palace. By 20th November the flotilla arrived in Suez whence the
collection of royalties were taken to Cairo, and at Ismail's
expense, invited to entertain themselves in the capital. Verdi's

specially written opera *Aida* was not ready in time and so instead *Rigoletto* was performed in the new Opera House to a glittering audience. Eugénie, rumoured to be Ismail's mistress, stayed for several days.

The English had at first dismissed the idea of the Canal as impracticable. Palmerston in the House of Commons had said, "it is an undertaking which I believe, in point of commercial character, may be deemed to rank among the many bubble schemes, that from time to time have been palmed upon gullible capitalists. . . . Her Majesty's Government has for fifteen years exercised all its influence at Constantinople and Egypt to prevent the execution of the project". But now the Canal was reality. The Prince of Wales congratulated De Lesseps: *"J'éspère que, depuis que vous êtes parmi nous, la nation anglaise vous a prouvé combien elle apprécie les avantages que votre grand oeuvre procurera à notre pays."*

In 1875 Britain was not slow to take the opportunity of purchasing shares in the Canal from an impecunious Khedive. Disraeli immediately sent an agent with a cash offer which was accepted, £3,976,582 for 176,602 shares. The house of Rothschild were commissioned to pay the money. With it Britain bought political influence in Egypt and the Sudan.

Ismail increased Egypt's debt from £4,000,000 to over £100,000,000 in a dozen years. Anglo-French intervention into Egypt's affairs made it plain that in order to restore credit some measure of control must be taken over the government. In 1878 Evelyn Baring made moves whereby Ismail became constitutional monarch with an English finance minister and a French minister of public works, but Ismail tolerated this only six months before dismissing the ministers.

In reply the English and French Ministers of Foreign Affairs wrote: "The Khedive is well aware that the considerations which compel Her Majesty's Government to take an interest in the destinies of Egypt have led them to pursue no other policy than that of developing the resources and securing the good government of the country . . . if the Khedive continues to ignore the obligations imposed on him by his past acts and assurances, and persists in declining the assistance of European Ministers, we must conclude that he deliberately renounces all pretension to their friendships."

Salisbury, the British Foreign Minister, wrote to Lascelles in the British Consulate recommending Ismail to abdicate: "If Egypt were a country in whose past history the Powers had no share and to whose future destiny it was possible for them to be indifferent, their best course would be to renounce at this point all further concern with the relations between the Egyptian ruler and his subjects. But to England at least this policy is impossible. The English Government is bound by duty and interest to do all that lies in their power to arrest mismanagement. . . . The sole obstacle to reform appears to be in the character of the ruler. His financial embarrassments lead almost inevitably to oppression and his bad faith frustrates all friendly efforts to apply a remedy. There seems to be no doubt that a change of policy can only be obtained by a change of ruler."

In accordance with these sentiments the Powers of Britain and France were behind two telegrams which arrived in Cairo on the morning of 26th June 1879, one addressed to the 'ex-Khedive' Ismail, and the other to Tewfik Khedive of Egypt. The point was made. Father met son, both with tears in their eyes, and Tewfik took over. Four days later Ismail left Cairo from the station where large crowds witnessed his departure. No diplomats came, only a passive crowd who had not yet realized what the Khedive's abdication would mean to Egypt. The train drew out and the black-veiled women of the harem wailed. The captain of the Khedive's yacht, the *Mahroussa*, had orders not to land on Ottoman territory and so Ismail sailed for Naples.

Crabités quotes an eye-witness account of the departure of the Khedive from Egypt: "The scene was so affecting that there were few among the spectators who were able to refrain from tears." The British Consul thus describes what took place at Alexandria. "The deck of the *Mahroussa* was crowded with officials and European residents who had come to take leave of Ismail Pasha. His Highness was met everywhere . . . with remarked respect and consideration. His features were marked by traces of strong emotion, but he bore up manfully, and was quite cheerful, addressing a pleasant word of thanks to everybody who took leave of him, and shaking hands cordially with many well-wishers."

He lived a quiet life in Italy, travelling to Paris where he had been educated, London and Brussels, before his request to return to Constantinople was granted by the Sultan, and he passed the remaining sad years in his palace of Emirgham on the Bosphorus. He died on 2nd March 1895 and was taken to Cairo for solemn burial. Thus finished the reign of Ismail the Magnificent, the smart, well-mannered prince whose qualities should have achieved a greater career but for his weakness in money matters and his lack of patience in judging others which led to hasty transactions with foreign concession-hunters and moneylenders. The results of these weaknesses paved the way for British occupation of Egypt.

Tewfik was twenty-seven when he became the new Viceroy of Egypt. He had been educated in Egypt and had never left the country. He grew up rather shy and unaware of the world outside but he understood well the needs of his own people. He liquidated the national debt; built schools; reformed the law courts; abolished forced labour, except for the control of the Nile flood; abolished flogging and more than twenty crippling taxes which his father Ismail had imposed on the fellahin. In 1880 the British Agent wrote: "Being anxious to learn how far the numerous administrative reforms made by the present government were producing effect in the country, . . . I requested reports . . . on the subject. The answer . . . is extremely satisfactory. It leads one to the hope that the condition of the fellah is at last permanently changed for the better, and that the misrule and oppression to which he has been subjected for centuries has passed away for good."

British occupation of Egypt was precipitated by the rising within two years of Tewfik's accession of a fellah officer who called himself Ahmed Arabi the Egyptian. Arabi had had a simple village upbringing of lessons from the Koran in the village school and instructions on military matters in one of Mohamed Ali's institutes. He was born the son of a sheik in the provincial town of Zagazig, and the people around him were the sturdy placid peasant stock of the Delta who had long suffered under Turkish masters. He was a figurehead supported by a group of astute military officers who gradually made more and more demands on Tewfik. He had natural intelligence and in his early career was blessed with good luck; he was a lieutenant at seventeen and lieutenant-colonel three years later. The year before Said died Arabi had accompanied him as A.D.C. on the annual pilgrimage to Mecca.

Arabi's chance to champion the people against the ruler arrived in September 1881 when Tewfik dismissed the popular Minister of War and installed his own brother-in-law in his stead. On the morning of 9th September Arabi occupied the Square in front of Abdin palace, placed his eighteen guns and paraded two thousand men. Tewfik immediately sent to Sir Auckland Colvin, the acting British Consul-General in Cairo, and asked his advice. He was told to stand firm and order the soldiers to disperse. When Arabi rode forward to the Khedive he was ordered to dismount and did so. The Consul-General whispered "Now's the time", but the Khedive replied, "We are between four fires. We shall be killed". Tewfik told Arabi to sheath his sword, which he did and then the Khedive's weakness came to the surface and Tewfik made the ineffectual statement which blatantly exposed himself to a hard, intelligent man like Arabi: "I am the Khedive, and I do whatever I like". If this spoilt prince had also stamped his foot no one would have been surprised.

Arabi made his reply: "We are no longer slaves; we shall not be handed from one master to another."

Tewfik made increasing concessions to Arabi until it became clear to Evelyn Baring, Lord Cromer, the British Agent and Consul-General, that "the end was not far off. It was daily becoming clear that Arabi could be suppressed by nothing but force. If no one else would use the requisite force, the task could necessarily devolve on England".

British and French fleets anchored off Alexandria in May 1882. Threat of bombardment from the ships aroused the mob to rioting on 11th June and about fifty Europeans were massacred. This rioting and Arabi's refusal to surrender led the British admiral, Lord Alcester, to open fire on 11th July at 7 a.m. against the Alexandria earthworks. The bombardment lasted ten-and-a-half hours. The French declined to support the British and after a few weeks of diplomatic exchanges a British force under Sir Garnet Wolseley was landed at Ismailia and defeated Arabi in a desert battle at Tel el Kebir.

It should be remembered what Ahmed Arabi the Egyptian had done for his people the fellahin. General Gordon wrote,

"As for Arabi, whatever may become of him individually, he will live for centuries in the people: they will never be 'Your obedient servant' again." Arabi was exiled to Ceylon.

Evelyn Baring, ninth son of a Member of Parliament, embarked on a military career, having passed through Woolwich Academy in 1858. This career took him to the West Indies, United States, the War Office in London and to India as private secretary to his cousin, Lord Northbrook. In India he was known as 'Overbaring'. In 1877 as a major in the Royal Artillery he was appointed British commissioner of the Egyptian public debt office. After another session in India, he was asked to re-establish order in Egypt when the Arabi revolt was put down. At the beginning of his career in Egypt which lasted twenty-five years Cromer said, "The Englishman came not as a conqueror but in the familiar garb of a saviour of society."

Baring belonged to what is now known as the Establishment, with the set views and manners of aristocracy of the period. He was a square-headed self-assured man. His superiority complex showed itself embarrassingly early in his reign in Egypt. "The Egyptians", he said, "should only be permitted to govern themselves after the fashion to which Europeans think they ought to be governed." In Egypt he became known as 'the Lord'.

Britain's Egyptian policy was not clearly defined but dictated rather by the course of events after the occupation. At first it was to restore the Khedive to power and then withdraw. Lord Granville, Foreign Secretary, wrote that Britain had undertaken "the duty of giving advice with the object of securing that the order of things to be established shall be of a satisfactory character and possess the elements of stability and progress". No reforms were contemplated at first but conditions later demanded them. The British were committed, in order to reach the 'satisfactory' state Granville desired, to undertake more in Egypt than they originally intended. The first problem was the Sudan, part of the Khedive of Egypt's dominions, which was then in revolt, led by a religious fanatic, the Mahdi.

Mohamed Ahmed Ibnel-Sayyid Abdullah began making trouble in 1881, when he was in his thirties. His origins are obscure but he was certainly a man possessed, with the gift of oratory and wild looks. He declared himself the reincarnation of the Prophet Mohamed: he hated Egyptians. He was a frightening, sensual man who combined an outward appearance of sweetness with an unmistakeable but indefinable depth of wickedness or madness in his eyes. First-hand reports of him say "there was a strange splendour in his presence, an overwhelming passion in the torrent of his speech". He "was strangely fascinating; he was a man of strong constitution, very dark complexion, and his face always wore a pleasant smile". There was nothing pleasant in the problems the Mahdi caused. His first main success was the capture of the Egyptian garrison at El Obeid, which supplied him with arms and money.

Colonel William Hicks of the Bombay Army led an expeditionary force of 8,000 men against the Mahdi in 1883. *The Times* correspondent, who accompanied the expedition wrote, "We march on a campaign that even the most sanguine look forward to with the greatest gloom." The expedition lost its way, ran out of water and had its supply line cut by the Mahdi before 50,000 Arabs fell on them. Little is known of the disaster that followed but perhaps two hundred survived.

Gordon was longing to return to the Sudan to deal with the Mahdi and public opinion clamoured in his support. When the plaudits paused for a moment however, a cool, firm opinion was heard in Cairo: Baring called Gordon "quite unfit" for the job. On 18th January 1884 Gordon met the Cabinet for a short sharp exchange: "Her Majesty's Government want you to understand this. Government are determined to evacuate the Sudan, for they will not guarantee future government. Will you go and do it?"

"Yes," Gordon replied.

He arrived in Khartoum by February and was "met with a wonderful demonstration of welcome on the part of the population", wrote the Consul. "The state of affairs here, since it was heard that Gordon was coming, gives every promise of the speedy pacification of this portion of the Sudan." Nearly a year went by of exchanges between Gordon, Baring in Cairo and Granville in London. Gordon suggested that peace could be made in the Sudan by the appointment to rule of Zobeir Pasha, a man whom he had once called "the greatest slave hunter who ever existed", and whose son Soleiman he had killed. Public opinion in Britain would not have this. Gordon wrote, "If Egypt is to be kept quiet the Mahdi must be smashed up . . . remember that once Khartoum belongs to Mahdi, the task will be far more difficult."

On 13th March 1884, the telegraph from Khartoum went dead. Gordon was cut off.

Gordon's death knoll tolled for the first time that day, to be rung intermittently with each new change for the worst through the following months of anxious waiting, waiting for relief from Britain or attack from the Mahdi, not knowing which would come first. Lord Wolseley, victor of Tel el Kebir, was on his way; the Mahdi camped outside the town: Gordon sat on the roof of his palace and watched and waited.

At 3 a.m. on 26th January Khartoum was invaded by the Mahdi and his Arabs. Gordon had been sleeping only three hours when he heard the screams and shots three miles from the palace, drawing closer. When the invaders broke into the palace yard Gordon fired the roof guns at them until they came so close to the building the gun could no longer point at them. He then changed into his white uniform, buckled on his sword and stood at the top of his stairs, pistol in hand until the first intruders ran up the stairs to him calling, "O cursed one, your time has come". Gordon was speared to death, his head hacked off and carried away in a handkerchief to be stuck in a tree for all to see.

The relief expedition was two days late.

Cromer as British Agent and adviser to Tewfik continued his work with colleagues in the administrative offices in Cairo. Scott-Moncrieff, Scott, Vincent, Wood, Grenfell and others ran Egyptian affairs. Improvements were made in aspects of the life of the fellahin, irrigation, justice, and education. In 1892 Tewfik died and Cromer quickly arranged for his son, Abbas, a minor, to be brought back to Cairo from Europe.

Cromer had always been on good terms with Tewfik but his overbearing manner did not go down with Abbas who had been educated in Europe and knew what manner of respect to expect. Wilfrid Blunt, the Irish orientalist, described a visit with Cromer to the young prince: "a quite unmilitary figure of proportions which made him look like a woman dressed up in man's clothes. He has, however, a very good manner in talking, and a pleasant smile, with brown eyes, and just a tinge of russet in his hair. He reminded me much of his grandfather Ismail, and has just the same sort of French accent, talking French well but not perfectly. He showed no sign of shyness, and treated Baring with easy politeness, without any sign of special deference; me he treated with considerable amiability. I shall be surprised if he does not give Baring trouble. He is said about here to be very anti-English but Baring will not hear a word of this, though I expect it is true." Blunt goes on to comment on the stern British treatment of the young Egypt on this occasion. "Baring's manner . . . was very abrupt, like that of a schoolmaster to a schoolboy . . . on our way back from the palace I remarked to him that I thought the Khedive would not bear driving with any but a very slight rein, his answer being that it was necessary to treat Orientals firmly. . . ."

Cromer's reforms won Egypt's race against bankruptcy and by 1888 he was able to relieve the taxpayers. The land tax was reduced, the salt tax and tax on local country produce were abolished. Extensive irrigation had raised agricultural output and in 1898 Egypt was in a position to begin her greatest scheme to date of control of the Nile, the Dam at Aswan. This barrage controlled 60 per cent of the Nile during the flood season from July to October, holding water for the critical hundred days in summer.

In the year the Aswan Dam was begun another event took place, further south in the desert. Sir Herbert Kitchener was marching against Omdurman: revenge for Gordon. The Mahdi had outlived Gordon by only five months and had died, either poisoned or from typhus or smallpox, on 22nd June 1885. His successor was the Khalifa Abdullah who settled in Omdurman and soon felt so secure that he dispatched a letter to Queen Victoria, summoning her to Omdurman to turn to the true faith: "Thy soldiers thought only of retreat from the Sudan with discomfiture and defeat, whereof they have had more than enough. . . . Thus hast thou erred in many ways, and art suffering great loss, wherefrom there is no refuge for thee save by turning to God the King, and entering among the people of Islam and the followers of the Mahdi, grace be upon him. . . . But if thou wilt not turn from thy blindness and self-will, continue to war against the hosts of God thyself, with all thy armies and war-like equipment. So shalt thou behold the end of thy work. Thou shalt be crushed by the power of God and his might, or be afflicted by the death of many of thy people, who have entered on war with the people of God, by reason of thy Satanic presumption."

By "Satanic presumption" the Queen was sending Kitchener to teach a lesson to this pocked-marked brown-faced nomad of the Baggara tribe of the West Sudan.

In *My Early Life*, Churchill wrote: "Nothing like the Battle of Omdurman will ever be seen again. It was the last link in the long chain of those spectacular conflicts whose vivid and majestic splendour has done so much to invest war with glamour. Everything was visible to the naked eye. The armies marched and manœuvred on the crisp surface of the desert plain through which the Nile wandered in broad reaches, now steel, now brass." The Khalifa's army, 60,000 strong, met Kitchener's 20,000 troops. Churchill, then riding with the 21st Lancers, continued: "Ancient and modern confronted one another. The weapons, the methods and the fanaticism of the Middle Ages were brought by an extroardinary anachronism into dire collision with the organization and inventions of the nineteenth century. The result was not surprising. It was the end of the Mahdi."

The British and Egyptian Governments signed an agreement on 19th January 1891, on the administration of the Sudan. Sir Reginald Wingate, who had been Director of Intelligence of the Army at Omdurman, was made Governor-General.

Two years later Cromer reported to the British Foreign Office on progress made in Egypt; that "the foundations on which the well-being and material prosperity of a civilized community should rest have been laid. . . ." By 1905 It was generally recognized in Europe that Britain was the dominant power in Egypt; France, Germany, Austria and Italy signed agreements to this effect. The situation thus clarified, Egypt enjoyed an increasing material prosperity and, in particular, freedom to control her financial affairs.

Ironically enough, with the increase in order and solvency, the cry of nationalism was heard the louder. The Nationalist Party under its leader Mustafa Kamil seized every opportunity to inflame anti-European and anti-Christian feeling. This feeling

was intensified after the Denshawai incident in June 1906 when,
after some British officers had angered villagers by shooting
on their land and disturbing the domestic fowls, a fight resulted
in the death of one of the officers, and excessive floggings were
meted out to the fellahin as punishment.

> O you mighty ones who wield supreme power,
> Forget not our loyalty to you and our affection.
> Have no fear in our fair Egyptian land.
> Disperse your guardsmen and banish all apprehension.
> Seek your pleasure far and wide,
> Shoot the lovely necklaced doves,
> And when you weary of your sport
> Then shoot the poor local rustics.
> Man's life is as cheap as beast's,
> And like to wild doves are we,
> Made of the self-same metal
> We too have our chains around our necks.
>   *Hafiz Ibrahim.*

In April 1907, for health reasons, Cromer resigned after
twenty-five years. No one would deny the progress made in his
time although there were still those who deplored the man's
manner: in his farewell address in the Cairo Opera House
he assured the Egyptians that his departure did not mean the
departure of the British. The Egyptian national poet, Showki,
commented on the going of Cromer:

> How shall we name this era, after you or Ismail?
> Were you born Pharaoh to govern the Nile?
> Or despot by conquest of the land of Egypt,
> Deferring to no one, never answerable?
> Master by might of our necks in servitude,
> Did you try the path to our hearts meanwhile?
> At your departure the land gasped in thankfulness,
> Freed from a pestilence too nearly fatal. . . .

Cromer was succeeded by Sir Eldon Gorst who had worked
with him for eighteen years. He finished his career with four
fitful years of growing nationalism and anti-British feeling.

Abbas was condemned by the nationalist poet Ali al-Ghayati
for his friendship with Gorst:

> Abbas!
> This is the end between us:
> Do not worry any more.

We shall not blame you any longer
You have accepted that we should live in chains
And be punished whenever we ask for life—
Your rapprochement with the foes
Meant nothing to us but torture.
Our hopes in you are gone.
Gorst means evil and wickedness
Our pens of peace shall therefore turn into
Lances of war.

Gorst died within a month of his resignation in July 1911 and was succeeded by Kitchener.

Kitchener was then sixty-one, with a long distinguished career behind him. Following the River War and the victory of Omdurman, only marred by his desecration of the Mahdi's tomb and the carrying off of the Mahdi's head in a kerosene tin as a trophy, after service in India, Japan, Australia and New Zealand Kitchener arrived back in Egypt on the day Italy declared war on Turkey in 1911.

This man with the grave face, the "heavy moustaches" and "the queer rolling look of the eyes" that Churchill reported, inspired Egypt to work to its own ends. Projects that caught Kitchener's fancy were blessed with his sustaining enthusiasm: courts, schools, sanitation, the new Ministry of Agriculture, village savings banks, the heightening of the Aswan Dam for the greater control of the Nile, land proportionment, and the establishment of cotton markets throughout the country. He was returning to Egypt from leave in England on 3rd August 1914 when a message from the Prime Minister came to him on the cross-Channel steamer asking him to go back at once. Next day Britain declared war on Germany. Kitchener did not return to Egypt. The Khedive Abbas was in Constantinople at the time and as his enmity for England was then quite open he also never returned to Egypt.

With Turkey's entry into the war Britain declared that: "In view of the state of war arising out of the action of Turkey, Egypt is placed under the protection of His Majesty and will henceforth constitute a British Protectorate. The suzerainty of Turkey over Egypt is thus terminated and His Majesty's Government will adopt all measures necessary for the Defence of Egypt and protect its inhabitants and interests."

Hussein, uncle of Abbas, became Sultan of Egypt and Sir

Henry McMahon succeeded Kitchener as High Commissioner. For each this was a short-lived reign. During the war years, while Britain fought in France, a growing nationalism in Egypt began prodding Britain in the back. In the middle of the war Wingate, seventeen years Sirdar and Governor-General of the Sudan, replaced McMahon. Hussein died in 1917, his only son Prince Kemal-ed-Din declined the succession as he preferred free time to hunt big game in Africa, and Fuad, sixth son of Ismail, became Sultan.

Fuad, eleven when his father had abdicated and gone to live in Italy, was educated in Geneva and Turin and later at the Turin Military Academy from where he passed out as an artillery lieutenant in the Italian Army, stationed in Rome. It was during this period of his life that he studied and was concerned with European affairs, an interest which stood him in good stead later in life, and he founded the firm friendship between the Italian and Egyptian royal families which was to last many years.

Fuad's patronage of scientific and intellectual associations revived in Egypt much of the work started by Ismail, and which had dwindled away with his abdication. Fuad made annual visits to learned societies in the European cities and applied his knowledge to the betterment of his own country. He was president of the Egyptian University; encouraged the education of Egyptian women, whose lives until then had been bound by restrictive tradition, realizing their value in the regeneration of Egypt; supported the Association Internationale d'Assistance Publique; supplied the explorer Hassanein with the means to travel unknown parts of the Libyan Desert; revived the Egyptian Red Crescent; presided over the Geographical Society; founded the Museum of Hygiene, and other societies including the Institute of Oriental Music, the Royal Society of Entomology, of Political Economy and Legislation and of Engineering. Until his fiftieth year he was considered more as a patron than a prince likely to rule the country.

On 15th January 1918 a child was born in Beni Mor, in Assiut province; his name was Gamal Abdel Nasser.

A new name in nationalism must now be noted. Saad Zaghlul was born of fellahin stock in 1860 in the Gharbia Province, educated at the village school and Al Azhar university in Cairo, he was editor of the official journal at twenty. Zaghlul had been involved in the revolt of Arabi, his principal forerunner in the race of nationalism. At twenty-four he was a judge, at forty-six Minister of Education and at fifty Minister of Justice, in which capacity he set the tone of his later dealings with the ruler of Egypt, then Abbas, by accusing him of corruption. After Armistice in November 1918 Zaghlul, leader of the Nationalist Party, asked independence for Egypt and proposed that he and a delegation, '*wafd*' in Egyptian, should make their appeal in London. This was refused. Russell Pasha, who served forty-four years as a police officer, described the mass hysteria which broke out in Cairo when Allenby admitted British politicians had made a mistake in preventing Zaghlul Pasha's delegation to London. For days the mob raged: "I don't think many people can ever have been in such a mob. It was composed of several thousands of the roughest elements of Cairo, all armed with something, . . . the whole mob was shrieking and yelling and waving their weapons in the air. Many of the crowd, with their heads back and their mouths wide open, produced no sound from their throats except a sort of dry whistle. Others had their beards and chests white with saliva and I saw several fall spinning to the ground in fits of mad hysteria."

Zaghlul and three supporters were deported to Malta and trouble increased. Within a week Cairo was isolated, railway lines were destroyed, telegraph lines cut, foreigners molested and at Dairut Station a British prison inspector, two officers and five other ranks murdered in a train by a mob.

The Egyptians sang of the British High Commissioner:

> Woe on us, Wingate,
> Who has carried off corn,
> Carried off cattle,
> Carried off children,
> Leaving only our lives.
> For the love of Allah, now let us alone.

Lord Allenby, commander-in-chief in Egypt, restored order temporarily in April 1919 and Zaghlul was allowed out of Malta. But the British Government were slow to act. Temporary quiet on the telegraph line from Cairo induced no urgency in London. The situation must clearly have been simmering, with occasional brutal murders or acts of sabotage to emphasize the unrest, but it was December of that year before a mission, under Lord Milner, left England to "enquire into the causes of the recent disorders, and to report on the existing situation in the country".

The situation was: active dislike of British rule; indignation at not being invited to the Peace Conference after the war; and increasing following for Saad Zaghlul, father of the people and enemy of the Sultan. Into this situation on 11th February 1920, Giumada 1, 1338, by the Arab Calendar which measures time from the death of the Prophet Mohamed, a son was born to Fuad. His name was Farouk.

Chapter 2

Early Tragedy
(11th February 1920—April 1936)

Farouk, officially Prince Said, was born two weeks prematurely. His mother Queen Nazli was to say of him in later years, "He was a monster, he was destined never to finish anything in his life—not his schooling, not his marriages, not his reign—not even his pre-natal development." When Dr. Mohamed Shahin Pasha announced the birth of a son to Fuad, the King gave him 1,000 pounds in gold, ordered 10,000 pounds to be distributed among the poor and 800 pounds to the mosques. One hundred and one cannon boomed in salute. The following notice appeared in *The Times* of 19th April 1920: "Cairo April 16th, Lord Allenby informed the Sultan this morning that the British Government had recognized his son Farouk as the lawful heir to the Sultanate."

Farouk was born into a country which had suffered invasion, flood and famine perhaps more than any other country in the world. In the fourth century B.C. the population of Egypt was estimated at seven million; in 1800 the French put the total at no more than two and a half million. This had increased to nearly fourteen million. The population was broadly divided into the fellahin who worked on the land, and the town people of the same blood, mainly Mohamedan or Copt;

> Muslims are sinners; Christians are perverse;
> Jews are confused; and Magians are worse.
> We are all sorted into two great kinds:
> Clever godless and stupid godly minds!

the Bedouins and nomadic Arabs; the Nubians; and the foreigners, Greeks, Italians, French, British, Levantines, and

Turks. Of the Egyptian character Pennethorne Hughes wrote:
"Facile agreement, corruption, wild inaccuracy, venality,
jealousy, and avarice are the faults of the Egyptian (the sloth
claimed against him is partly a symptom of disease). Politeness,
affability, a sense of humour, are his virtues."

Of all adults 60 per cent worked on the land. In 1920 the
cultivable land amounted to about eight million acres, of which
five and a half million were cultivated, in the three seasons of
the year, summer, flood and winter, by the two principal
methods of watering; perennial supply by canal, or seasonal
flooding of the basins along the Nile. High land near the Nile
not serviceable by canal was fed by the immemorial shadufs
worked by a fellah, or sakias, water wheels lined with earthen-
ware pots, driven by a blindfolded buffalo.

> I have laboured since dawn and my arms ache to their bones,
> He who knows but this knows well the language of groans.
> O weight of my destiny, falling, falling ever.
> You must be raised, and I must go on drawing from the river.
> Hissa Ho!
> O Shaduf, your rump weighs more than sorrow.

Cotton, sugar and rice in summer, wheat and barley and flax
in the winter were the main crops. Egypt was then the world's
third producer of cotton, mainly from the Delta. Cotton occupied
over a third of the land and half the working life of the Nile
Valley people. Cotton ginneries, sugar refineries and rice mills
formed the basis of industrial Egypt. Trade with Great Britain
and the Empire, which took a third of Egypt's exports and
supplied half her imports, formed the basis of her commerce.

The day Farouk was born the sun came up as usual over the
desert, dispelling the cold clear night and sending home the
marauding foxes from the edges of Cairo to their lairs under the
pyramids. The Nile moved slowly on its muddy way, broken
and gushing at the Aswan sluices but settling soon into a placid
river. Feluccas, with their sails the same shape as those on the
wall paintings in the tombs at Thebes, moved slowly on the
water, helped by a northerly breeze which passed over the water
to disturb the waves of sugar cane and the date palms. The
fellahin padded their way between their little fields and the
breeze caught their long blue and white cotton galabieh. In the
towns people crowded people, tarbushes bobbed amid fezes

and muslin veils, bicycles avoided donkeys. In Cairo and Alexandria, Port Said, Rosetta, Damietta, in Tanta, Damanhur, Zagazig, Belbes and Mansura, in Medinet-el-Fayum, Beni Suef, Minia, Assiut, Akhmim, Suhag, Girga, Kena and Luxor, Esna, Edfu, Aswan and Korosko iced water sellers increased their trade as noon approached. Coffee and tobacco followed the sweetmeats after the mid-day meal and the Egyptians retired as the full fierce sun burnt the features of Rameses at Abu Simbel, and the dunes and cliffs of the Rift Valley, glinted on the polished pink syenite obelisks at Karnak and drew curses from foreign tramp captains negotiating the Canal at Suez. When the sun had disappeared below the western desert, as quickly as it had risen that morning, darkness quickly hid the cotton fields, the Coptic graveyards and Byzantine ruins. The pyramids pointed at the moon. Mosques collected slippers at their doors as the faithful filed in. The bazaars sounded to the brass and silver workers' hammers and the clink of cheap glass and jewellery. Roman dishes and lapis lazuli things and amber were sold next door to strings of bean rosaries. Hookahs were passed round and smoke blew through one moustache after another while the eyes followed beautiful brown-eyed girls, women at eighteen, distinguishing a form which moved beneath the close fitting cashmere vests with flowing sleeves, gold embroidered jackets, full silk trousers and pink stockings. Shish kebab spattered over charcoal fires and the pleasures of the towns began for those who knew where to find them, the rope-players, jugglers, the fire eaters, glass eaters and live serpent eaters, the Ghawazi dancing girls and their low class imitators in the cheaper booths who moved obscenely before a still audience. Male dancers, dressed like the female Ghawazi, went through the same movements for those who preferred perversion.

It was an ordinary Egyptian day like any other, and yet the thoughts in the minds of the people were not settled. A new prince should have given some cause for celebration but Egypt had problems. Many thought the British had been there too long, independence was the consuming motion of the time. Relations with Great Britain were at their lowest ebb. The Milner Mission which had carried on its investigations under a veritable state of siege (while in the Hotel Semiramis protection was afforded the mission by armed guards at every door,

machine guns at the street corners and snipers on the roof) left
Egypt in March 1920 having investigated every department as
best they could under the conditions, and with proposals prepared. Zaghlul and seven other delegates went to London to
discuss the future of Egypt. This was in June 1920.

It was in no doubt that Zaghlul represented the majority
feeling of Egypt. Unlike the rebels before him, the ill-mannered
Arabi, he was a statesman. He led the party founded after the
departure of Cromer in 1907, a middle class nationalist party
started by Mustafa Kamil who declared at the time: "A new
spirit has been born within us. More than ever before we now
realize that nations cannot rise without themselves, struggling
for their own cause. We cannot win independence by help from
others. We have to work for it ourselves."

Milner was wise enough to realize that "no settlement could
be satisfactory which was simply imposed by Great Britain on
Egypt, but that it would be wiser to seek a solution by means of
a bilateral agreement". But the vacillation of Whitehall delayed
any agreement, and Lloyd George completely misunderstood
the Egyptian situation. Zaghlul was the popular idol and as
Sirdar Ikbal Ali Shah wrote in his biography of Fuad "at that
time Egypt would cheerfully have seen the Dynasty washed
away in the Nile floods and a new Egypt, revolutionary and
fiercely self-determinate, rise in its stead with Zaghlul presiding
over a new Washington".

Through 1921 arrangements dragged on amid growing unrest from the people. On 18th May a mob besieged the palace
in Cairo. King Fuad, who believed "that no man born of the
people could give effective leadership because of the personal
element which is so strong in Egyptians", during the Zaghlul
inspired riots against him, said, "I draw distinction between no
man, I honestly strive to do my best . . . I work all hours of the
day. I work harder than any fella, and—this is the result."
On 20th May two police stations were burned down in Alexandria, Cairo mobs again moved in the streets and on 22nd May,
Alexandria, as though in competition with the rioters of Cairo,
turned its fickle opinion against Europeans as an alternative to
the monarchy, attacked thirty and murdered fourteen of them.

Prime Minister Adli Pasha and a delegation went to London,
Zaghlul stayed at home, and when the mission failed, over the

question of British troops remaining in Egypt, Zaghlul called a public meeting in Cairo. The British prevented it and violent reprisals followed, two British soldiers were attacked in Cairo and Europeans murdered in the streets. Lord Allenby in Cairo, with whom Fuad kept close counsel, wrote to the Secretary of State requesting that he treat the matter "as one of extreme urgency". However six weeks lapsed and more murders were committed before this declaration made by Allenby on 28th February 1922:

"Whereas His Majesty's Government, in accordance with their declared intention, desire forthwith to recognize Egypt as an independent sovereign State, and whereas the relations between His Majesty's Government and Egypt are of vital interest to the British Empire; the following principles are hereby declared:

1. The British Protectorate over Egypt is terminated and Egypt is declared to be an independent Sovereign State.

2. So soon as the Government of His Highness shall pass an Act of Indemnity with application to all inhabitants of Egypt; Martial Law, as proclaimed on November 2nd, shall be withdrawn.

3. The following matters are reserved to the discretion of His Majesty's Government until such time as it may be possible by free discussion and friendly accommodation on both sides to conclude agreements in regard thereto between His Majesty's Government and the Government of Egypt:
   (*a*) The Security of the communications of the British Empire in Egypt.
   (*b*) The defence of Egypt against all foreign aggression or interference, indirect or direct.
   (*c*) The protection of foreign interests in Egypt and the protection of minorities.
   (*d*) The Sudan.
   Pending the conclusion of such agreements the *status quo* in all these matters shall remain intact."

On 15th March 1922 His Highness the Sultan of Egypt proclaimed Egypt a sovereign independent State. He himself assumed the title of His Majesty the King of Egypt. One hundred and one guns fired from the Citadel in Cairo.

Zaghlul sought to oust the monarchy. King Fuad wished to remain friends with Great Britain and wanted British troops to help him stand up to Zaghlulism. To add to his problems the dreaded Society of Vengeance, under direction from its gaoled leader who still succeeded in sending out his sinister instructions, began its atrocities once more; the British Inspector of the Cairo city police was murdered in daylight; a British colonel was shot through both lungs, outside the Consulate; a British official at the Ministry of Agriculture was attacked and wounded with his two drivers while driving in his carriage; and finally three students assassinated Professor Newby Robson of the Law School, in a Cairo main street.

In 1923 Zaghlul was brought back from where he had been exiled and within a week was attacking the King and constitution, the British and the Liberals. In the elections in 1924 Zaghlul won an overwhelming majority and, aged sixty-four, was invited by Fuad to form a Cabinet. On 15th March, the first Egyptian Parliament was inaugurated by the King.

"Zaghlul's policy", Ikbal Ali Shah said, "induced bloodshed, but he himself was vigorously opposed to violent measures outside the purely political field. He was kindly, and even humorous, and he exercised a personal spell over friends and enemies alike. At heart he was not an anti-British fanatic. All he wanted was a complete break with Great Britain, and among his intimates he would frequently speak of the days when he worked with amity with British officials. He had the greatest liking for the temperament of the British as represented by the individual. He was at war with things British, and not with the British."

In late 1924 an attempt almost succeeded to murder Zaghlul; he escaped and went immediately afterwards to London to negotiate with Ramsay MacDonald. He was asking withdrawal of British troops from Egypt, withdrawal of all British control and advice, and withdrawal of British claims to protect the Canal. Having listened to his demands, but with no hint of compliance, Ramsay MacDonald announced that Zaghlul Pasha "is returning shortly to Egypt in view of the inclement weather".

A storm was certainly brewing, and burst on 19th November 1924 when Sir Lee Stack, Sirdar of the Egyptian Army and Governor-General of the Sudan, was mortally wounded by revolver shots in broad daylight while driving near the Ministry of Education in Cairo. The assassins got away in waiting cars. Indignation overtook Great Britain and within three days a virtual ultimatum was handed to Egypt demanding an apology, punishment, prohibition of public demonstration, a fine of £500,000, withdrawal within twenty-four hours of all Egyptian troops in the Sudan, appointment of a British Governor-General in the Sudan, increased irrigation in the Sudan, and maintenance of British lawyers and financial advisers in Egypt. Zaghlul resigned.

New elections were held in 1926 when the results were Wafd, under Zaghlul, 144 out of 201 seats, the Liberals 28, and the King's Party of Union 7. But Zaghlul did not take office. Two of his colleagues had been tried with complicity in the murder of Sir Lee Stack, and acquitted. The judge immediately resigned, some whispered because he considered the verdict a miscarriage of justice. Zaghlul was a sick man, and told the High Commissioner he would never take office again. He died aged seventy-four on 23rd August 1927. King Fuad received the news in England.

Zaghlul Pasha was succeeded by Nahas Pasha, a lawyer by profession, born in 1876 at Samanoud in the northern Delta. Educated in the Egyptian Government schools in Cairo he had taken his degree in 1900, and became a judge in 1904. Most professional Egyptians were ardent nationalists and after the First World War Nahas immediately joined the newly formed Wafd party. In 1919 he was dismissed from Government service for taking part in politics; from then on he became one of the most active members of the party. After the troubles of 1921 Nahas had been with Zaghlul and three colleagues on their exile in the Seychelles for two years and in January 1924, when Zaghlul was selecting his cabinet, Nahas was made Minister of Communications. After the murder of Sir Lee Stack Nahas continued to work as a lawyer, as well as secretary of the party, and was one of the counsel who defended and won the case for Nokrashi and Ahmed Maher in the murder trial.

Nahas Pasha's personal honesty and character were never questioned. He was an eloquent, persuasive speaker in Arabic and French. He was a tall man with a striking face which clearly showed all his emotions when he was addressing an audience.

He had a cast in his left eye which gives the unnerving impression, from his photographs, that he was able to watch those to his side as well as those in front. Legend has it that once he bumped into Allenby on some stairs and angrily gasped, "I wish you would look where you're going," to which Allenby replied, "I wish you would go where you're looking." He was on the whole a likeable, attractive man with a sense of humour and pride of appearance. Nahas became a dominating personality in Egyptian affairs for over twenty years.

Nahas Pasha's first appointment as Prime Minister lasted only a short while. He broke off treaty negotiations with Britain, in order to placate the extremists in his party, and then drew a deep breath for his ensuing battles with the King. The first was short-lived: Nahas presented for royal approval a Bill which allowed heavy penalties against any politician who violated the Constitution. Fuad refused to sign it. Nahas resigned. Fuad abolished the 1923 Constitution and effectively nullified the Wafd domination of Egyptian political life. The King had his say in Egyptian affairs for five royal years from 1930, but the strength of the people was growing.

In 1934 Fuad suffered an attack of pleurisy but even when lying ill he fought to keep a tenacious hold on government. He forbad any news of his illness to be made public but within a few weeks the people ceased to believe the 'mild influenza' story put out to them. Wild rumours went about that the King had been dead for months. When Fuad was unable to leave Egypt to unveil a memorial to Mohamed Ali in Greece the truth had to come out. The illness had left him with a poor heart, a much weaker man than before, unfit to face the problems which were almost upon him.

Students of the Moslem University in Cairo, hitherto royalist supporters, performed a *volte-face* and secured, by striking, the appointment of a Wafd rector. The tide was on the turn; a new wave of Wafdism flooded the political beach. "The Wafd", stated Lacouture, "was the expression of the entire people, of which in the fullest sense it was the delegate. Any attempt at defining it would involve a complete description of Egypt. It contained all the generosity, intellectual muddle, good nature, contradictions and mythomania of its millions of supporters. It united the unlimited poverty of some and the insultingly bloated fortunes of others, the demand for change and the demand for conservatism, reaction and movement. There was something spongy, lax and warm about it which is typical of Egypt.

"The Wafd seemed to bring all the possible Egypts together; that of the lords and that of the fellahs, intellectuals and agitators, Christians and laymen: on the one side black morning and evening dress, well-rounded stomachs and tarbooshes, and on the other the *galabiya* of the poverty-stricken. Few men who have played an important part in modern Egypt have not spent at least a short time in the Wafd."

The will of the people, however, began to express itself outside the Wafdist party: a religious movement, later to wield political power, sprang like a bamboo shoot from a seed bed of discontent. In 1928 the Moslem Brotherhood was founded in Ismailia, at first as a rival body to the Y.M.C.A. "The Organization did not long retain a resemblance, either in spirit or objective, to the Christian body," wrote Desmond Stewart. "Led by a man of more genius than principle, it suddenly proved the most popular force in Egypt: its beanstalk growth was due to its tap-root to the Islamic heart of the Egyptian people . . . all the ills of modern Egypt consisted in the betrayal of Islam. The road to ruin lay in imitation of the West; the road to rebirth lay clearly sign-posted by the Koran . . . which . . . should be imposed as law on the whole people."

Hassan el Banna was leader of the Moslem Brotherhood, a man of unshakeable self-confidence based on fanaticism. While still a student he had a passion for founding societies, one of which he modestly called "the society for the Prevention of Sin". This was El Banna's message:

"In our Egyptian Society, the norms of morality have been smashed and the standards of virtue have crumbled away. The instruments of destruction appear on all sides. Young men and women, families and individuals, bodies and souls, are all shattered, calling for the most urgent reform and restoration. Any such restoration can only come about if we reform the very sources of culture and law, if we reform the exploitation of leisure-time, and if we combat abominations." In the atmosphere of mystery with which he surrounded himself, he created the impression that he had mighty forces at his disposal. Followers of El Banna increased. The Moslem Brotherhood, a limited nuisance to Fuad, was to so establish its intricate network of power cells in the following twenty years that it became Farouk's worst headache.

On 12th November 1935 the student Nasser was with thousands of his fellows who demonstrated in Cairo, shouting: "O God Almighty, may a calamity overtake the English," reminiscent of an earlier cry heard in Egypt: "O God All-Glorious, destroy the Ottomans!" Two of his friends were killed in the riots. He himself received a blast of shot in the forehead. Next day his name appeared in print for the first time, in *Al Gihad* (The Struggle). A year later he was sent to Cairo where he obtained his Secondary School Certificate with distinction from Al Nahda Al Misria School. He showed an interest in law and the history of great men.

On 3rd October 1935 the British Minister in Addis Ababa sent a telegram to London reporting the first bomb to drop in an Italian air raid against Ethiopia. The bomb landed on a house in Adowa containing hospital stores and flying the Red Cross flag: invasion by a blacksmith's son, Mussolini, had begun.

The Italian invasion of Ethiopia made it essential for Britain to be able to defend the Suez Canal: aggression by Mussolini brought Britain and the Egyptian Nationalists temporarily together. Yet it seemed likely that the Egyptians would be willing to tempt Italian invasion of their own country if this would wring concessions from Britain in the negotiations for an Anglo-Egyptian Treaty. The Egyptians saw strength in unity and formed a United Front: the Wafdist Nahas, the Liberal Mahmoud, the Shaabist Sidki and the royalist Yehia. On this remarkable, if temporary, consolidation of views the Egyptians founded their position for negotiation with Britain of the 1936 Treaty.

Conversations opened in Cairo on 2nd March 1936 between Sir Miles Lampson, the British High Commissioner, and the Egyptian Delegation: there were four main points which had remained outstanding for settlement since Egyptian Independence in 1922:

1. Security of British Imperial communications in Egypt.

2. Defence of Egypt against foreign aggression.

3. Protection of foreign interests and minorities.

4. The Sudan.

The first person to handle Farouk after his birth was an English midwife named Lucy Sergeant who bathed him and passed him on to a peasant girl from the village of Govcala in Turkey, specially selected by doctors to breast feed the young Prince. Her first plentiful feeding of the infant must have set the quantity of his appetite for the rest of his life. As a baby, she later recalled, he was voracious, he was good and seldom cried, and grew so quickly that it was almost noticeable from day to day.

Farouk is an appellation of Omar, the second Caliph after the Prophet. Omar el Faruk is claimed to have so successfully administered justice in his time that he was able to sleep by the roadside without fear of attack from any enemy. Farouk means 'One who distinguishes between right and wrong'. Farouk's upbringing was shared with his four sisters and parents in the various royal palaces. The distance between Cairo and Alexandria was the width of his world. Abdin, an enormous stone palace of some 550 rooms, the official residence of the rulers of Egypt since its construction in 1863 by Ismail the Magnificent, was his principal home. The palace was divided into two major wings: the *salamlek*, the King's quarters, offices and reception chambers, and the *haramlek*, where the Queen and her daughters lived in semi-seclusion, attended by the Ethiopian Rizah Aga, Fuad's chief eunuch.

The persons intimately concerned with Farouk in his earliest years were his midwife, governess and mother. The midwife was Lucy Sergeant, whom he feared at first but later regarded with such affection that he sent her a telegram on her birthday practically every year until the end of his life. Ina Naylor, widow of a Yorkshire doctor, was his governess and nurse from his fourth to his fifteenth year. His mother, Queen Nazli, thirty years her husband's junior, had married Fuad in 1919. He had divorced his former wife in order to marry Nazli and had suffered a bullet wound in the throat from Prince Ahmed Safatin, the indignant brother of the woman he gave up. Nazli was the daughter of a noble Franco-Egyptian family, descended from 'Soliman Pasha the Frenchman' who had married the daughter of Sherif Pasha, Egyptian Prime Minister. Schooled in Paris, she was a dark-eyed beauty who had first attracted Fuad one night at the theatre. Through Lady Graham, wife of an English adviser to the Government, Fuad learnt who she was and Lady Graham arranged a party for them to meet.

King Fuad, whom he called Papa, Naylor and Queen Nazli were authority in young Farouk's world. Naylor was hired by Fuad and a bitter rivalry developed between her and Nazli, becoming a conflict of the boy's affection. Farouk once hurt his mother when she asked him why he more readily kissed Ninzy (Naylor) and he replied, "Because you wear too much rouge."

The sisters nearest to him in age were Fawzia (Wuzzy) and Faiza, and then Faika and Fathia (Atty). He was devoted to them. They called him Luky, which name stuck after a baby sister's early attempt to pronounce Farouk. Farouk had an elder sister Fewkia twenty years older, from Fuad's first marriage. King Fuad, who adored his mother, Ferial, believed that the letter F brought him luck. Farouk later perpetuated this habit of choosing names beginning with F for his own children.

Farouk played in the palace rooms, in the Byzantine room, the Suez Canal room; and crawled under Louis XVI beds. On his second birthday his parents gave him only instructive presents, illustrated albums and toys that demanded a certain amount of attention in their use. Fuad imported mechanical toys for the child, from Berlin, Paris and London; Farouk spent his time dismantling them. One day in the Ras el Tin Palace he had just successfully put out of commission his new electric train. He rang for the palace electrician, Francesco, to mend the thing. Francesco's nephew, Antonio Pulli, who had recently arrived in Egypt as an emigrant barber and electrician from a small town in the Italian province of Lecce, came to help and soon had the train clicking busily along its tracks. On this minor piece of electrical engineering success by Antonio Pulli was based a lifelong friendship; Pulli became the *eminence grise* with a major influence on Farouk.

He grew up six months of the year in Cairo, in Abdin and

Kubba Palace at Heliopolis, in the cooler season from October to March. When summer came everyone retired to the beaches of Alexandria, to Ras el Tin and Montazah Palaces. All the palaces had magnificent grounds, lawns shaded by palms and jacaranda, decorated with oleander, flamboyants and flaming bougainvillaea, with gravel paths to grottoes and low marble walls leading between beds of cannalillies, petunias and phlox, salvias, stocks and hollyhocks, sunflowers, cineraria, sweet peas, climbing nasturtiums and geraniums. Hawks, hooded crows, egrets and fantail doves fluttered near the fountains and the pools and streams. A herd of a hundred gazelles roamed the gardens of Montazah beside the sea where Fuad built his son a schoolhouse beside the beach.

When old enough to start learning he was wakened at 6 a.m. After breakfast he studied from 9 a.m. until 11 a.m. and again until luncheon at 1 p.m. The early afternoon until 4 p.m. was a rest period and then he would return to his books and desk, sometimes until 9 p.m.

At an early age he met and dealt with the English: the governess, King Fuad's chauffeur, his chemist Titterington, known as Titters, who tasted his food, his A.D.C. Colonel Castle-Smith, even the five English motor-cycle outriders. He soon learnt the art of being elusive and avoiding authority, slipping away to avoid his mother and governess, for clandestine meetings with a member of the garage staff. They became such friends that the garage hand was eventually promoted to colonel.

He was an open, healthy-minded boy, but no judge of character. As a child he was fairly fit, but suffered from a weak chest, poor eyesight, and abscesses in his delicate ears. He liked nothing more than a good joke and probably inherited his sense of humour from his father. When Naylor introduced the delights of April Fools' Day into the household and invited the King to come and see the newly-born twin camels in the stables, and fooled King Fuad into believing her, he ably responded by issuing a return invitation to her to come and see the eclipse of the moon with him that evening. She declined, to the King's joy, because there actually was an eclipse on that 1st April. One of Farouk's early tricks, played on his father, was to ask him to stand still for his photograph. When Farouk pressed the camera trigger a three-yard-long green snake leaped from the lens.

Life in the palace was still based on the ancient Turkish manner. King Fuad, who had abolished the veil in 1927 (it was introduced by Mohamed Ali when he noticed a wife of his flirting with one of his officers) still kept five young Turkish girls in his harem. Their principal duty, however, was to iron the yashmaks. Five eunuchs controlled the haramlek which was kept locked every night from 9 p.m. to 4 a.m. The chief eunuch's striped trousers, frock coat and red tarbush were a sign of the times, progress from the days when eunuchs were employed solely to protect the girls of the harem from unauthorized attentions of men. Eunuchs were slaves, but this description can be misleading unless one understands that slaves could become very important. Madame Tugay tells a story of the chief eunuch, who had the title of Excellency, of the Imperial Ottoman Palace: "When Emperor William II, accompanied by the Empress Augusta, paid Sultan Hamid a state visit, it was said that the Empress, who knew nothing about eunuchs, was told that the chief eunuch was a very important personage indeed. So she, wishing to be amiable, spoke to him through her interpreter and asked whether His Highness's father had also been a eunuch."

Farouk was a fair, girlish boy with blue eyes. He never spent an hour in the company of another boy but grew up surrounded by women. Having no brothers the only boys he ever met were those who came to his birthday parties. He never went to theirs.

Mrs. Naylor adored her charge. She was called out to look after him from the age of three (King Fuad's telegram to her read "Prepare at once to proceed east") and for the next fourteen years she dominated Farouk's life. There was seldom an occasion when she was not present with him, and he, very susceptible to advice, and with an excellent memory for what he was told, learnt well from her. Unfortunately this susceptibility of Farouk's did not have the additional quality of discernment between good and poor advice. This dogged him all through life: if one man was convincing enough Farouk would believe him, his opinions would then remain unchanged until another of stronger character came along to influence him.

He swam, rode his horses Sammy and Silvertail (who was reared on a bottle) and climbed palm trees with instruction from his French gymnast. He had a fencing master, and Mr. Hathway, an English master who came every day to teach mathematics and reading. The tutors reported to Mrs. Naylor on his behaviour; if it was bad he was sent to bed early while Naylor rested on a couch in his room to make sure he stayed in, supervision which he once overcame by sprinkling the couch with sneezing powder. On another occasion he left a note on her pillow saying, "I will try to be a better boy tomorrow."

Ninzy introduced more English delights into the oriental household, paperchases, treasure-hunts, and feasts every Christmas when she arranged for a Christmas tree and toys to be sent from Hamleys. When Farouk was nine his portrait was painted by de Laszlo and when the artist asked him to sign his autograph book Farouk asked if his governess could sign it also. When it was explained diplomatically that the album contained only royal signatures, Farouk was insistent, "If Mrs. Naylor mustn't write her autograph, then I will not write mine." De Laszlo then had a commoner's signature in his book.

Princess Nimetullah, youngest of the Khedive Ismail's fourteen children, used to visit her brother Fuad regularly three times a week at the Koubbeh Palace, which he preferred to the Abdin. She was very fond of her nephew Farouk, who warmly returned her affection. At the age of ten or eleven, one day, when he happened to be alone with this aunt in his mother's private drawing-room, he pointed to a large photograph of Queen Nazli, and said: "Aunty, my mother is so good and so beautiful, can anyone be like her?" He was the darling of Nazli and her ladies-in-waiting who spoiled him outrageously. He became an obstinate boy. Queen Nazli hoped to maintain her hold on him after he had ascended the throne and, without going as far as Agrippina, Nero's mother, she permitted his weaknesses, his love of pleasure and flattered his vanity. The Queen had some influence on him against his father, posed as a martyr, and complained that she was virtually a prisoner in the Palace. (Though he loved his wife, King Fuad imposed certain restrictions on her activities. In the season, she went to the opera and plays, visited exhibitions, performed certain duties of royalty, such as being present at the opening ceremony of hospitals or schools, and called on the senior princesses of the royal family.)

Nazli enjoyed dabbling in the occult and it is said she repaired nightly to a wise old woman whom she kept in the palace to hear her incantations over a smoking cauldron. Farouk went with her and stayed there until the early hours of the morning. The consequence was that after months of this the boy's damaged nerves made him quite unstable and unreliable. He was unable to get to sleep before three o'clock in the morning and on discovering this fact some of his relations sought some means of occupying his time between a normal bedtime and when he could get to sleep. They hit on a method, by teaching him to gamble.

Farouk's education was sadly neglected. He was like his mother, not intellectual, and uninterested in books, whereas his father possessed a fine library and had founded the Cairo University while still a prince, and the Alexandria University after his accession. Farouk shirked his lessons whenever possible. In this he was aided and abetted by his mother who sent orders to his tutors to report favourably on her son's progress in his studies. These monthly reports were regularly submitted to King Fuad who believed them, until the deception was discovered and Farouk sent to England.

Farouk was not strong, of average intelligence, not brilliant but kindly and affectionate. His schooling had started when he was six, with an hour's Arabic and an hour's English a day, increasing to a full day's work when he was eight. Study, and then play was Fuad's policy and some have blamed him for keeping his son at his desk too long. Intent on keeping his son slim Fuad put Farouk on diets which Farouk later remembered had made him so hungry he had eaten the cat's dinner. He was pampered. When he kicked a ball someone brought it back; when he swam someone followed in a boat. And yet he grew up with his own manly qualities. Early in his teens he looked a handsome, fit Prince. He was taken to see the Tutankhamen treasure, which was discovered when he was two years old, and to the Coptic Museum in old Cairo. On one occasion he had to attend an official tea party. Mrs. Naylor did not go but beforehand impressed upon Farouk that he was not to show his customary big appetite for food, and to leave some for the poor. At the reception he ate little and when pressed to take more by Sir Percy Lorraine of the British Embassy his reply was quite emphatic: "No thank you, Mrs. Naylor said I was to leave some for the poor."

His principal hobbies were fishing and photography. Most of his spare time at Montazah was spent in fishing; many times all the breakfast and lunch fish for the nursery dining-room came from his rod. He was a photographer from an early age, and in addition to several cameras for still photography, he had a Ciné Kodak, a present from his father on his twelfth birthday. Motoring was another of his hobbies. His first car was an Austin Seven, also a present from his father when he was eleven years old. This he learnt to drive in a few days under the tutorship of a trusted English driver and from then on he was permitted to take his sisters for a weekly drive in the grounds. His second car was a Fiat, a present from the King of Italy, and then a Morris racing model, a present from his father when he was fifteen.

In his early teens he had monthly pocket money of £5 from which, for a while unbeknown to his parents, he donated £2 to a poor family and £2 to poor school children for their books. He was concerned with the people round him. When a stablehand was dismissed from the palace for attempting to sell a diamond tiepin which Farouk had lost while out riding, the prince declared he would never again wear jewels when riding to avoid the risk of putting temptation in the way of poor people. When an old gardener was about to be dismissed as he could no longer work, Farouk, then aged nine, made the observation, "If he is too old to work here, he is too old to work anywhere and he must live," and asked if the man could be kept on.

Fuad said when he himself was a Prince: "It is nothing to be a Prince, it is something to be useful," and he set his son a strict curriculum of studies—history, geography, mathematics, physics, chemistry and sports. He introduced him as early as he could to the ceremony which accompanies the position of a monarch: at the age of twelve Farouk took his father's position for the first time at an official function, the R.A.F. display at Heliopolis, impressing everybody with his self-possession. In 1933 he was appointed Chief Scout of Egypt. In 1934 he inaugurated the International Postal Congress in Cairo on behalf of his father and from then on he often appeared in public, a young man, as observers noted then, with "discerning tact and a direct and winning manner. He has a neat wit, and it amuses him sometimes to tease those around him with some play upon words or a riddle revealing both his sense of the appropriate and his fluent command of the English language".

By the time he was fifteen Farouk was a serious boy, respecting and a little frightened of his father. At parades and receptions he would stand in just the same manner as the king, holding his gloves and with a serious bearing. He enjoyed the more light-hearted occasions of visits to the zoo, football matches, fencing tournaments, and Boy Scout parades. Whenever appropriate his sisters accompanied him, dressed identically and immaculately, looking beautiful in their white picture hats, dresses edged with fur, white socks and shoes. Whenever they were with him Farouk's hand was seen gently bringing them forward, making sure that two shy girls should not miss anything.

His upbringing made him a sincere follower of Islam, sub-mission to the will of God. Five times a day Farouk prayed on the rug in his room, and washed his hands, feet and hair in the Moslem manner. The strongest bond Farouk was ever to have with his people was religion.

With each birthday the number of his presents grew. His early birthdays were good collecting times for books and he eventu-ally had five hundred of an educational nature. Other gifts interested him more. He was given so much that it is easy to see how his collecting instincts were aroused. When he was shown his father's coins and stamps this confirmed him as a collector for life.

Fuad insisted Farouk should master Arabic. He wanted to make his son an Egyptian: he understood the weakness of being regarded as an outsider. Fuad's enlightened policy prevailed despite the general superiority felt by the Turks over the Egyptians, who felt inferior, and jealous of the Turks. An Egyptian could not marry a Turk, the only way to progress for an Egyptian was in the government, and gradually Egyptians took over. This was due to King Fuad.

When Farouk was fourteen the King applied to send him to Eton but he knew no Latin and was refused. After several reversals of decision Fuad and his advisers decided finally in 1935 that the Prince should attend a course of higher education in England. Seeming older than his age he was entered for the

Royal Military Academy at Woolwich where Fuad felt his bearing and manly qualities could be given wider scope than at public
school. Farouk arrived in England on 18th October 1935 and
took up residence in Kenry House, Kingston Hill, Surrey.
Among his suite were his Oxford-educated tutor Ahmed Hassanein, the explorer; Aziz el Masri, as military tutor; Saleih
Hashim, professor of Arabic and Islamic science; and Doctor
Kafrawi, as personal physician. Several English teachers were
asked to help with special subjects; and Regimental Sergeant-
Major W. H. Parker became his fencing and combat tutor, to
tell later his favourite story of waking the Prince early in the
mornings for two miles' sharp walking.

Aziz el Masri, a Circassian, who had had a distinguished
military career and had been in charge of the Cairo police
training school before being appointed tutor to Prince Farouk,
was anti-British and pro-German. In England he resigned over
some dispute with the other tutors.

Hassanein had returned to Egypt after Oxford at the outbreak
of the First World War and became secretary to General Maxwell. He was an excellent liaison officer between Egypt and
England. King Fuad promoted his exploration in Libya where
he was the first man to cross from the Mediterranean southward
to al Darfur and for this he was presented with the Gold Medal
of the Royal Geographical Society. In 1923 he was First Secretary to the Egyptian Legation in Washington and later Fuad
promoted him on the palace staff to Assistant Chamberlain. His
extravagant wife's debts had to be paid off by the British before
he could come to England. Once there he undoubtedly trained
Farouk well at first but later began to abuse his position; he
combined personal charm with an ambitious and unscrupulous
nature, and began to spoil the boy.

At the entrance examination for the Royal Military Academy
Farouk sat with pen poised waiting for the answers to be given
to him. (Evidently this had been the procedure when he took
trial papers in Cairo.) No one could help him. He failed. The
truth of his education at last was out, and King Fuad was
furious.

Thus Farouk never received a proper education in the company of other boys, and in genuine competition with them. Those
who had spoiled and pampered him were responsible for the

character he developed. Farouk's ability to convince those who met him that he was intelligent stems from his grasp of incidental, isolated items of general knowledge: he could never hold a long and penetrating discussion, and lived on his wits.

At one of his luncheons with King George V, when the King inquired why Farouk's notepaper bore the symbol ∓ to represent Farouk Fouad, the prince replied, "For economy." Farouk met Edward, then Prince of Wales, and they went to a Rugby International at Twickenham and Soccer matches together. After only a few months in England in 1936 Farouk attended the funeral of King George V.

When he arrived in England he had spent a few days in London and in a jeweller's window had seen brooches and other objects made of the mounted wings of a large tropical butterfly which were of a lovely shade of blue. He admired them so much that he bought appropriate presents for his parents and sisters and had them sent to them in Egypt. From then on he sent presents home by virtually every post.

As his tutors' control laxed the Crown Prince became more and more elusive, disappearing on his own by bicycle to shop in Kingston—Bentalls was one of the most attractive stores outside London—and to the local people he was known as 'Prince Freddy'. He also liked to explore the Charing Cross Road bookshops.

For two afternoons a week he attended the Military Academy, the rest of his time taken up by lessons and sport at Kenry House, and visits to British institutions. At the Motor Show "he was very animated, talking and laughing a great deal, and often went out of his way to look at things that attracted his attention. . . . Prince Farouk had probably the unusual experience of finding himself in a crowd, rubbing shoulders with all sorts. . . . He seemed to find nothing strange in the experience but was entirely self-possessed and, incidentally, displayed very charming manners, with a smile and a thank-you for everybody. . . ."

Early in 1936 King Fuad's health deteriorated sharply; for three years he had wasted from his former self. On the night of Monday 27th April it was clear that Fuad was dying and Farouk telephoned the Prime Minister, Ali Maher Pasha, from England, promising to return to Egypt by the shortest possible route. Despite slightly more hope on the Tuesday Farouk prepared himself for the worst. A week before he died Fuad had a vision in which he saw three chairs: in one sat his old friend King George V, in the other Cromer, the third chair was empty. The vision ended when George V sent Cromer to fetch Fuad.

For four days Fuad had fought his illness, rallying again after each relapse. On Wednesday morning his doctors reported another rally "due to his astonishing will power"; he talked a little to them and listened while the news was read to him from the morning newspapers and then his heart suddenly failed and he died peacefully at 1 p.m. The Prime Minister received the news during a cabinet meeting and made an announcement to the public at 2 p.m. Nine hours later Farouk was proclaimed King of Egypt; the cabinet telegraphed its loyal support and ardent wishes for a prosperous reign.

The Prime Minister made a Proclamation to the Egyptian nation, extolling the virtues of the late monarch: "King Fuad's prodigious efforts for the country had harmed his health. Nevertheless he had struggled against death with great will power, and his last thoughts were for his country. . . . The most direct homage Egypt can now render is to turn towards his son Farouk, giving him the confidence and affection felt for his father. The Egyptian people", the Proclamation continued, "had loved Prince Farouk since childhood and were confident that the new King would march in the footsteps and follow the example of his illustrious father."

Fuad had had to take second place when popular nationalist feeling made Zaghlul virtual dictator of Egyptian politics after the First World War. Fuad bore this humiliation well, until after the murder of Sir Lee Stack when the Royalist Party, the Ittehad, came more into the open and the King was able to exert his authority. However, when Lord Lloyd was appointed British High Commissioner the Wafdist and other parties appealed for a return to recognition of their opinion and Fuad's ambition to exercise his own personal rule was thwarted. Fuad was pre-occupied with his personal desires: his measurement of his own achievements for Egypt tended to be numbered by the number of Royal Societies that he founded. His support for the specific was afforded at the cost of the general; the Egyptian University flourished under his patronage but the organization of State education for the people was chaotic.

Lord Lloyd paid this tribute to King Fuad: "The death of His Majesty King Fuad removes a very considerable figure from the stage of Near Eastern events. His remarkable abilities, his untiring energy, and his mastery of minute detail—as well as an exceptional understanding of every intricacy of Egyptian politics with which he was so conspicuously endowed—all these combined to make him a dominating influence in the Nile Valley."

From Italy Signor Mussolini sent a telegram of condolence to the Egyptian Government. Obituary notices in Italian papers emphasized the part Italy had played in Fuad's political and military education and the impression Italy had had on his thoughts and tastes. The difficulties of Egypt's political position were described in tendentious language and the proclaimed independence of Egypt as a farcical formula. British interference in Egyptian affairs is, the papers stated, "continuous, annoying, and brazen faced".

On Thursday afternoon, 30th April, the wooden frame covering the body was taken from the Koubbeh Palace to Abdin Palace with military ceremony. Draped in the Royal Standard of Egypt it was drawn through the streets escorted by Egyptian Lancers of the royal bodyguard whose blue and red, yellow and red, and green and red pennants fluttered from the lances in the sunshine. It took two hours from 5 p.m. for the procession to reach the Opera Square from Koubbeh Palace. The European communities gathered on verandas, roof tops and balconies, to see the cortège pass, and the streets were packed with people, including a large crowd which followed the gun carriage and overtook it in Station Square, throwing all into temporary confusion which was the more difficult to clear, as the solemnity of the occasion had subdued the soldiers and onlookers and precluded the use of curses or shouts which could have overcome any more cheerful chaos. People called out quotations from the Koran, and chanted "The King is dead and now is in heaven". At the Abdin Palace the Prime Minister and Cabinet received the body which lay in state until 10 a.m. the following morning.

The funeral drew the largest crowd ever seen in Cairo, waitng expectantly, early on Friday morning 1st May. The funeral procession was not ostentatious, in accordance with ancient Moslem custom; the coffin was carried on a simple black gun carriage, draped in the Egyptian flag embroidered with a crown. Bands marched but did not play and before the coffin marched lines of Egyptian soldiers in khaki uniforms and red tarbushes, following came the Ulema and Prince Mohamed Ali and Ali Maher. It took the procession two hours to walk four miles to the mosque where it paused outside while sacrificial oxen were slaughtered, their blood spotting the coffin.

Farouk stayed indoors at Kenry House, Kingston Hill, where sympathizers called all day on 29th April, making final preparations for catching the train from Victoria. He had decided to return by rail through France to Marseilles and, travelling incognito, to board the Peninsular and Orient liner *Viceroy of India* which would call specially at Alexandria to land him. Before leaving London Farouk had half an hour's private conversation with King Edward at Buckingham Palace when he was offered a British warship to take him home, but he declined.

The train left Victoria Station at 1.53 p.m. seen off by the Duke of Kent, Mr. Eden, Egyptian students and the Egyptian colony in London. A guard of honour of the Seaforth Highlanders were drawn up at Dover Marine Station for inspection by Farouk before he boarded the French mail steamer *Côte d'Azur* and was escorted across the channel by H.M. Destroyers *Scimitar* and *Scout*. A special room was arranged on a platform at the Gare de Lyon, Paris, and Farouk left his train to receive a deputation from the President. At Marseilles he met the British Consul-General, the Prefect of the Bouches du Rhône, and the Mayor of Marseilles and immediately went on board the *Viceroy of India*, due to sail at midnight. On 3rd May a salute was fired as the *Viceroy of India* arrived at Malta; from there on it was non-stop to Egypt where he would land as King. One can imagine his thoughts as he stared out from the liner across the water to the yet invisible coast of his country. We may be sure his intentions were of the best, to be reflected in the words which he contemplated and which he would utter within a few days in Cairo, aspirations for the future of his country.

The death of Fuad when his son was at such an impressionable age was the first great tragedy of Farouk's life. His father,

whose portrait before his illness shows a man with firmer
features than one would look for in an Oriental Sultan, an im-
perious angle of the head, waxed upturned tips to his moustache
and a fullness of neck that one expects, could one say, in an
English sergeant-major, chose an explorer and Army generals
to train his son and a British military career for him at an age
when to remain in the heat of Egypt would have encouraged him
in indolence: he wanted European barracks rather than oriental
palaces for his son at that age, a training the boy was not to have.

Chapter 3

No More Auspicious Opening
(6th May 1936—July 1937)

Alexandria was astir early on the morning of 6th May 1936. Flags which had been at half-mast were raised to the masthead. Ships in the harbour were dressed overall and sailors on the British warships stood by at their stations. H.M.S. *Ajax* relinquished its escort as the liner carrying Farouk approached the harbour, and the *Amir Farouk* fired a royal salute to the accompaniment of guns from Port Saleh and the British Navy. The King transferred to the royal yacht *Mahroussa* and then by launch to the Ras el Tin Palace quay. The royal standard broke over the palace, the Egyptian Army guard of honour presented arms and the band played the national anthem and within a few minutes the King was driving to the station in an open Rolls-Royce with the Prime Minister Ali Maher Pasha. Crowds lined the route, Girl Guides and Boy Scouts, soldiers, policemen and firemen, men and women in their thousands, white turbaned theological students, Wafdist Blue Shirts, Young Egypt Green Shirts, workmen's syndicates, and children shouted "Long Live Farouk King of Egypt and the Sudan", "Long live the King of the Nile". A measure of the delirious welcome was the number drowned or killed in the crush.

Fellahin waved to the King's train on its journey to Cairo where Farouk shook hands with many of the 3,000 notabilities waiting on the red-carpeted platform, banners waved "King Farouk—King of Egypt and the Sudan", people climbed the fountains and trees, shouted from balconies and rooftops and cheered as the party left to pray at his father's tomb in the Mosque of El Rifaii, surrounded by the Royal Bodyguard in their blue, white and scarlet summer uniforms. As the procession passed crowds rushed into the street stirring up the sand which had been laid earlier, until everything was seen through a haze of dust. Later at about 5 p.m. the King, followed by the Princesses and Queen Nazli, drove from Abdin Palace to Koubbeh Palace. The dust and the din had died, a new reign had begun.

The day after his return Farouk broadcast an eagerly awaited message to his people. The speech was his own: "It was Allah's will that I be deprived of a last meeting with my father. I start a new life which I embrace firmly and with goodwill. I promise that I will dedicate this life to your service and to the continuous efforts for your prosperity. With my own eyes I have seen your love and attachment for me, and I say to you that I intend to maintain this solidarity for the sake of our dear Egypt. I believe that the greatness of a king is in the greatness of his people. I want to bring reforms and in this Allah will help me."

Fuad, whose debts had had to be paid off by the British when he became Sultan, left something over £10 million to Farouk, in land and investments abroad. He inherited the estates of Faroukia, Edfine, Ismailia, Mariout and Zafaran. King Fuad had laid down that the succession should rest in his own direct descendants, and not, as previously, in the eldest male relative of the Sultan (under which system Prince Mohamed Ali, Farouk's uncle, would have become ruler of Egypt). The Egyptian Constitution safeguarded the monarchy; two articles forbade any proposals for the amendment of the monarchical system of government. Other articles conferred important prerogatives on the king: the right to dissolve and prorogue the parliament; the right to create and grant civil, military and other honorary titles; the appointment and dismissal of the army officers; and the nomination of two-fifths of the senators.

As Farouk was then only sixteen the Cabinet was faced with a task of appointing a regency. According to the Law of Succession the new king was due to attain his majority in August 1937, eighteen Moslem or lunar years from his birth and although he would then be able to rule without a regency he would not attain his civil majority until his twenty-first lunar year. The new Egyptian Parliament met on 8th May 1936 to nominate a Council of Regency and appointed Prince Mohamed Ali, the heir presumptive, a popular and affable prince of distinguished appearance and manners; Aziz Pasha Izzet, who had married Fuad's niece, and had spent three years as Egyptian Minister to the Court of St. James's and a year as Minister of Foreign Affairs, known as an excellent diplomatist with charming manners; and Sherif Pasha Sabri, the junior member of the Regency, Queen Nazli's brother and then Under Secretary of State for Foreign Affairs.

Prince Mohamed Ali, author of *Breeding of Arabian Horses* and owner of one of the world's largest studs, was the younger son of the Khedive Tewfik, and grandson of the Khedive Ismail. He was well known in international society, where his strong sense of humour and outspoken manner charmed his wide circle of friends. A large part of his palace was arranged to house his collections which included many exquisite specimens of Turkish art, forming the largest and most complete group of rugs, illuminated manuscripts, embroideries, ceramics, and jewellery ever assembled in private ownership. The Prince was remarkably handsome, dark, with fine drawn aquiline features, though he was of delicate health, and never married. The Aga Khan wrote of Mohamed Ali: "He is a fascinating and many-sided personality . . . he exerted for long a quiet, soothing but very powerful influence, largely behind the scenes, in Egyptian life and politics . . . his energy and vivacity are as great as his spirit is sensitive and his intellect powerful. . . . He speaks several languages, ranging from Arabic and Turkish, through English, French, and German. . . . His detailed historical knowledge of Egypt . . . is truly phemomenal. . . . All his life he has been a great admirer of Britain, and of the British character and way of life, and a staunch supporter of Anglo-Egyptian friendship. . . ."

It was partly Mohamed Ali's friendship with the English, and possible collusion with the Wafd, that inspired Ali Maher, to whom Fuad had entrusted the undertaking to ensure that Farouk became King, to get Farouk back to Egypt quickly after Fuad's death. Mohamed Ali later admitted that he had wished to keep Farouk in England for at least two more years but that the unfortunate influence of Ali Maher to the contrary swayed him. Nazli, jealous of the English, who had never been allowed by Fuad to have any influence on Farouk, wished to have him at home with her. She opposed his return to England.

In 1936 *The Times* wrote: "The new reign could have no more auspicious opening, nor one better calculated to advance the tasks of internal government in Egypt, than the successful conclusion of the treaty now under negotiation, settling relations with Britain upon a new and permanent footing of mutual advantage and fortifying Eygptian security and independence."

One of the Regency's first tasks was to refuse the King permission to build a new station for Montazah Palace in Alexandria as the royal train used it but twice a year, to which Farouk replied with his customary caprice by knocking the old station down with a lorry and hiring his own workmen to build a new stone station, consisting of a long platform, a covered section in the middle and a sentry box at each end.

In the May election the Wafd party won as usual and Nahas Pasha as Prime Minister headed a delegation to Britain of seven Wafdists and six prominent politicians from other parties. Most of the negotiating of the Anglo-Egyptian Treaty had been completed in Cairo with the British High Commissioner, Sir Miles Lampson; the signing was to be in London. Lord Avon later recalled in his memoirs that all thirteen members of the delegation signed the document, unusual, but a method of sharing the responsibility and making it difficult for any Egyptian party to evade it later. He also recalled how, as the party was large, with several wives in London also, and as it was a fortnight after the twelfth of August he sent for a number of grouse from Yorkshire to give the delegation at luncheon. This was not successful; on asking later how lunch had gone he was told the Egyptian ladies had "complained of being given old crows to eat".

The 1936 Anglo-Egyptian Treaty abandoned one of the four points reserved in the 1922 Declaration of Independence: the protection of foreign interests and minority groups in Egypt, but it retained the other three: imperial communications, the defence of Egypt, and the Sudan. At the same time Britain agreed to remove her forces from Cairo and Alexandria to the Canal Zone; to allow immigration into the Sudan; and to sponsor Egypt for membership of the League of Nations.

A month before the Treaty was signed Farouk was guest on board H.M.S. *Queen Elizabeth* in British naval farewell exercises. The Treaty, signed on cream parchment tied with blue ribbon, recognized Egypt a country of equal status with Britain. It was devised with the aim of "consolidating their friendship, their cordial understanding, and their good relations". Of the restricted garrison force to remain in the Canal Zone (an imperial thorn in the flesh of Egypt) the numbers were not to exceed 10,000 land forces and 400 air pilots.

The Treaty was ratified by the Egyptian parliament by 202 votes to 11: praise for it was unbounded in the British and Egyptian press, and says Tom Little, British troops in Cairo were greeted "with cheers instead of brickbats and Nahas was received home like a conquering hero".

Mohamed Neguib, in *Egypt's Destiny*, took a broader view of the Treaty and its effects: "It reduced the status of the British High Commissioner to that of ambassador and established a British military mission to the extent necessary to ensure the defence of Egypt without further assistance from the British Army except 'in the event of war'. In such an event the King of Egypt was obliged to make available to the King and Emperor of Great Britain 'all the facilities and assistance in his power, including the use of his ports, aerodromes and means of communication, and to take all the administrative and legislative measures, including the establishment of martial law and an effective censorship necessary to render these facilities and assistance effective' [*sic*].

"It was hardly an ideal treaty from the Egyptian point of view in as much as it authorised a limited British occupation for another twenty years. But the new relationship established between the two countries was so much less inequitable than any previous Anglo-Egyptian relationship that the treaty was received in Cairo with rejoicing."

Neguib, understandably, believed that the British after the Treaty were seeking some means of re-occupying Egypt at their first opportunity. Although he claimed himself not insensible to the growing danger of war then hanging over Europe, he accused the British of attempting to re-occupy western Egypt on the pretext that another war was imminent. In 1938 when the British requested permission to send two battalions to Mersa Matruh in order to "acquaint them with the terrain", Neguib refused permission. Weight was added to his argument when he discovered they were the two same battalions who had evacuated the town after the Treaty, and must both have known the terrain quite well.

G. S. Hoare wrote in *Fortnightly Review* in 1936; a "still unknown factor in the Egyptian political scene is King Farouk . . . it seems improbable that he can, on his own initiative, play any important part in his country's affairs for some years, but he will represent the monarchy, and . . . his word, whoever inspires the utterance, will be all-powerful, for Eastern ideas of monarchy are not ours. He will have advisers to guide him, and these men, whoever they are, will be of high importance to Egypt. . . . King Farouk . . . has only to inherit a little of his father's intelligence, courage and acumen to be able to select both his advisers and his servants from the best elements of the country. Indeed, one of the outstanding characteristics of King Fuad was the unerring wisdom which enabled him unfailingly to pick out for what has been termed 'the Palace group' men of exceptional ability." Farouk, it transpired, was not blessed with that "unerring wisdom".

The *Egyptian Gazette* wrote on 1st January 1937: "King Farouk is already the most popular figure in this country, impressing everybody with his fine qualities, his kingly yet modest and pleasing bearing, and his obvious interest in and love for his country, King Farouk seems destined to play a very important role in his country's future. His public appearances . . . have shown him to be almost western in his lack of ceremony and his desire to mix with his peoples."

Of his religious outlook Sheik Mustafa el Maraghi, Rector of Al Azhar Mosque, intellectual headquarters of Islam, said: "He is a reverential King, full of zeal for Islam, likes to read on religious subjects and to understand their lessons, and pay his respects to Allah. What I like in him is his great faith and vast aspiration for the future of Egypt and its progress, so that it can take its proper place among the nations and peoples of the world. He is the first King of Egypt who has direct contact with his people."

From the eulogistic utterances of the King's contemporary subjects come the occasional clear facts, like hard fruit from a mass of blossom. The Prime Minister of the Lebanon admired the intelligence of Farouk and declared that he was in spirit, "not only the King of Egypt, but King of all the Arabs". Makram Ebeid Pasha, a leading politician, said of him, "he inherited dignity from his grandfather and father, in his infancy he was a child, but in his youth he became a man. Farouk is courageous and wise, patient and democratic, with a great love for his people. His true democracy is mirrored in the manner in which he celebrates his birthday, because instead of having festivities in his honour, he uses the occasion to visit the poor and sick and to leave charity with them."

At about 10 a.m. on 2nd January 1937 Farouk left Koubbeh Palace, accompanied by Hassanein and motored to the quay at Heluan. He was to spend a month touring upper Egypt and this occasion was another excuse for the people to show their respect. The streets and the Opera Square of Cairo were crowded as the King's car negotiated the route via Sharias el Kubba, Malika Nazli, Kasr el Nil, Soliman Pasha, Kasr el Aini, and Misr el Kadima. Men, women and children, schoolboys and students chanted "Long Live our Beloved King". School bands struck up the national anthem and the King was treated to the same verse many times as his car slowed. The author is indebted to Sir Edward Ford, King Farouk's tutor from August 1936 to June 1937, for the loan of his diary written on the royal tour of Upper Egypt from which the following extracts are made:

Saturday, 2nd January 1937. The roads were posted all along the way with flags and decorations and banners, and at places there were carpets and coloured awning suspended by the roadside in what is a characteristic Egyptian style. The road too was covered with sand in patches to make smooth going, and the populace was already assembled at each village, the women beginning their wild lu-lias and the young girls dressed in bright colours, nearly all of them in scarlet. The schools obviously were on holiday, and occasionally one saw a small troop of well-disciplined boy scouts. At Heluan, there was a large concourse, including the Mudir of Gizeh, the Sheikhs and notabilities of Heluan and the district, all in a special multi-coloured marquee. There was a considerable detachment of the Royal Bodyguard, well turned-out but with an arms-drill that would make a Guardsman laugh. Some scouts were there too, and police, soldiers and a large crowd from the district. The kindly, distinguished Rector of Al Azhar was there, carrying a lovely silk scarf over his long black robe: Nahas Pasha, the Prime Minister (perhaps a little resentful of the many signs of the King's popularity, for the whole place was garlanded with flags and banners and thronged with people) was talking with a pleasant cheerfulness to the Court Pashas. Russell Pasha, the Commandant of Police, made a fine figure in his uniform, his tarboosh adding about 4 inches to his 6 feet 3 inches. Soon the Regency Council arrived, Prince Mohamed Ali with Aziz Izzet Pasha, followed by the king's uncle Cherif Pasha. The usual salaams and hand-shaking followed. Prince Mohamed Ali, never at a loss for words, was soon going from one person to another, finally lighting on Nahas, with whom he seemed to be exchanging confidences. Was Nahas complaining of the King's popularity? There seems perhaps to be the beginnings of a dangerous rivalry between the King and Nahas Pasha: the latter is very jealous of the former, who perhaps is dominated more by his father's pre-Treaty conception of the Monarch rather than what it is in form now, namely a constitutional one. It is important therefore that he give his Premier the impression that they are engaged on a common task.

The Prince wears his tarboosh on one side at a rakish angle, has silvery side-whiskers, a white moustache, and generally has an air of Turkish distinction, that practically no Egyptian can boast. Aziz Izzet looks, and is, a courtly Turkish gentleman with European manners and a touch of nobility about him. He might be found any day in a London Club and taken for an old-established member. Cherif Pasha is said to have a sturdy common-sense: he does not look distinguished and resembles his sister the Queen in having a row of large protruding upper teeth.

The next wave of cheering heralded the arrival of the Queen, accompanied by the four Princesses, all dressed alike in white turned-back hats and grey tweed coats and white stockings. The Queen wore an ugly brown velvet hat, and an undistinguished coat and skirt. She smiled and shook hands unaffectedly.

Amidst tremendous cheers, hand clapping and shrill cries from the women, the third batch of red cars with their motor cyclist outriders drove up, and the King descended followed by Hassanein Pasha. He stood to attention for the Egyptian National Anthem and then shook hands with the Regents, the Prime Minister and the local notabilities and went on board, followed by the suite. We started almost at once.

Every village seemed to have poured out its whole population on to the banks, which were gaily decorated with flags and a few arches. Those Arabs who had horses brought them down to the bank, and, carrying a flag on the end of a lance or a stick, followed the yacht along the shore, their horses leaping and prancing about and occasionally breaking into a wild gallop along the mud or sand. There were a few camels too, trotting with their impudent, superior look upon the shore while their riders waved their pennants. And, at each place, the crowd, arrayed at first in some species of order, schoolboys in one place, girls in another, women again in another, ranged in a continuous line upon the bank, went wild as the yacht passed, broke their ranks and, still shouting, ran some of them half-a-mile or a mile along the bank keeping level with us.

The King's tour is technically 'unofficial', but four large paddle steamers and two motor launches are required to carry the large party that accompanies him. One boat contains a whole detachment of the Royal Bodyguard, which arrives first at every place and forms a Guard of Honour. Another has two Under-Secretaries and the Government representatives on board. A boat precedes the flotilla up river with the Chief Irrigation Officer of the Nile on board marking out the course. Another boat carries cows and gemoosses for milk.

The boats travelled by day and anchored every night. It was very cold at night and froze hard, leaving the top decks with a layer of ice on them in the early morning. Even in the day time, the temperature was low out of the sun, and the following north wind kept the boats cool. Among Sir Edward Ford's companions on board were

his co-professor, Ahmed Bey Youssef; Mourad Mohsen Pasha, Keeper of the Privy Purse; Hassanein Pasha, Comptroller of the Household; the King's physician, a common-looking little fat man, but genial enough, Dr. Kafrawi by name; and Omar Fathi Bey, the chief A.D.C. Their minds are filled with few thoughts except those of preferment, and the main, if not the sole, preoccupation of these Court officials is that they shall not do, nor seem to do, anything which could possibly offend His Majesty. Few of them have much work to do, and still fewer have any recreation or hobby. They are very courteous, at least to those who have any chance of being useful to them. The sycophancy that is the order of every day is repugnant to a European: but with them it is almost a necessity. This accounts for the loathsome familiarity of the King's personal servants.

The 'Household' contains two barbers. Their duty is, every alternate day to shave H.M. One was appointed by King Fuad to look after the young Prince, who began shaving at thirteen or fourteen. Nobody is ill, except the Queen who has need of radiological treatment. But there are three doctors on board, and one chemist, besides two sailor assistants, who sit and dispense with him. Of the two tutors, the Arabic one occasionally gives His Majesty a lesson, and more regularly the Princesses. I am never asked to do anything! Every other night His Majesty has a cinema performance on his deck. Only Mourad Mohsen Pasha, Hassanein Pasha, Dr. Kafrawi and Omar Fathi Bey have ever been invited to join the Royal party for such entertainment.

At Beni Souef the King left the ship as usual on a red carpet up steps specially built for the occasion, through a triumphal arch, into his scarlet Rolls-Royce, and drove off amid wild cheering from a

crowd that had now lost any semblance of order. Equally voci-
ferous was the host that awaited His Majesty's arrival at the ground
where the Fête was to be held. Two special pavilions had been
erected there, one for the Queen and Princesses and their Harem,
and the other for His Majesty. After the National Anthem was
played there was the usual scramble for places among the retinue.

The Fête Sportive consisted of boxing bouts, fencing, gym-
nastics, running races, scout marches and a form of fencing with
sticks common in Upper Egypt and Soudan. This was a most
picturesque sport, two men in turbans and gallabias of different
blues walking round each other at a distance of about five yards
and brandishing their sticks in the air, and suddenly sinking to a
'knees-bend' position, and continuing to stalk each other menac-
ingly round an imaginary circle. The object for the striker is the
other man's head, and doubtless many have been broken in the
process. One will aim at the head of the other who defends himself
by holding his stick with both hands above his head and warding
off the blow. The performance is accompanied by much waving of
the arms and flowing of the gallabias.

At the end of the performance the two Mudirs (Governors) of
the adjacent provinces of Beni Souef and Faiyyoum were preparing
to assemble their 'Notables' to present them to the King. These
latter, except for the Sheikhs, who are dressed in their turbans and
long flowing gallabias, were all dressed in the ceremonial dress of
a redingote and tarboosh. But they had not counted with the mob,
which had been gradually encroaching on to the field and had
almost rendered impossible the race of one mile round the course.
As soon as they expected that the king would go, they rushed on to
the ground, swept among the scouts who were formed up before
His Majesty and surrounded the Royal Box. Even the stand, where
I had been sitting with the notables, was invaded, my feet trod
upon, my shoulders used as a support and my tarboosh crushed. A
cloud of suffocating dust arose from the stampede and His Majesty
was only able to move away, when, with a desperate courage, some
soldiers, of whom there were far too few in attendance, by beating
about wildly with their sticks, cleared a space in front of the box. . . .

The boat was put in turmoil one evening by two extraordinary
whims of His Majesty. He sent down one of his servants to the
Captain and Engineer and told them that he wanted two things
done in his bathroom. The first was that, in the lavatory, a permanently open ventilator should be changed into one which he could
manipulate at will, by strings, so as to open or shut it. The other
was that, instead of having a hot and cold tap for his bath, he
should have one tap only, connected with both the hot and cold
pipes, so that he could obtain the mixture he required by simply
turning one lever, as in most shower-baths. This may be easy
enough to do at short notice in a palace at Cairo but in a boat on the
Nile late at night, it is not so quickly done. Some patchwork

arrangement was fixed up by the Chief Engineer and his two assistants (all three Englishmen), but the result was not successful and two days later water was leaking from the Royal deck right through into ours, from pipes which had burst through undue pressure after being stopped.

One morning the boat procession ran across a flight of duck. Farouk stopped the yacht and went off in a launch after them with Colonel Omar Fathi Bey and Hussein Sabri Pasha. It was then about noon, the duck were flying high, there was a lot of steam craft on the river and shouting groups of people on the banks, so he had little hope of shooting. Ford then recalled an interview he had had with King Farouk four days previously when he told His Majesty that

> the report published in the newspapers, and obviously given to them, that he had brought down 208 duck on his first duck shoot (more than any of the really good shots who were out with him, and 65 more than Sir Miles Lampson, a highly experienced gun) was not being believed in Cairo, and that it would be much better if he did not try to bluff but trusted more to his natural modesty and simplicity to impress people. Farouk's answer was that he was not sure of the 8 but that he himself had certainly shot 200 with his own gun! The facts apparently are that, shooting very well for a beginner, he brought down 40 or 50 duck but that there were two or three good Bedouin shots behind him who put the rest into his bag.

Farouk was not a good sportsman, and used special aids such as rapid fire repeating or magazine guns to promote good results. When off form he was known to throw valuable fowling pieces into the lagoon.

> At another riverside stop the King visited a cotton ginnery factory. As we were driving to the factory, two or three Bedouins with their wild Arab horses (which they ride beautifully) dashed along by the side of the cars, knocking one of the motor-cycle escort off his cycle and kicking over a policeman who was trying to keep the crowd back. The way they dashed at full gallop in between the procession of cars, waving sticks, kicking a mudguard here or a buffer there, but apparently under control, was a wonderful, if rather alarming sight. Less pleasant was the slaughter at the roadside of three bullocks. They lie there, with their legs tied, until the King passes, when their keepers slit their throats and practically sever their heads. As we passed their jugular veins were spouting blood and all their gullets were open, while there was still just enough life in their legs for them to be making a despairing kick. . . .

His Majesty came to lunch today. He was cheerful and friendly: I sat on his left. He is not easy to talk to, as he is apt to interrupt any conversation with puns and jokes. He likes also to make an 'impression' rather than to talk naturally. He is at his best chaffing or talking lightly on current things, but he does not evince much personal interest in the people to whom he talks. I commented on the palm branches twisted into arches, which the villagers had erected in his honour on the bank. He said it was like 'Palm Sunday', and then asked if I had ever heard of 'Ice Cream Sundae'! Towards the end of the meal, in boyish mood, he made Mourad Mohsen Pasha, who was sitting on his right, turn away from him on some pretext, and then picked the handkerchief out of his pocket.

Mallawi. Before lunch, a performance of wild-looking but obviously controlled, galloping was given by local Bedouin riders. A large square was cleared between the Museum and the tents where the royal party was to lunch, across the middle of which these horsemen dashed at full gallop on gaily caparisoned horses, which pulled up within a few yards, just in front of the people. They ride in iron stirrups with wide flat bottoms, which look like shovels or scoops: their saddles are backed, so that it is difficult to fall backwards (although one rearing horse threw its rider). Their bridles are festooned with decorative balls of wool or similar stuff. After these spectacular dashes, they began to dance, each horse in turn following the drummer, who can get him to dance and prance, throwing his head the while, and can even make him sit down on his haunches and finally on all four legs. Two or three men with pipes play the same air monotonously for some ten minutes, an air of some two or three phrases only, but the drummer keeps up a vigorous rhythm beating his big drum with a stick enveloped in cloth, while there is also a man who plays a small drum. Now two of the horsemen raise their sticks and begin a mock fight, rather like the stick-fighting of the Soudanese on foot. The horses prance round, and, when the sticks clash, one of them rears, the rider is thrown and there are many cheers.

A picturesque ceremony occurred after luncheon when a local saint, an old man in sheikh's clothes and a long beard, was presented to the King. He has a considerable reputation in the locality as a savant and 'a religious' (in the Old English phrase) and, as he was brought up the King went to meet him, a gesture that was tremendously appreciated by the crowd. The sheikh then recited the Fatha, or the opening of the Koran, to the King, prayed for blessings upon him, extending his hands as if to receive them from heaven, while at the end I saw that Hassanein and those few who were immediately near made a gesture like washing the face in receipt of the sheikh's benediction. Then the King embraced him upon both shoulders, and, amidst great cheers shook hands and said farewell. When the old man rejoined the crowd to be taken back to his house, everyone crowded round to touch his hands and receive some of his heavenly blessing and he could hardly be got away in a car for the throng. His Majesty had played his part with a simplicity and dignity, which was wholly charming, and it must have made a big impression on the people there.

Manfalout, Friday 8th *January.* In the morning, long talk with Hassanein Pasha. We have many talks together, as I sit next to him for most meals and his reminiscences of Oxford are a delight to me. He has a quick wit, great courtesy, an interest in all subjects, and is a quite unusual type of Egyptian. Slim, sharply featured, with a sallow colour and grey hair brushed straight back from a high forehead, he has an unmistakably Bedouin look. There is said to be Scottish blood in his ancestry, and this makes him fairer than most Egyptians. He has keen, penetrating eyes, never looks sleepy, and has an air of refinement that the coarse looking Egyptian type entirely lacks. He has never had political inclinations, and, though he is a firm believer in Egypt's right to govern herself and a fervid Moslem, he is quite without that aggressive conceit which marks other ambitious men in this country. Although his culture and his intellect are occidental, his mentality and nature are of the east. He has an eastern courtesy, and, in conversation, an eastern way of leading you off the path you have selected by a sympathetic evasiveness. I found this, this morning when I went to him to tell him of a talk I had had a few days previously with His Majesty in which I had frankly told the King some ways in which I thought he was failing. (The chief grievance was his unpunctuality. I also urged the folly of trying to bluff, to create a bubble reputation, which sooner or later must burst. His Majesty did not like my saying these things, told me he would not have allowed me to say them if he had known me less well, and denied strongly that he had ever bluffed.) Hassanein seemed to approve what I had said, though he suggested that it was no good talking like that to His Majesty now. His Majesty *was* King, and must be coaxed and wheedled: one must appeal to his pride, to his good sense, rather than reprove or admonish him. The Pasha had sometimes had to do so, but he had now found 'a more excellent way'. The Pasha himself was insecure of his position: he thought it likely that His Majesty would reject one who had had to act, so to speak, as his schoolmaster, especially when the inevitable intrigues started. The King, he told me, was very elusive, and often could not be found even in the palace. He receives most of his information and gossip, even on political matters, from his Berberine servants. He was no longer a boy, and had become a King. And he had the idea that a King must be perfect: therefore he must not be 'found out'. That is why he must have the reputation of doing everything. His people expected that. No one must be allowed to prick the bubble.

As to my job, I complained that I had never been given an opportunity even of trying to do it. I neither lived in the Palace nor saw the King more than once or twice a week if I was lucky. Hassanein showed a certain sympathy, and told me that His Majesty intended to go first to Switzerland at the end of February and then to England. I expressed the hope that he would not travel with too large an entourage, and that in England he would meet young men of university age so that he could always be able to claim among them friends, when he came to England. You never 'get' much out of Hassanein, who makes no promises but is an extraordinarily quick, sympathetic and adroit responder to complaints. But at lunch-time, when we had been talking for over two hours, I felt I had advanced a step.

The tour lasted a month and took Farouk as far south as Aswan. Everywhere he was greeted by crowds, children put on gymnastic displays, officials and their wives put on their best clothes and manner, tea with officials was complemented by dinner with the King on board his yacht, Farouk toured the sites of antiquities and ordered his car to slow through the crowds. He never left without a message of thanks and a donation to the poor of the place. "Touching quantities of cheap flags had been hung across the road and the mosques and any respectable building had been illuminated, the whole place was *en fête*, and occasionally a stray 'Vive Le Roi' would be shouted for sheer joy."

A month later the all white Royal train ran slowly into Cairo from Aswan at the end of the tour. This had been Queen Nazli's first opportunity for freedom since her husband had died. Her Chamberlain Hassanein had been with her throughout the tour. The ladies-in-waiting took turns to accompany her and the first of them to return to Cairo was asked by a senior princess whether the Queen Mother was well. "I have never seen Her Majesty so well or so happy," said this lady, with more frankness than tact. "She is radiant and dances every night."

In this year, 1937, Nasser entered the Military College where he was noted for his "exemplary conduct, his self-reliance and his serious outlook . . . his outspokenness and his rebellion against colonialism".

Chapter 4

My Beloved People
(July 1937—1939)

In April 1937 Farouk returned to Europe, this time accompanied by his four younger sisters and Queen Nazli, to see some of the places he had had to miss when last there. He went to stay at the house where he had received the news of his father's death a year before, Kenry House on Kingston Hill. Much had happened in that year and it must have seemed a very different atmosphere to a seventeen-year-old, responsible King who had left the place as a sixteen-year-old schoolboy.

Edward Ford, still attached to King Farouk as English tutor, accompanied the Royal Party and initiated much of the tour of England. The author is indebted to Sir Edward for allowing him to quote further extracts from an account which he wrote at the time:

We left Egypt on 27th February on the P. & O. Liner *Viceroy of India*. The whole suite consisted of thirty-two persons, bringing 7 tons of luggage and over 250 pieces—this excluding what had been sent on direct by sea to England. The King kept himself largely to himself and his servants—up on the Captain's bridge where he was berthed. (He had the captain's quarters.) He behaved well—though he was very restless, and liked wandering alone all over the ship, and on to the second and third class decks, particularly when dancing was on in the evening. The Queen walked about the decks as any ordinary passenger might—hoping to see the gay life, dancing etc. of which she had often heard and read, but never tasted.

At Marseilles the King was presented with a beautiful pair of skis by an old merchant who had done trade with Egypt. They still retain their virginity, for, during three weeks at St. Moritz, he never once put them on. He went about three times on the ice-rink, but had no sooner learnt to stand up on his skates than he refused the help of his admirable instructor, and made an absurd sight 'scooting' along on his right foot. He once rode in the snow, spending much of the time snowballing two girls who were riding with us. Snowballing in fact was the only winter sport which he indulged to any extent—and this was done indiscriminately, at Hassanein Pasha, at his Berberine servants, at the Swiss Minister, and Maitre d'hôtel and any girls in the party—particularly on any expeditions which he undertook by car, by train or sleigh. Instead of spending his time on snow or ice, he would lie in bed till lunch-time, and then go out in his car in the afternoon to the village and buy watches, medals etc. at jewellers' shops in and around St. Moritz, have a large tea at one of the Conditorei cafés, and come back to the hotel to play at the gambling machines, where a 'lucky dip' produces a briquette or a watch. He must have spent quite a sum on those machines, and had shelves full of these fairly worthless trophies. He rarely lunched before 2.15 or dined before 9.45. Most of the suite would wait religiously for two hours or so, often to be told at the end that he had dined upstairs! Hassanein almost confined his attentions to the Queen, and the King took the doctor, the A.D.C. and his Arabic tutor as his chosen companions, in that order of favouritism. Always too he had a detective, and his private cinematographer.

After dinner, the King and his mother would adjourn to the bar where there was dancing. This they both enjoyed, especially the Gala nights, which later became frequent, when little puff-balls were distributed, which the King spent hours in throwing at the other guests, particularly at any girl with whom he wishes to dance. Unfortunately, he showed poor taste in his choice and his friendships led to a good deal of gossip in the hotel. I can think of little good that our visit to St. Moritz did, except to the little princesses, who entered into the winter sports with spirit and enjoyed every minute of it.

I tried to enlist the support of his uncle Hussein Sabry Pasha, as one who clearly had a certain position with the King, not to flatter him but to speak to him frankly, to encourage him to be punctual and to be careful whom he became friendly with; but his answer was, frankly enough, that, though he was the King's uncle, he was his guest on this trip, and clearly could not say that sort of thing. Hassanein was little more helpful, but as usual, dilated on his own difficulties, saying that at the moment the King did not want even *his* advice. I told him frankly that had it not been that we were going to England where I thought I might be of some positive use I would resign at once. The King refused all encouragement to take part in winter sports, stayed up late at night with worthless companions, and could never get up in the morning. It seemed to me that the quicker we got to England the better, and I urged Hassanein not to delay. He agreed, but immediately proceeded to arrange a long programme of Swiss visits. The technique of Hassanein is simple and effective. He always agrees, sympathises and combines with what one says. Had he not the same difficulties with the King himself? But he avoids giving any promises or apparently taking any positive action.

I suggested to him that, if he were really in agreement with me about certain aspects of the King's life (as was Sabry Pasha), then we three might go together to His Majesty, and say to him that unless he really acted upon our advice, we would no longer be responsible for him and would tender our resignations from his suite. This suggestion received scant consideration.

The next three weeks we frittered away in Geneva, Berne and Zurich. The King started to buy medals and coins, at first indiscriminately by weight, but later with a little discretion, and watches too, and the hotel foyer bristled with a crowd of men, who were partly detectives, and partly dealers. From what I gathered there were not lacking intermediaries between the King and the dealers who demanded commissions on what he bought.

In Switzerland, M. Martin was attached to the King by the Federal Government, in his capacity as Swiss Minister in Turkey and Egypt, to show Switzerland to their Majesties. He arranged a full programme of events, but nearly lost his reason as he saw them one by one postponed, cancelled, shortened or altered. The King was booked to visit a chocolate factory from Berne one afternoon. He cancelled the visit at luncheon time on the grounds of tiredness, but spent the afternoon in looking over two other buildings in Berne itself with full publicity. At two other factories, visits timed for 10.30 and 11.0 were fulfilled so late that the workmen had to be kept on beyond their luncheon hour at noon, with a promise of double pay—and at one of them, only after a speech of encouragement had been made to them by the managing director. At the Swiss Cavalry School, where he was forty minutes late, the band got their own back by playing the Egyptian National Anthem over five times in succession and keeping him at attention for some three or four minutes!

During this time, the King, except for these various expeditions, kept himself to his rooms in the hotels. There he sorted his medals and coins, ate chocolates, fed at his own times and was generally inaccessible to his staff. Only the doctor was invited in; only Hassanein had the right to enter. Queen Nazli grew increasingly worried about him. After asking for it for nine days, I finally managed to get a talk with her, in which I urged that we should get quickly to England. As a result I left Switzerland with instructions to make certain preparations for the King's visit, but not to make any definite arrangements.

It had been arranged for the Queen to be at Ballardcombe with the princesses, while the King was at Kenry House. But she insisted on being with the King, and the small Kenry House had to be stretched to contain Queen, lady-in-waiting, maid etc. as well as the King's immediate entourage. This only lasted some ten days (during which the Queen had four different beds) before the journey up and down to London became too tiring for her, and she took up quarters in the Egyptian Embassy.

The King made a poor start by refusing, on the grounds of an engagement, an invitation from Lord Derby to his box at Epsom for the Spring Meeting, on the second day after his arrival. He had, and would make, no engagements at that time, and spent the afternoon in his bedroom. He also refused an offer from Sir Philip Sassoon of hearing and even viewing the coronation ceremony on television and watching the procession from his house in Park Lane. He seemed to think that, if as a monarch, he couldn't be in the Abbey, he would not be anywhere else as a private individual The result of it was that the whole party, twenty-five strong, including the little princesses, who were blissfully happy in their garden and on their horses in Richmond Park, moved to Paris for a week over the coronation period.

Little had happened in the three weeks before their departure to Paris. The King had attended several auction sales, in which, under the name of his detective Dyer, he used to bid personally for such lots as struck his fancy. He tried several cars, and paid visits to antique dealers, tea shops, and theatres. He saw over the Mint, and I arranged for him to hear most of a criminal trial at the Old Bailey where he lunched with the judge (Lord Finlay) and the Alderman and the Sheriff in waiting. (A man and his wife were charged with the manslaughter of their two infant children.) He showed a keen interest in the trial and stayed on the bench by the judge's side for the whole afternoon.

With his mother he was the guest of the Government at the Naval Review. There he caused some ill-will by keeping all the distinguished guests waiting a quarter of an hour for him before dinner—at the end of which time a message arrived that he was dining in his cabin. It was thought that he might be feeling ill, but that impression was at once dispelled when at the end of dinner he was found changed and cheerful on the deck.

Two weekends were arranged for the King at the express request of the Secretary of State for Foreign Affairs—at Wilton with the Pembrokes and at Boughton with the Buccleuchs. The Wilton weekend was an undoubted success, for he impressed the older people there with his gaiety and spontaneity, but it was noticeable that he did not feel really at ease with his male contemporaries. At Boughton, where the Foreign Secretary and Mrs. Eden were themselves guests, he behaved most inconsiderately in suddenly deciding to go for a swim some twelve miles away at 8 o'clock in the evening. Dinner for the whole party, including the Foreign Secretary, was put off for an hour and a half, and a good deal of trouble caused to his host and hostess.

The Queen insisted on coming to both of these weekend parties. They were originally arranged for the King to meet contemporaries. But the Queen got the idea that Hassanein was conspiring to estrange the King from her: and there was a very real danger at one time that the King would cancel his acceptance of both invitations. However, both the hostesses graciously asked the Queen as well, and her charm undoubtedly gained admirers and she in no way interfered with the King's pleasure. In fact, her influence with him now, though perhaps greater than that of anyone else, is very remote.

I had always hoped, and had often suggested that the King might spend at least one term as an undergraduate at a British University —preferably Oxford, since both Hassanein and I had been there and knew several of the dons etc. I had received from Mr. H. A. L. Fisher, the Warden of New College, an intimation that he would be very glad to have him there, if I would accompany him. As a whole term was now out of the question the Warden agreed to a fortnight's residence. I enlisted the support of the Egyptian Ambassador, and wrote to Hassanein, when he was in Paris, to tell him of the possibility. But the Pasha was unable, or unwilling, to help, and it was only with some difficulty and at only two days notice that he finally was induced to give instructions for a three-day tour of England to include both the old universities, Stratford-on-Avon, and Birmingham.

The first visit was to Cambridge. At 3.30 the King set off by car from London with (as usual) his servants and detective. Hassanein and I were to follow immediately—but the Pasha had not yet told me what our plans were at Cambridge. At 3.35 the Queen decided that she would accompany the King. She had not been asked and was not expected at any of the places which we were to visit. As she was unable to stand the strain of a car journey, we had to go by train, and there was no train before 5.30 which we could catch. The Pasha, either to obtain or pay out money, said that he had first to go to Kingston and left. The lady-in-waiting was by now almost broken down by strain and weariness, and excused herself from coming. The maid had not packed. The detective spent an hour on the telephone reserving carriages and accommodation at the hotels, and only the Queen and I arrived in time to catch the train. At 5.45 the Vice-Chancellor (in bands, cap and gown) was standing at the gate of his College ready to welcome the King of Egypt to Cambridge. Thus robed and thus ready he stood—for one and three-quarter hours, till 7.30, when the King drove up. The comedy, or tragedy, derived its point from the fact that for once the King *had* arrived in Cambridge on time but he had neither Hassanein nor me with him and no conception of what had delayed us or that the Queen was following him. He had spent his time buying puppies and we found him in a hotel.

This was a not untypical example of the way in which our arrangements, if they could be called such, were made and executed. One must say in fairness that nobody could show greater ability to pretend that nothing untoward had occurred than the King. However late, he would enter smiling, and engage with men as formidable as Lord Rutherford in easy, friendly conversation. I believe that the Vice-Chancellor completely forgot the inconveniences and difficulties in the presence of so much youthful charm and acumen. The King behaved well at Cambridge, showed great interest in the Museum and Library, and left the impression behind of a precociously intelligent young man. It was amusing to hear him pretend here, as at Eton also, that he had actually been at Woolwich. On being shown an undergraduate's rooms, he said, "Ha, very comfortable, nothing like the bare rooms we lived in at Woolwich."

From Cambridge to Stratford-on-Avon, where he was given loud cheers. They 'held' the play ten minutes for him, but he was a good twenty minutes late for it. He went round behind the scenes afterwards, said nice, simple commendatory words about the play *Cymbeline* "which", he added, "I thought exceedingly dull when I read it: but you made it most interesting". I don't think he had ever even heard its name before that night. Next day the party drove to Oxford.

I was becoming rather anxious about two new characteristics of the King: first, his careless indifference to his mother: secondly, his association with his servants (his detective, valet etc). And on this drive, we came upon him at Woodstock having tea in a small 'pub' with his valet, his chauffeur and his detective. I talked to Hassanein about it. Hassanein said that it was one of his greatest worries, that he had even challenged the King with it and asked him why he preferred his servants' company, and he had replied, "They don't nag at me." It was a repellent sight to see him slapping his Italian valets on the back, or to find them meekly submitting to having their tongues painted with black ink by him before going in fancy dress to a Servants' Ball at Kingston. And I determined on a suitable occasion to tell him of the dangers of encouraging those who might try to exert influence without having any responsibility. At the moment, it is probably true to say that he enjoys himself more in his rooms and with his books (though he doesn't read them) and medals, and in the company of his servants than, in that of his family or his chosen advisers.

At Oxford, apart from keeping the Vice-Chancellor waiting half an hour for him in the lounge of the Randolph Hotel, the King behaved well and showed a similarly intelligent interest as he had at Cambridge. In the afternoon, he went up the Cherwell in a canoe with Mr. Longden, Senior Censor of Christ Church, while Hassanein punted the Queen with the President of Magdalen and his wife!

In company, the King asks intelligent questions, and makes continual jokes of a mainly poor quality. He shows far more knowledge than one would expect him to have, and he has a very accurate memory. He talks mainly of himself, in rather boastful terms, occasionally telling stories of exploits as imaginary, though not so highly fantastic, as those of Baron Munchausen. He makes the occasional mistake of 'telling the expert', as with the fingerprint specialist at Scotland Yard, but generally with knowledgeable people he deals well. With his contemporaries, bluff does not succeed, and I think he feels aware of it. His great efforts to establish himself as a man of the world who knows and has seen life do not carry great conviction with younger people.

During a full day at Eton, the King was shown over the school buildings by the Provost and Headmaster, took great interest in a small collection of Egyptian antiquities in the library (to which he has since added some books), watched the Eight practise and a cricket game on Upper Club, had tea alone with two boys, heard the organ with much interest, and finally received the cheers of the whole school which was assembled for Absence. It was a most successful day.

He paid visits to Buckingham Palace for luncheon and Marlborough House to be received by Queen Mary, and went on a fine spring day to Wembley, together with the King and Queen, to see Sunderland beat Preston North End in the Cup Final. When he went with his mother to listen to questions in the House of Commons, he asked to see the Library but was told that while the House is sitting only Members of Parliament are allowed in the Library, with no exception. However, in the House of Lords he was able to spend some time examining the treasures of the Peers' Library.

I doubt if it can be said [Ford wrote] that Farouk's visit to England has left him many friends here. He does not seem to me to have the capacity for making friendships easily, or to appreciate that they involve a give-and-take. He has, however, had the chance of becoming acquainted with a very great variety of people.

With me he became very friendly towards the end of his time here in England, but I became simultaneously aware of a good deal of hostility, or possibly jealousy, among his Court towards me. Even so, he would very rarely ask me to accompany him alone to anything, and I had terribly few opportunities of talking to him alone for any length of time. Thus it was extremely difficult to let him know directly of any criticism to which he was becoming exposed except through Hassanein. Hassanein's eyes are on the future, and I think he dislikes doing even the gentle amount of scolding which he can hardly avoid. He was largely preoccupied with the Queen, who liked to have him as her escort to a theatre and restaurant almost every night.

When summing up what he had done for Farouk Ford admitted it amounted to little.

Perhaps the most that I could say is that I am aware that he feels a little restraint in my presence, and I think he believes that I am working disinterestedly for him. In England, he even began to disregard his favourite 'Yes-men' a good deal, and it would be difficult now to point to anyone who has much influence over him.

The Queen is being hard pressed, she told me, to provide a mistress or mistresses for the King. I suggested to her that she would do better to wait until he is a little older, when she had much better help him to choose a good Queen. At the moment, the King is only just beginning to appreciate female charm.

At sixteen years of age (Sir Edward Ford recalled for the author) Farouk was a mixture of a boy of ten and a man of twenty-two, and one never knew which would emerge predominant. He liked to present himself as someone with wide experience of life, and disliked it when the illusion was exposed. Once, when Ford noticed a row of silver cups laid out in a room of the Palace and inquired what they were he replied, "Oh, just a few trophies I won for sporting events, when I was young." Ford noticed a price tag in each of them; they had been sent by a jeweller for him to select one to give as a prize to the Alexandria Yacht Club. "Ah, I had you nicely there," said Farouk with considerable aplomb.

On another occasion he asked Ford to admire a new tie which he was wearing. Ford said he thought it handsome, but "too loud". About a month later, Ford appeared at the palace wearing an I Zingari tie. "That really *is* too loud," said the King. When Ford gave him a piece of English oratory to read as practice for a public occasion, he took the book to the end of a big hall in the palace and read it in a loud, clear voice. Ford commended him. Farouk said, "That was very good, I liked that. I liked it very much—especially the bit about 'Let the best man win'." Ford murmured something about that particular phrase being something of a cliché, but Farouk insisted that he recognize its merit. "I'm so glad that you thought it good," said Ford. "It is very good," persisted Farouk. "Don't you agree?" "Well, all right, yes," said Ford, anxious not to discourage this newly found enthusiasm on the part of his pupil. "I'm glad you agree," said Farouk with a smile, "because I put it in myself!"

Such incidents were endearing, more so than the glee with which Farouk would turn the hose-pipe on his tutor as he was dressing after a swim. As to his actual tuition, this took the form of reading together in English, H. G. Wells's *History of the World*, Hendrik van Loon's books, etc., and then getting Farouk to write a precis or short essay on the passage. But the pupil was expert at diversions. He would press a bell under his desk and a servant would appear and be told to bring sweet drinks or chocolates or perhaps one or two specimens from one of his incipient collections—anything to create a distraction.

Farouk left Europe again on 20th July 1937 having, among other experiences, had his first taste of gambling and continental night life. *The Times* reported thus: "The King of Egypt left Marseilles last night for Alexandria in the Egyptian steamer *El Nil*, after having been officially seen off by the authorities."

Five days later, and three days before he was due officially to ascend the throne, Farouk arrived at Alexandria after five months away. Coastguard ships, aeroplanes of the Egyptian Army and a host of small craft came out to meet his steamer which docked at 8 a.m. Twenty-one guns fired, hooters and sirens honked and screeched and welcoming thousands broke into a storm of charging and cheering. "Egypt", it was reported then "is making great preparations for Thursday's celebrations, and it is already evident that the country intends to give proof of intense love for and pride in the young monarch, who has already captured the imagination of his subjects." Cairo continued to prepare for what in Europe would be called a coronation; in Egypt there was no crown and no religious ceremony, but a simple parliamentary procedure when the King would stand before both Houses of Parliament to take his Oath of Loyalty to the Constitution which would then authorize him to rule the country, having reached his majority at eighteen lunar years. Lunar years being eleven days shorter than solar years means he was seventeen and a half at the time.

The city had never seen anything like it: two million people took advantage of fare reductions to descend on Cairo by train, steamer, felucca, bus, camels and donkeys. For three days Cairo's population was tripled; tons of mutton and beef were roasted and given out in the city parks. Prices of food and drink rose sharply, the stall proprietors soon appreciating the fast piastres to be made from their visiting country cousins. All the illuminations were lit on the evening before, as a test, and the brilliant spectacle exceeded all expectations. Visiting Arabs attempted to control their nervous horses among the diplomatic limousines and the gharries in the town.

Nahas Pasha made arrangements for the accession ceremony. At one stage it was suggested Farouk should wear the golden fillet which was once worn by Tutankhamen, discovered in 1922 in the Valley of the Kings. However, the Egyptian people, when they were the subjects of Turkey, had grown accustomed to seeing each new Sultan invested with the sword,—"A Caliph dies— not one man weeps, or cares. Another takes his room—not one is glad"—the sword of Osman girded on him by the head of the Mavlevi Dervishes. Accordingly Nahas decided to use the jewelled sword of Mohamed Ali but although all possible corners were searched it could not be found. Nahas Pasha's contribution to the arrangements were eventually made, a red limousine for himself and a gold coach for Farouk. Cairo went crazy with decoration. Triumphal arches spanned the main streets and the Egyptian national green bedecked the buildings, the flags of Egypt, green with a white crescent and three white stars. The town of Beni Souef, a hundred miles away, selected twelve good runners to carry an address to the King.

At about 6 a.m. on 20th July 1937 detachments of infantry who were to line the route began arriving from their barracks at Abbassieh and the city was filled with the noise of bands and marching feet and a great stirring of the thousands who had slept out in the parks and on the pavements all night. By the time the distant booming of guns announced that the King had left the Abdin Palace every available vantage point was taken.

Queen Nazli wore a magnificent white dress and was only semi-veiled, and the princesses, the oldest of whom was sixteen and the youngest seven, looked charming in simple white frocks and large white hats. Wearing a uniform of red, white and green and grasping the baton of field marshal, King Farouk rode to the *Barlman* Parliament in his coach, flanked by barefoot runners and Royal Guards in their white, blue and gold uniforms and red fezes. The temperature was 104°F.

The ceremony at the Chamber of Deputies was timed for 9 a.m. Inside, where an air conditioner had fortunately been installed, it was cool, and bright with the assembling audience. On the ground floor were the Senators and Deputies, the politicians of Egypt, of whom it has been said, to quote John

Marlowe, "personalities are more important than policies and personal jealousies more powerful than party loyalties". Some of them gained office by buying votes for anything from 25 piastres to £2 a piece and, once in office in this building, practised their politics in such a hubbub that the satirist Jarvis was induced to write rules for their behaviour, one of which stated that "not more than twenty-five members shall address the House at one time". Most wore official evening dress but some were in Arab robes, almost all wearing the bright green sash of the Order of the Nile. In the first gallery the British Ambassador and Lady Lampson (she hardly reached to his shoulder in height) headed the Diplomatic Corps, the uniforms and dresses made a colourful display amidst which only the scarlet coat and white plumes of a British major-general, and the white and gold *hattar* and *ikal* and dull brown kaftan of the Saudi Arabian representatives could be distinguished.

At 8.45 a.m. tremendous cheers, deep shouts of men mingled with the shrill ululations of the women, and the engines of an Egyptian squadron overhead, announced the arrival of the King. Four mounted police officers and a company of police, with white coats and yellow and red pennants, followed by the Egyptian cavalry, more sombre in their khaki uniforms, mounted on chestnut horses; the royal bodyguard in white coats, gold braided, blue breeches with a broad red stripe, and red and blue pennants. The Grand Chamberlain and the Chief of the Royal Khassa, and the Regency Council preceded the royal coach in which Farouk rode beside Nahas Pasha.

Nahas Pasha addressed the assembly in his usual able fashion; "There are days", he began, "which for great occasions . . . are always remembered with great joy and pride . . . His Majesty King Farouk's reign has been an augur of prosperity and happiness to the dear Fatherland . . . during his reign Egypt has achieved her liberty and independence . . . the Capitulations have been abolished . . . Egypt has joined the League of Nations. . . . Such being the prelude to his reign it is therefore no wonder that the people should be hopeful of a happy future full of success and victory. . . ."

On Thursday, 29th July 1937 (Gamadi Al Oula 1356) King Farouk I of Egypt and the Sudan attained his majority and officially ascended the throne, taking the oath "to observe the

Constitution and the laws of the Egyptian people, and to maintain the national independence and the integrity of its territory". In his speech he promised:

> I shall have the interest of the country at heart before all other matters. We are all children of Egypt, and we all belong to the country. We are all her soldiers and her servants, and the King is the first servant of the country. I believe that the greatness of a King can come only from the greatness of his people. And the King must have faith in this and be ready to sacrifice for this. The poor are not responsible for their poverty, but rather the wealthy. Give to the poor what they merit without their asking. A king is a good king when the poor of the land have the right to live, where the sick have the right to be healed, when the timid have the right to be tranquil, and when the ignorant have the right to learn.

Every town in Egypt had been equipped by the Government in recent weeks with a radio loud speaker so that the people for the first time could listen to their King:

> My beloved people, I send you my best greetings and I would have liked to have shaken hands with every one of you, in order to express to you the depth of my gratitude and the profoundness of my love . . . it gives me pleasure on taking up my constitutional powers to announce to you that I have taken upon myself to respect the constitution and the laws of the country . . . I undertake to devote my life and efforts to the service of the country, and to strengthening its power and making its people happy . . . I tell you frankly that the glory of the fatherland necessitates the co-operation of all classes of the people. . . . And if it is Allah's will to lay on my shoulders at such an early age the responsibilities of kingship I, on my part, appreciate the duties that will be mine, and I am prepared for all sacrifices in the cause of my duty. . . . My noble people, I am proud of you and your loyalty, and am as confident in the future as I am in Allah. Let us work together. We shall succeed and be happy. Long live the fatherland.

Accession meant more celebrations for Cairo. Peasants from mud villages stared open-mouthed at the buildings of the city, guns boomed and every pole was draped in green and white. Celebrations continued for three days, Nazli gave a party for wives and daughters, there was a banquet and His Beautitude Anba Youannis, Patriarch of the Coptic Cathedral, gave thanks, Farouk said his prayers at El Rifaii, lunched with the Ulemas and dined with the Prime Minister in Zafaran Palace; and the Egyptian Army was reviewed on the large parade ground at Abbassieh. The poor had received donations, soup at official kitchens, fireworks and music. Farouk then retired to the cool sea breezes of Alexandria.

At this time he might have gone from strength to strength; his reign was founded on a firm basis of good relations with Britain, popularity with his people and a promising marriage. Could anyone at that time have surmised that all these could come to nought? Was youth to be his downfall, or poor or evil counsel from his advisers, or some deficiency in his character? The first year of his reign saw the consolidation of his popularity. He was respected by the politicians, by the professional, commercial and cultural leaders of Egypt; the fellahin liked him. Government buildings, private homes, hotels, bars and shops throughout the land carried his portrait. At that time the Egyptian author Mohamed Altabii wrote of the King, "He acquired admiration and respect for his person, without recourse to his crown. He is intellectually mature, has vast culture, and is well equilibrated in his speeches", and a little later, "The love of the people for Farouk rises daily, and this from a people that has always been disappointed in its leaders. Only one person has not disappointed them, and the entire country has placed its faith in him. That man is Farouk, for in him we find that the interest of Egypt is above all other interests."

At about this time the Moslem Brotherhood became more definitely political. Hassan el Banna, who sent letters of exhortation to Farouk demanding of him a pure life, the dissolution of all political parties and the establishment of an Islamic constitution, described his movement in what were now recognized as his customary eloquent terms: "a salafite movement, an orthodox way, an athletic group, a scientific and cultural society, an economic company and a social idea". He demanded the Koran as the sole code of living, riddance of all foreigners and the freedom of all Arab-speaking people. Forceful speeches were gaining him tens of thousands of idolizing followers. He needed action to realize his ideals and he started collecting arms and hiding them away up and down the country. He began to speak of the *Jihad*, or holy war; Farouk remained unaware of the short, snub-nosed Supreme Guide's real potential.

The political pattern within Egypt was further complicated, it added to its colour by formation of the Wafdist Blue Shirts encouraged by Nahas and the Royalist Green Shirts, youth

movements modelled on Mussolini's Black Shirts, which had one
of their first open street clashes on 26th June 1936. In 1937
Nahas was shot by a Green Shirt, but survived.

On 15th November 1937, before Farouk returned to Cairo
from his summer palace, there were student riots in the Opera
Square between Wafdist supporters and the opposition. Three
days later Farouk inaugurated the first session of a completely
independent Parliament and in his speech from the throne made
a lengthy recital of what his government would do for the
country; the improvement and expansion of the army; better
social services in the provinces; and amelioration of the lot of
the fellahin. Nahas Pasha promised to curb all student demonstrations, whether for or against him, as these were exaggerated
abroad and injured the tourist trade.

In December 1937 *The Times* reported on the ministerial
crisis in Egypt: "There is little doubt that much of the present
tension is due to incompatibility of temperament between the
leading actors on either side and that reciprocal misunder-
standings have been aggravated by deliberately spread misinter-
pretations of the intentions of both parties," and continued,
"It is regarded as more probable that the King will entrust
Dr. Ahmed Maher, President of the Chamber, with the task of
forming a new Cabinet."

On 21st December Makram Ebeid Pasha, Minister of
Finance, narrowly escaped injury in a royalist student riot
outside Abdin Palace; dissensions between Farouk and his
advisers, Nahas and his Cabinet were coming to a head; there
was growing enmity between Farouk and Nahas. The Wafd refused to disband its Blue Shirt student troublemakers; it was plain
to the King that they should go: so soon after independence and
acclamation of Egypt's maturity it became obvious for all to see
that, at heart, those involved in running the country were grind-
ing their own axes: Egypt itself could get along as best it may.

On 23rd December 1937, after an exciting meeting which
began with cries of "With Nahas to the end", a vote of confidence in him as Prime Minister was carried almost unani-
mously, the most important abstainer being Dr. Ahmed Maher.
On 30th December Farouk acted, dismissing Nahas Pasha and
appointing Mohamed Pasha Mahmoud, whose first act was to
disband all coloured-shirt movements, although only three weeks

later the Young Egypt Society, the Green Shirts, violently anti-British and anti-Nahas, held a meeting in Cairo.

On 14th January 1938 there was a picturesque ceremony at Abdin Palace when 127 officers and 2,300 soldiers, representing the Egyptian Army, paraded before the King, mounted on a white Arab stallion, and recited in unison their allegiance, "I swear three times on Allah, his Sacred book, and his prophets, on my faith and honour as a soldier, to be the loyal, faithful servant of His Majesty, our King Farouk the First, and of his government, to obey all his august commands and all his orders... to execute on land, sea, and air, and beyond the borders of the Nile Valley, to be against those who oppose him...."

When Farouk returned from England he still lived with his mother and sisters Fawzia, successful one, Faiza, winner, Faika, extraordinary, and Fathia, good luck charm. Shortly after returning to Cairo, Farouk in his customary style of sudden decision drove fast in an Alfa Romeo to Alexandria and asked Safinaz Zulficar to marry him. She said yes: he was seventeen, she fifteen. The date was set for a year later, 20th January 1938. Early in the engagement Farouk decided to follow the example set by his father of giving all his family names beginning with F, and changed Safinaz's Persian name which meant 'Pure Rose' for an Egyptian name meaning 'the only one', Farida.

It was uncertain what arrangements would be made for the wedding for although there had been a slight relaxation in the strict Moslem practices since the death of Fuad, to have held a fully westernized wedding, with the bride present, and followed by a large reception, would undoubtedly have antagonized local religious leaders and neighbouring Moslem states, particularly the Mijaz and the Yemen.

Few people may witness a Mohamedan wedding, which is more a business contract entered into between groom and bride's father. Farouk waited, in the black and gold field-marshal's uniform, in a small room in Koubbeh Palace. Opposite the King was the bride's father, Judge Youssef Zulficar, vice-president of the Mixed Court of Appeals at Alexandria, in morning coat and red tarboosh. Sheik Mustafa el Maraghi was there to give religious sanction, together with three other sheiks, all in purple robes and white turbans.

The Royal Chamberlain handed the bride's father an envelope

containing a cheque as half of the royal dowry, the other half to be paid in the case of a divorce. The Judge then put out his right hand and pressed thumbs with Farouk while El Maraghi threw a cloth of green silk over the hands. Judge Zulficar offered his daughter, who at this stage, contrary to Moslem tradition, instead of waiting in her father's house, was peering at the ceremony through a grille:

"I betrothe to your Majesty my daughter, Farida." Three times Farouk answered: "I accept her betrothal to myself from thee, and take her under my care and bind myself to offer her my protection, and ye who are present bear witness." Copies of the marriage contract were signed and a white flag was raised on the palace roof as a sign that the bridegroom had shaken hands with his father-in-law. King Farouk descended the palace steps, preceded by tarbooshed pipers. One hundred and one guns began to salute, waiters moved among guests with rose water and honey. Gold caskets and boxes of chocolates were given to the immediate witnesses of the ceremony and a cashmere shawl to El Maraghi.

Farida, still breaking Moslem custom, posed for her photograph, and without a veil, in a flowing white satin wedding gown supplied by Worth of Paris. Nervous pages and bridesmaids fluttered around her while officials at the salute edged in different directions to get a better view.

Many of the dresses were embroidered with precious stones and on the train of one dress a verse of the Koran was embroidered in gold. Farouk gave Farida a three-strand diamond necklace which had been on show at the Paris Exhibition in 1937. Other presents included, from the Suez Canal Company, a silver table service and an antique Turkish watch; from France, a Sèvres porcelain dinner service, tapestries and hand mirror for Farida; from Italy, an alabaster statue of the Emperor Diocletian; from Hitler, a Mercedes-Benz sports coupé; and from Great Britain, a pair of shot guns. King George also sent a complete sports outfit of racquets and golf clubs for the King and magnificent jewellery for the Queen. The Hellenic Minister presented a copy of the head of Queen Berenice of Cyrene, the Consort of Ptolemy III, who ruled in Egypt 247–222 B.C., and invested His Majesty with the Grand Cordon of the Order of the Redeemer. Ataturk sent a solid gold box inset with diamonds, and hand embroidered linen; Arabia sent a 'number' of Arab stallions; the Prime Minister of Egypt presented an ivory tusk mounted on gold; the Princes and Nabils of Egypt gave the Queen a tray of pure gold, goblets inlaid with diamonds, a coffee set of pure gold, a jewelled rosary which once belonged to the Turkish Sultan Abdul Aziz, and the veil of Brussels lace presented by the Empress Eugénie to the three daughters of the Khedive Ismail on the opening of the Suez Canal. The Jewish community gave Farouk a casket containing the Psalms of David inscribed on silver sheets; and the Grand Rabbi opened a fund for the feeding of poor children.

The event recalls Prince Mohamed Ali's description, recorded by Emine Foat Tugay, of his own mother's wedding presents, "In a vast drawing room, the bride's jewels were displayed on cushions of silky scarlet velvet, tiaras, bracelets, earrings and drops, diamond aigrettes and other ornaments, all gold set with the most precious stones, but chiefly with diamonds. . . . Two other large rooms were lined with shelves of various precious stones, goldsmiths' work set with jewels, gold and silver plate glittering with precious stones, censers with shining golden chains, amber mouthpieces for pipes, chubouks in gold and enamel set with diamonds, huge gold and silver trays, some plain, some inlaid with gems, bejewelled lamps, toilet sets with diamond-studded brushes and combs, in short a display of such dazzling magnificence that the spectator was tempted to ask if some Aladdin had not, thanks to his magic lamp laid under contribution, the fabulous treasures of the djinn. . . ."

Cairo had a fairground atmosphere. At Abbassieh the Royal Khassa had erected a marquee where butchers carved meat and cooks prepared bread, rice, soup and sweetmeats for the poor. (A hundred thousand poor people were fed from ten marquees at Farouk's request; between them they consumed 100 tons of meat.) Booths nearby shook and sounded with the concert parties, bands, acrobats and the gulla-gulla men inside.

Bands of young men, shouting, cheering and dancing took up the centre of all roads while bedouins bedecked in finery steered their caparisoned Arab horses through the mob, waving swords and firing volleys into the air. Every water-cart of the Tanzim Department had been painted green for the day; any vehicle that moved was covered in a close wrapping of urchin arms clinging to the sides for free rides. Tram conductors could not board their own vehicles for the crush, youths performed the *dance du ventre* on the roofs. Crowns of cardboard and paper were the motif of the day and by night these shapes were picked out by strings of lights. Opposite the Semiramis Hotel firework rockets shot over the Nile and all its boats, bobbing with up-turned faces. Thomas Cook's vessel and the Anglo-American Nile and Tourist Company's S.S. *Puritan* held receptions on board. The Red Crescent and the Kasr-el-Aini hospitals slowly filled with casualties. All British troops were given a holiday. The Rio Cinema had a huge portrait of the king, crowned, out-lined with six thousand bulbs; the Pharaonic Mail Line erected figures of ancient gods, sixty feet high, handing the King and Queen the Cup of Happiness and the Wine of Life, and fights broke out in the post offices over the commemorative postage stamps when stocks ran out: celebrations, excesses on all sides.

Queen Nazli had chosen Farida for Farouk. She wished him to make an early marriage, not to one of the many princesses avail-able, but to a girl less well born than herself, and whose parents would have to depend on Nazli's favour. Ostensibly to be a companion for the young princesses Safinaz Zulficar had accom-panied her mother, a lady-in-waiting to Nazli, during the royal party's travels abroad. Farouk had been given every oppor-tunity to fall in love with this girl, which he did. However, all did not work out quite as Nazli had planned. Farouk's wife Farida lost all semblance of subservience and placidity. She be-came a Queen, equal in standing to Nazli, and conflict soon arose.

The press in Egypt and Britain acclaimed the King's popu-larity: "Every occasion that could be found to give vocal expres-sion to the feeling of loyalty and affection, which seemed to animate everyone, foreigners as well as Egyptians, was seized with alacrity." The months after the honeymoon passed quietly enough; when Cairo became too hot the King and Queen retired for the summer to Alexandria. In August the Duke and Duchess of Gloucester, on their way to Kenya by Imperial Airways, had tea with King Farouk, and in the same month Farouk had his first aeroplane flight when he flew over Alexandria for half an hour in an Egyptian Air Force plane.

On 16th September 1938 *The Times* reported the projected visit of Farouk to the Western Desert and the opening of a new road to the west from Alexandria which would "eventually provide a link with the great Italian road along the coast of Libya, but perhaps at this stage its greatest interest will be in providing possibilities for camping excursions".

On Thursday, 17th November 1938 at 8.30 p.m. a salute of forty-one guns fired simultaneously in Alexandria, Cairo, Port Said and other towns informed waiting Egypt that Farida had given birth to a daughter. Farouk, who had gone to Cairo to attend a service on the last Friday in Ramadan, flew back to Alexandria and landed on the special airstrip in the grounds of Montazah Palace where the Princess was born. He named her Ferial, signifying light, the name of his grandmother. Seven-day celebrations were announced with military parades, fireworks and concerts, free food and clothes for the poor, sweetmeats for children and £1 to every baby born that day.

Neguib related how, when his own son was born in 1938 he wanted to name him after the great Sultan Salah ed Din but that his wife, "in the belief that it would bring him luck, wanted to name him Farouk". Neguib argued against it and suggested, if the baby was to be named after a king, to call him George as "the King of England has always been luckier than the King of Egypt". The midwife settled the dispute by registering the baby's name as Farouk, without asking his father. Neguib, of course, was later to dislike George and Farouk; it must be an unfortunate family affair that the name Farouk stuck and even his father forgets sometimes to call him Salah ed Din.

When his son was a few months old in the summer of 1938 Neguib recalls how he first met King Farouk: "I had just been promoted to rank of Major and was temporarily in charge of the Military Museum in Cairo. . . . Farouk, whose acquisitive instincts were even stronger than his father's, had decided to start a private arms collection of his own. I was ordered to drive down to Alexandria, where he was spending the summer, to present him with two truck loads of exhibits. Farouk was eighteen at the time and I was thirty-seven. It was a very hot day, and the King was taking a bath when my man and I arrived at Montazah Palace. We were told to unload our trucks and await His Majesty in the palace garden. Although we were in full uniform . . . Farouk chose to appear before us naked from the waist up, wearing nothing but a sun helmet, slacks, and sandals without socks. . . . I was struck by the flabbiness of his muscles and the rolls of fat on his chest." Neguib stayed at Montazah Palace for six days. Farouk showed interest in the guns and wanted to know how he could acquire the oldest guns in Egypt. These were the original Krupp cannons of 1871, which Ismail had bought and four of which remained at Giza. Farouk requisitioned two for his collection. Soon after this in the autumn of 1938 Neguib was a graduate of the Staff Officers' School. Farouk came to present graduates with their diplomas and despite his plea to follow his example of only saluting the King, Neguib's fellow graduates all knelt and kissed the King's hand. This, one of his first open acts of defiance, Neguib disguised by appearing confused and shaking the King's hand instead, "so hard", he claimed, "that he winced".

In the summer of 1939 Neguib visited England for the first time in his life, on a two months' military study tour. He then recorded not uncommon observations of an imperial nation: "It made me realize . . . how differently the British behaved in England from the way they behaved in Egypt . . . they were so considerate I found it hard to believe they were the same people. . . . If they had only been as considerate towards Egyptians in Egypt, they would have aroused far less antipathy"; but then, too, Neguib continues in typical vein, "they would have realized the folly of attempting, in the twentieth century, to maintain a nineteenth-century imperial relationship with a people who have always resented their unsolicited tutelage".

Early in 1938 questions were asked in the press concerning Farouk's friendliness to Britain; to date Britain had regarded him as a young man who had enjoyed his short six months in England, and his subsequent visits to Stratford and the playing fields of Eton, and whom they thought was sensibly influenced by the old friend of Britain, his former tutor Ahmed Hassanein, but then the King had dismissed his government and unrest swept Egypt. But the *Nation* reported "the ratio of royal to civil power is a domestic issue. . . . Europe's chancelleries are worried about something quite different: Does the action of King Farouk foreshadow a changing foreign policy at Cairo which will replace London with Rome as guardian, policeman, and adviser?"

Italy and Great Britain were in bitter rivalry for Mediterranean supremacy: Mussolini was aggressive, Chamberlain wishing to bargain; Farouk knew, however, that if he inclined towards Rome, Great Britain's attitude would harden; the British had no intention of letting go the Suez Canal. What Admiral Mahan had written in 1900 still held: "Egypt in military situation approaches the ideal; for to a local concentration of forces, defensive and offensive, operative in two directions, towards Gibraltar or towards India, it adds several streams of supply, so diverse in origin that no one navy can take position to intercept them all . . . if the Mediterranean be blocked, the Red Sea remains, always the shortest route to India. . . . The truer solution for a state already holding Malta and Gibraltar, would seem to be to grasp Egypt firmly, to consolidate local tenure there, and to establish in India, Australia, and the Cape sources of supply of ammunition and arms, against the change of temporary interruption on the side of England." Egypt was the strategic centre of the British Empire: as early as 1934 Mussolini had declared: "We must have Egypt; we shall be great only if we can get Egypt."

In 1935 the Duce increased his Libyan garrison to some 50,000 men, and built a trans-Libyan highway. In the same year Great Britain transformed the desert port of Mersa Matruh into a strong flank against invasion from the west; the Egyptians built a railroad from Alexandria–Fuka to Mersa Matruh, an extension of seventy-eight kilometres completed in seventy-seven days. In 1936 Anthony Eden was asked in the House by a Liberal Member of Parliament if he would "state the nature of the plans for an Italian attack on Egypt which were found in the Italian Staff plane that crashed in the Sudan in August, 1935. . . .'

Mussolini arrived for an official visit to Libya on 12th March 1937, to open the 1,200-mile coast road and address Egyptian journalists: "The road is a new tie between two countries, from remote times on friendly terms, which today can be strengthened and enlarged. Tell your traders that the Italian Government and the Italian people wish to live in the most cordial friendship with the Egyptians."

From 9th to 11th May Marshal Italo Balbo, Italian Governor of Libya, paid a visit to Egypt for conversations with Farouk and Mahmoud Pasha. Balbo emphasized Italy's friendly feelings towards Egypt and declared that Italy had no territorial designs whatever on Egypt. He declared that Italy only wished for an improvement in economic relations between the two countries and he condemned "mischievous foreign propaganda" for disturbing Italo-Egyptian relations. He attempted to explain the massing of troops in Libya solely because the terrain there provided a good training ground. . . . Count Galeazzo Ciano, Italian Minister of Propaganda and son-in-law of Mussolini, wrote in his diary for 2nd September 1937:

> The navy is very active—three torpedoings and one prize. But international opinion is getting worked up. Particularly in England, as a result of the attack on the destroyer *Havock*. . . . The row has already started.
> The Duce pretends to have a bone to pick with Egypt about her armaments. When I proved to him that they only exist on paper, he replied that he meant to provide himself with a subject of dispute for the right moment. "Egypt will serve my purpose. We must begin now to say that it is Egypt who is troubling the waters."

Mussolini's threat by land from the west against Egypt depended on Britain's naval control of the eastern Mediterranean; any Italian mobile force moving along the Libyan coast road would be within the range of British naval guns. To counteract this Mussolini took two measures: by ordering a new quota of submarines which would give him more of these vessels than held by any other navy; and by building roads further south in the desert, up to the Egyptian border. In September 1937 the London *Daily Herald* correspondent in Cairo reported that the Italians were organizing mechanized forces for desert service made up of equal numbers of air-borne, motorized, and camel-mounted troops, while great stores of food, fuel and munitions were being dumped along the strategic roads. Italy's Savoia–Marchetti 79 and the new Piaggio 32 bombers of the Regia Aeronautica were ready to fly over the rock and sand below; desert did not impede the possibility of air attack.

In 1938 Italy had naval bases in the Dodecanese Islands of the Aegean and at Tobruk, only sixty miles from the Egyptian border and less than 450 miles from Port Said. In Egypt the British Military Mission was quickly transforming the 13,000 strong army to a mechanized force twice that size, with a supporting air force. The pressure was on; meanwhile life in Egypt continued as normal.

"At tea-time, the Alexandria Sailing Club is full of smart women on one of the three terraces as though it were a theatre. The western sea-front which opens before them provides a diversion . . . for their dreams. The background is too far away to be of interest: Agamy, the Mex desert, the tanneries . . . the tanks of the Vacuum oil, the funny aerial trucks of the very smoky coal quay, the dense crowd on the marine quay and beyond, their beloved and blamed town with its domino-like houses set up in rows along the water's edge. This is all very far away, but it is a pleasure to look at the spruce *Mahroussa* with its green-edged white hull, its yellow funnel and shining brass work, awaiting Royal pleasure. Even the old-fashioned, black and white training ship, the *Faroukia*, its masts and sails erect against a lovely pale sky, is worth a glance. On the right is the smart Sailing Club and the Rowing Club. . . ."

> "I have followed the capes, where you sing, O sea,
>   In groves of palm and acacia,
>   You who wear like bright points of embroidery,
>   Dekhaila and Alexandria."

Meanwhile in Cairo: "Ministers and Diplomats have their time well filled. Lunches, teas, dinners. Like the departed Fregoli, they must know when to appear in lounge suits, black ties or tail coats . . . there is not a hostess who does not dream of receiving an ex-President of the Lebanon, a Lord, a big game hunter, a member of the French Institute, an Excellency or Gaby Morlay. All is grist to the mill. Receptions are most ostentatious; often with the help of the famous confectioner Groppi. The guests only stay a short time, having three or four invitations for the same afternoon. They complain, but they are delighted, and, every evening, for a rest, there is dancing in the cabarets and hotels until the early hours of the morning." So wrote Fernand Leprette.

Foreigners were most welcome in Egypt, and they found Egypt an irresistible temptation to visitors; once they had been in Egypt nearly everyone wanted to return. An Englishman visiting Cairo in 1937 wrote that the winter season there was going to be gayer than it had been for years. "King Farouk is passionately interested in Egyptian antiquities, but he also likes giving parties. And a party at the Royal Palace is a real event. The gorgeous gardens, the uniformed A.D.C.s, the Royal

Guards, the string orchestra, and the Arab music provide glamour which even Hollywood cannot emulate. More than a thousand guests will be invited to each of the *soirées* that the young King will give. There will also be dinner parties, banquets, and possibly a Court Ball. King Farouk is showing himself more and more in public—and every Friday he drives in state to a different mosque."

The visitor went on to describe the foods and sports available: "Lamb kebab and spiced salad; bread of the Palace, a cake steeped in honey and topped with cream; konafa, a cake of fine macaroni dipped in sugar, mulakhiya, cucumber with yoghurt and mint, pigeon stuffed with green wheat, a soup of sliced herbs mixed with boiled meat, rice and garlic; vegetables stuffed with rice, raisins and meat, Turkish fashion; vine leaves stuffed with rice; baklava; and the blood oranges, tangerines and sugar cane.

"At Gezira is situated the world's best country club with squash courts, polo, tennis courts, bowling greens, croquet lawns, and a 5,250 yards golf course with grass greens and turf fairways. . . . Racing takes place on Saturdays and Sundays, at Heliopolis and Gezira. . . . Good duck shooting is available only for the rich man, but snipe, quail and sand grouse offer plenty of sport."

"Step into Egypt at Marseilles," said the advertisements, "you can be there within a week." Shopping in the Mouski, a drive to the Pyramids, an aperitif at the Semiramis bar, luncheon at Mena House, the Royale Cinema, Tutankhamen treasure at the Museum, the Coptic Museum, excursion to Sakkara, or to Luxor: Egypt before the war. This life was shortly to be shattered; an era was passing.

In the palace Antonio Pulli was no longer an electrician but had been given the title of bey; he was the King's closest confidant. He and other Italians, Ernesto Verucci, Pietro Garo, including Kavatis, keeper of the royal kennels, were granted Egyptian nationality by royal decree. Farouk maintained an Albanian bodyguard, Circassian body servants and Nubians as general servants. The two Albanians always accompanied him, together with Pulli on his forays to various night clubs, now becoming more frequent; if Farouk liked the look of a belly-dancer Pulli did the procuring and later she would be shown up the palace back stairs. Farouk saw less of Farida who remained in the *haramlek*. Pulli saw the girls out again, drove them home and paid them off.

Pulli now accompanied the King everywhere, ready to answer, supply, bring, fetch at a moment's notice, day or night. Rumour had it that Pulli could sleep standing on one foot, so he became known as 'the Stork'. Farouk's eye for women roved the night clubs and hotel bars.

Farouk and Farida decided to spend the Spring Festival, Shem el-Nassim, in 1939 on a cruise, boarding the 6,000-ton *Mahroussa* from Ras el Tin Palace in Alexandria. When the family returned they spent a few days on the beach before catching the train back to Cairo. Baby Ferial enjoyed the sea and onlookers were pleased to see this outwardly happy family group. On return the King was confined to Abdin with chicken pox.

Early in 1939 Farouk felt the force of his own power. He was now acting as a King and in his statements there is an element of personal, unaided authority, in his photographs a forthright air. He was heavier in the chest and face. On 20th January 1939 as he left a mosque in Cairo the congregation rose and hailed His Majesty as Caliph and Commander of the Faithful. That this acclamation was based on fact was denied a few days later and in any case, the King's aspiration to the position of Caliph, though undoubtedly desired by certain Moslem students of Al Azhar University, would have been very premature.

In the same month Farouk made another short tour of Upper Egypt, when he completed the second heightening of the Aswan Dam by laying the last stone. A month later Egyptian Army officers were strongly reproved by Farouk when they voiced their discontent at newly introduced lower rates of pay. Farouk broadcast to the Egyptians on the occasion of the Moslem New Year, on 20th February 1939, and in a notable speech declared that if he had not inherited all his father's sterling qualities, at least he had inherited the most outstanding: "Like him, no one can influence me." He added that once he had made up his mind on a course of action he carried it through at all costs; "It is my self-confidence and reliance on Allah which inspires my actions, although this does not prevent me from seeking the views of experienced men." He exhorted the youth of Egypt to work hard and respect the law and he further asserted the need for a strong Egypt, prepared "to impose respect for her on anyone attempting to interfere with her dignity".

Farouk supported unity of Arabs; in this cause he hoped his sisters would be of use. He hoped to marry Faiza to the son of King Abdullah of Jordan, and to arrange the engagement eventually of his daughter Ferial, to Faisal of Iraq. Fawzia was pledged in marriage to the heir to the throne of Persia, Prince Reza Pahlavi. Farouk saw himself as a symbol of Moslem unity and grew a pointed beard, resembling those worn by el Maraghi and the Grand Mufti of Jerusalem.

On 15th March 1939, Egypt's Independence Day and birthday of the Shah of Persia, the ceremony of wedding contract between Fawzia and the Shah was held in Abdin Palace. The delegation from Persia included the President of the *Majlis*, Minister of Justice and the Chamberlain and, after a ceremony at the Mosque Qusun, at which Farouk led the prayers, el Maraghi made a pointed speech to the Persian Crown Prince: "I express the fervent hope that there will be a permanent reconciliation between the two most important sects in Islam. . . . It comes at a moment when all Islam must unite. This union has been sent to us by Allah."

On 6th April 1939 Goebbels was in Cairo for one day, during which he visited the Pyramids at Sakkara, and the Citadel before taking off for Rhodes next day.

In August 1939, when war in Europe was virtually inevitable, Mahmoud Pasha, old and in poor health, retired as Prime Minister. Ali Maher Pasha, formerly Chief of the Royal Cabinet, took his place. When war was declared the new Egyptian Government immediately fulfilled its obligations to Great Britain under the 1936 Treaty. Martial law was declared and diplomatic relations with Germany broken off. Egypt, however, was not actually at war with Germany; her resources were pledged to the Allied cause but she was not bound to enter the hostilities. Egypt's position was anomalous: had she declared war on Germany, then, in the event of Allied victory, she would have been entitled to a place at a victory conference table and to a share in the bounty; if the Allies lost she would have been at the mercy of the enemy. In any case Egypt's military contribution to the Allied cause at the beginning of the war could not have made a significant difference to the outcome.

Chapter 5

Ultimatum
(23rd February 1939—5 p.m. 4th February 1942)

On 23rd February 1939 Count Ciano wrote in his diary:
"Attolico has sent a very interesting account of his conversation
with the Egyptian Minister to Berlin, Mourad Pasha. He speaks
in the name of his King, who declares himself to be anti-British,
and asks whether, in the event of Egypt proclaiming her neutrality and Great Britain attempting to intervene, directly or
indirectly, the Axis will be ready to support King Farouk. This
matter is so serious that I felt bound to make a number of
reservations, even though the source of the information is very
reliable. In agreement with the Duce I authorized Attolico to
continue his conversations and to make it clear that any effort
to weaken the ties between Egypt and London finds approval
here." Hitler sent gifts to Farouk.

On the evening of 1st September 1939, the day Germany
attacked Poland, the British Ambassador in Cairo, Sir Miles
Lampson, saw Ali Maher. The Prime Minister undertook to
honour the clause in the Anglo-Egyptian Treaty of 1936 under
which Egypt guaranteed to come to British aid and Ali Maher
was appointed Military Governor: Egypt honoured her agreement to stand by Britain through the war. On 13th September
Farouk visited Mersa Matruh to inspect the Desert Air Force
and the 7th Armoured Division. Two months later at the opening of Parliament Ali Maher proclaimed: "Egypt, which seeks
peace and believes firmly in its benefits . . . could not do otherwise than fulfil her duty."

Ali Maher was the son of that Maher Pasha whom Cromer
had called "a bad adviser, a cause of strife, and an obstacle to

harmonious co-operation" between the British and the young
Khedive Abbas II. A personally ambitious man, Ali Maher had
considerable influence over Farouk and early in 1940 it was
plain that the Prime Minister was encouraging the King to
maintain diplomatic relations with Italy, in the face of British
objections. It was not difficult to influence a young man who was
taking growing offence at the manner in which he was treated
by Sir Miles Lampson, Lord Lloyd comments when writing of
Cromer's treatment of Abbas II fifty years earlier could easily
describe the relations which had developed between Farouk and
Lampson: "There was a considerable school of thought which
held, and not without some justification, that the Khedive was
what he was largely because of the method which Cromer had
used towards him. It was agreed that at his accession Abbas's
position *vis-à-vis* the overshadowing position of the great
Consul-General had been one of great difficulty for a young and
sensitive ruler, and that by no means enough had been done to
help and encourage him."

By Farouk's twentieth birthday on 11th February 1940,
Egypt, situated at the cross roads of Europe, Africa and Asia,
on a maritime trade route, air lines and oil lines, had become
the centre of a crisis of international ramifications. Polson New-
man wrote: "The destiny of the civilized world may be decided
under the shadow of the Pyramids. . . ."

Lugol wrote of the King on his birthday, in the *Bourse
Egyptienne*: "In the times in which we live, this auspicious day
represents more than a date, for in the Valley of the Nile, the
person of the King stands for stability, continuity in the government, certitude for the morrow. As a constitutional King, carrying on the great traditions of a dynasty which has transformed
Egypt, His Majesty King Farouk I is the living symbol of the
aspirations of his people, and it is to him they turn in time of
difficulty. Charitable, clear-sighted, the patron of science, letters
and sport, he has never ceased to give his encouragement to all
good causes. He has given lavishly to the Red Crescent, to the
Welfare funds of the Egyptian and British forces. . . ." The
Arab papers of the day praised the King for helping Egypt to
keep its Moslem spirit and oriental character.

In March and April 1940, Marshal Balbo passed through
Cairo, ostensibly to and from a hunting expedition. In April

Nahas Pasha sent a request to the British in which he asked three questions, taken by the Foreign Secretary to be a statement of Nahas Pasha's conditions for the furtherance of Egyptian co-operation with the Allies throughout the war: that all troops would be withdrawn from Egypt when war ended; that the Sudan question should be reconsidered; and that Egypt should have a place at the Peace Conference table. This was a time for bargaining: in April Ali Maher had several interviews with the Italian Ambassador, Mazzolini.

In the winter of 1940 and spring of 1941, Goering and Raeder were pressing Hitler to join Italy in attacking Britain's bases in the Mediterranean and Middle East, to capture the Suez Canal and the Persian and Iraq oilfields. It was proposed that one German army group should move through Gibraltar to Tunisia; one through Yugoslavia to Anatolia; and the third, a centre prong of the fork, through Italy into Tripolitania to conquer Egypt.

Four battleships based on Alexandria, two in Gibraltar, 55,000 British, Indian and Commonwealth troops and 200 aircraft in the Nile Valley amounted to Britain's slight defensive power in the Mediterranean. But this slight power was in the hands of three daring commanders; Cunningham, Wavell and O'Connor.

On 22nd May 1940 Wavell, who had taken up his command in Cairo in August 1939, and had since then held a 'watching brief', signalled to the Vice-Chief of the Imperial General Staff: "Italy seems to be hesitating on the brink. . . . What his [Mussolini's] action against this country will be, no one can tell. I think it is quite likely that he will make no direct attack on it, at any rate at first. We can detect at present no signs of aggressive attitude, or of Fifth Column methods. What the Egyptians will do is also doubtful. The Government has been, and is continuing to be, very helpful, but recent events in the West have undoubtedly shaken them for the time being."

Within a week, if Wavell could have known, he was proved wrong, Ciano's diary for 30th May 1940 read: "The decision has been taken. The die is cast. Today Mussolini gave me the communication he has sent to Hitler about our entry into the war. . . . The Egyptian Minister speaks on his own responsibility of an eventual proclamation of neutrality by his

Government. I encourage him. I do not believe that Egyptian neutrality would make a great deal of difference in the game, but, nevertheless, it might have a certain advantage."

On 11th June 1940 Italy's declaration of war was delivered to the Egyptian Council of Ministers and next day the Egyptian Chamber of Deputies held a secret four-hour session at which a resolution was passed "approving the policy of the Government tending to give all possible aid to the Democracies fighting for right and justice". Six days later the first Italian bomb fell on Egypt.

It was unfortunate for Lampson that he had a young Italian wife when, after the Italian declaration of war, he had to demand that Italians should be expelled from Egypt or interned, and Italian firms confiscated. Ali Maher was reluctant to agree to this and Farouk was ordered to dismiss him and his Italian advisers, not without first some pointed remarks from the court that if their Italians were to go Lampson's ought to go also.

One day in 1940 a meeting took place in Cairo between Colonel Anwar el Sadat, a young officer with Nasser in the Egyptian Army, and General Aziz el Masri, who had just been dismissed as Chief of Staff of the Army, a move demanded by Lampson for el Masri's known pro-German sympathies. The meeting was held in a clinic belonging to Dr. Ibrahim Hassan, Vice-President of the Moslem Brotherhood. Aziz el Masri's services were regarded as "eminently valuable to the revolutionary movement". At this time, el Sadat continued: "The Egyptian regime was sinking further and further into decadence under a King who was selfish, uneducated to his royal task, and surrounded by men of tarnished reputation.

"The General knew this unworthy sovereign well, for he had been his tutor in England in 1936. He told me of his vain attempts to give Farouk the type of solid education which would fit him for the royal task which would one day be his. It was a waste of time. Farouk had already fallen under the evil influence of two intriguers, Omar Fathi and Ahmed Hassanein, who, in order to enjoy the favours of the future King, flattered his every caprice, taking him into London's night clubs and places of ill-repute and bringing him home dead drunk in the small hours of the morning.

"Now the old patriot," El Sadat wrote of the General's feelings shown at this meeting, "though full of sadness, affirmed his faith in the regeneration of Egypt. His hopes lay in the young officers of the Army."

The Times wrote in mid-1940 of the prevailing feeling in Egypt: "At heart Egypt stands behind Great Britain and hates and fears the Italians, but at present the country is bewildered, and urgently needs a proper lead." Meanwhile the Italians were planning. On *11th July* Ciano wrote: "Mussolini is good humoured . . . and optimistic about the approaching action in Egypt." *27th August:* "Mussolini says that Keitel also thinks that the taking of Cairo is more important than the taking of London." *9th September:* "The drive against Egypt has suffered a new delay. . . . Never has a military operation been undertaken so much against the will of the commanders." *11th September:* "The beginning of the attack on Egypt is confirmed for tomorrow . . . General Carboni . . . says that our advance as far as Mersa Matruh is easy, and that it is possible to reach Alexandria." After weeks of uncertainty the attack on Egypt began on 14th September.

On 2nd January 1941 Nahas Pasha, still indignant that the Treaty he had signed in 1936 seemed to favour Britain and not Egypt, sent a memorandum to Farouk complaining that the war was causing economic hardship, interfering with production and with trade. "Egypt", he claimed "has risked her strength and wealth and indeed her freedom and political life in aiding her ally. She has gone beyond mere performance of her Treaty obligations." The Egyptian Army in 1941–2 were in charge of defending the Suez Canal and the delicate task of detecting mines dropped into the Canal. Egyptian anti-aircraft crews were responsible for defending their towns against air raids.

The Egyptian Army certainly played its part, although its members were good material for the satirists of the day. "The Egyptian Army", wrote Jarvis, "is probably the largest Army in the world. . . . The word 'large' is connected solely with bulk and waist measurement, and here the Egyptian Army stands forth as the premier military force of modern times. Seniority is entirely by weight."

Eden, as Foreign Minister, was in Cairo in March 1941 for

conferences with British officers, Smuts, and the Egyptians, to discuss sending the greater part of the Army of the Nile to aid Greece. Churchill sent a telegram to Eden that week: ". . . while you are on the spot you should deal faithfully with Egyptian Prime Minister, Farouk, and anyone else about our security requirements. It is intolerable that Roumanian Legation should become a nest of Hun spies, or that the Canal Zone should be infested by enemy agents. I am relying on you to put a stop to all this ill-usage we are receiving at the hands of those we have saved."

In May 1941 the Germans invaded Russia. The Egyptians looked to either side and saw an Axis nutcracker which would squeeze them from both directions, from the west and the north-east. Up until this time one could say the Egyptians supported an Allied victory but with the advent of the nutcracker situation many began to have second thoughts. Fifth Column whispers sowed suspicion between Farouk and the British. For him to remain loyal to Britain, and to honour the Anglo-Egyptian Treaty, demanded much of the King. *Foreign Affairs* wrote in July 1941:

> It requires not only a sense of loyalty, but also tact, forbearance and mastery of the niceties of psychology for King Farouk to be able to adhere to the Anglo-Egyptian accord of 26th August 1936, when there is bound to be an undercurrent around him attempting to force him into the arms of the Axis. We may assume that Moslem extremists continually tell him that he should capitalize the well-known antagonism of Fascism and Nazism to Jewry in order to join forces with them to assure the preservation for Islam of Islam's Holy Places. But he has not listened to such counsels. . . .
>
> King Farouk's unchallenged position as a devout Mahomedan, and as a man whom the Moslem leaders throughout the world trust, makes his loyalty to his Treaty obligations a matter of outstanding importance, not only for the defence of the Suez Canal, but in preventing uprisings in favour of the anti-Jewish Axis powers throughout the entire Near East, North Africa, Moslem India, and other lands.

In 1941 a poor grain harvest caused considerable hardship in the country. An order went out to restrict the acreage for cotton (down to about a fifth) and plant cereal instead. Farouk himself presided over a Council of Ministers to consider the problem and immediately ordered the reserve stocks of maize in the Royal Domains to be distributed among the fellaheen.

1941 was a disturbing year for the British. In the Middle East Rashid Ali led a revolt in Iraq. Egyptian Army officers made contact with the German Headquarters in Libya and acted in harmony with them. El Sadat wrote: "The rebellion in Iraq acted as a kind of safety valve which prevented an explosion. It was the first sign of the liberation of the Arab world. . . . Now seemed to be the golden opportunity for General Aziz el Masri. No one could do more than he to hold the Egyptian forces together and to win vital German support for the Arab cause. . . . We, the young officers, wanted to attack the British and make Egypt a second Iraq."

To the young officers' surprise Aziz el Masri refused to share their enthusiasm. One day in March 1941, an agent of the Wehrmacht sought out Aziz el Masri at his home and gave him a message from Germany. The Germans, it said, thought highly of the General's patriotic activities, and they would be happy to make use of his military experience in collaboration. He had only to make his plans known and Germany would see to it. El Sadat received a shock at this stage: Colonel Moussa Loutfi, chief of the Egyptian C.I.D., told him that his activities were known and that the British Intelligence Service had him under close surveillance. El Sadat warned El Masri. They decided to accept the German overtures and planned the General's escape from Egypt. The Germans recommended an air strip near Gabel Rozza on the Oasis Road. "Their choice", wrote El Sadat later, "showed they knew our deserts perfectly. No doubt the German 'explorers' who visited Egypt shortly before the war had contributed something to that knowledge."

A rendezvous was fixed for dawn on a certain Saturday when a German aircraft should pick them up, but their car broke down on the way. El Masri made one more attempt to escape. He arranged with a Squadron-Leader Zulficar to use an Egyptian military plane to fly him to the German lines, but on take-off the plane hit a post and crashed. El Masri survived but was imprisoned on a charge of conspiring against the State.

"I still think," wrote El Sadat, "that if ill-luck had not so dogged our enterprise, we might have struck a quick blow at the British, joined forces with the Axis, and changed the course of events." What was more sure was his final comment on these events: "The formidable reserves of violence in the Egyptian people remained latent and suppressed. It was all the more certain that revolution would come."

One section of opinion in Egypt held that war should be declared: that by fighting as an ally of Britain now would save Egypt from a compromising position after the war when, if Britain had fought to protect Egypt, and won, then the British would be able to impose what conditions they liked on Egypt. British occupation of Egypt was painfully obvious to the Egyptians: G.H.Q. was in Cairo. Wavell and Auchinleck wanted to move it into the desert west of the Pyramids but the priorities of war never allowed the time, and the physical expression of British Army occupation remained in Cairo in a structure named Grey Pillars, known to those who appreciated the ill-feeling it caused as "the grey pillars of unwisdom".

Egyptian harbours and towns filled with British and Allied troops. When food supplies ran low a system of rationing was installed under an Anglo-American organization, the Middle East Supply Centre. Such interference with the life of Egypt was resented by the Egyptians: this resentment, coupled with the fact that from the Egyptian Army Chief of Staff downwards there was increasing inflexion to the Axis cause, forced the British to deal firmly with Egyptian politicians.

To the British soldier the Egyptians were "wily oriental gentlemen"; for short, "Bloody wogs".

> "Howling hell of every breed,
>   Every colour, every creed,
>   Indigo Nubian,
>   Swarthy Greek;
>   Overall that garlic reek;
>   Shouting vendors seeking trade,
>   Beggars sleeping in the shade;
>   Clanging tram;
>   Raucous horn;
>   'Backsheesh!'—from the newly born;"
>   *J. Broome.*

Shepheard's Hotel was social headquarters in Cairo (as the building had once been G.H.Q. for Napoleon's troops) for officers who summoned the suffragi and ordered their gin adams, SB's (Suffering Bastards) and limoons, and waited an interminable time for it to come. As they said of Rommel at the time, "Wait till he gets to Shepheard's; that'll hold him up."

Practically every soldier who served in the Middle East has his own story of those days. This is one of the best:

King Farouk had been involved in a collision between his car and a British Army vehicle. At the Court of Inquiry the British Officer in charge called the lorry driver to give his evidence, which began as follows: "Sir, I was driving at 16.30 hours on the road in the direction of the Canal Zone when I saw a big sports car approaching with two wogs. . . ."

"Stop, close the court! Sergeant, take that man away; teach him how to give his evidence in a proper manner."

When the inquiry reassembled the driver was recalled to give his evidence, having spent a full ten minutes under the earnest tuition of his sergeant who endeavoured to instil in the man the correct phraseology to be used. He began again: "Sir, I was driving at 16.30 hours on the road in the direction of the Canal Zone when I saw a big sports car approaching. This car was driven by His Majesty King Farouk of Egypt and another wog. . . ."

Neguib wrote: "Of no country did the British demand more than they did of Egypt during the war, and of no country's interests were they less considerate. . . . Their troops marched through the streets of Cairo singing obscene songs about our King, a man whom few of us admired but who, nevertheless, was as much of a national symbol as our flag." Farouk was never so popular as when he was being insulted by British troops:

> "King Farouk, King Farouk,
> You're a dirty old crook,
> As you walk down the street
> In your fifty shilling suit.
> Queen Farida's very gay
> 'Cos she's in the family way,
> etc."

loud and clear, to the tune of the Egyptian National Anthem.

The troops told stories against the King and the Egyptian Army: One day Farouk asked his Egyptian Generals how long it would take the British Army to surround Cairo. "Two hours, your Majesty," they replied. "And how long would it take them to capture us all?" asked the King. "Two and a half hours, your Majesty."

Neguib continued: "They molested our women, assaulted our men and committed acts of vandalism in public places." Neguib's feeling for the Allies cannot have been strengthened the day three drunken South African soldiers hit him on the head with a beer bottle and stole his wallet.

Throughout the months of battle in the desert an effort of almost equal strength was put behind the propaganda beamed from London and Rome. B.B.C. transmissions to Egypt were made more popular when a famous Egyptian crooner was hired to sing love songs in between news items and propaganda pieces; whereas the Axis propaganda described pro-British Egyptians as 'Pasha Pigface' and 'Pasha Fathead'. The propaganda promised the fellaheen a 'new order' of freedom. Alan Moorehead made the criticism that British propaganda, which could have done so much to help was, compared with the German, "childish and inept. . . . The British Empire was hawked through the mud villages of the Delta like a second-hand motor car".

To promise the fellaheen a 'new order' shows how ill-informed were the Axis propagandists. The lot of the fellaheen of Egypt has not changed for centuries and they were little affected by this war in their deserts. Habib-Ayrout, perhaps the best authority on the people of Egypt, wrote of them, "The fellaheen have changed their masters, their religion, their language and their crops, but not their manner of life. . . . The fellaheen owe their astonishing uniformity and stability to their close association with an element no less uniform and stable, namely the soil of Egypt. There has grown up between these two a bond which is at once firm and elastic; a balanced and self-sufficient interdependence which no crisis or government can disturb."

> "Thus do they, sir; they take the flow of the Nile
> By certain scales i' the pyramid; they know,
> By the height the lowness, or the mean, if dearth
> Or poison follows: the higher Nilus swells,
> The more it promises: as it ebbs, the seedsman
> Upon the slime and ooze scatters his grain
> And shortly comes to harvest."

While the 19 million poor people continued their normal lives the few rich got richer in the high-life of the cities. "Practically all the wealth", wrote Moorehead, "was gathered into the hands of less than 5 per cent of the people. There were Greeks, Levantines, Jews, Syrians, French, British and Italians of fabulous wealth. They took rich profits from the war and gambled heavily at the races, on the stock exchange and on the property market. . . . Prices trebled and all the display of monopoly and wealth came crudely and flagrantly to the surface."

Early in the war Farouk had to bear the largest burden of responsibility and judgment he had yet been forced to undertake: in order to continue as monarch he had to be popular with the people; he could not achieve this by showing too much friendliness to the British, particularly as their fortunes were then at a low level; he could not, on the other hand, be hostile to the force which occupied Egypt; and, in case that occupation was changed for a German force, as many considered imminent, he had also to appear to be sympathetic to the Axis cause.

One British officer in Cairo in the war described for the author his one and only meeting with Farouk. Five officers shared a bachelor flat and one of their members was suspected of having an affair with certain ladies of the court. The fact was that he had invited two ladies to tea and for Moslem women of the royal court to visit a Christian army officer's apartment was, to say the least, an adventure, and bound to be misconstrued. One afternoon a knock came at the door while the five officers were deep in their chairs and detective novels, pipes smoking. One Englishman opened the door to a bearded man in uniform, and asked him in. At this time Farouk was growing his beard but had not yet appeared with it in the press. The officer who opened the door knew Farouk well but the others did not recognize him and remained in their seats, until a slow awareness of who their visitor was brought them to their feet. In course of conversation, which was mostly hard luck stories of his ill-treatment by the Americans, particularly Cordell Hull, Roosevelt's Secretary of State, who would not give him an aeroplane, and by Lampson, Farouk produced a packet of cigarettes which he offered round. The cigarettes looked peculiar, and when the suspicious British held them up, proved to be hollow, so the King offered to explain their use and out of the cigarette came a contraceptive. At this stage, squeals and yells came from the servants' quarters below but Farouk forbade anyone to go and discover the cause. When the King had left, the officer who had invited the ladies to tea found that Farouk's men had twisted the arms of the servants to tell them where the women were and what went on. This was the purpose of the King's visit.

Farouk loved shooting. He occasionally invited high-ranking British officers to join him on early morning duckshoots, but his excesses could not be called sport; he had a passion for killing. One apocryphal story tells how Farouk suffered from nightmares in which he was chased by a lion. He sought the advice of pro-Axis el Maraghi who told him, "You will not rest until you have shot a lion." Whereupon Farouk shot two, at the Zoo, but the nightmares continued. "Fool," said el Maraghi, "the lion that chases you is Britain." On one occasion, Farouk visited the Wadi Rishrash, once one of the finest game reserves in Africa, founded principally by Hassanein and Russell Pasha, and having first made elaborate preparations to ensure his success, shot the animals.

Lord Chandos, Oliver Lyttelton, then British Minister of State, wrote in his memoirs, "The King . . . when he wishes—which was not always—could be charming and courteous", and recalled how even on a hot evening Farouk called to see him dressed in an English tweed suit "unannounced and incognito, drank copiously of very sweet orangeade and talked of his days at Woolwich".

During the first three years of his marriage King Farouk was so much in love with his wife that he gave her a gift every single morning. These presents included priceless jewels, furs, Paris dresses and objets d'art. He bought a large agricultural estate from his private fortune and made it over to her name. The Queen's jewels, too numerous to be contained in a jewel case, were kept in a special chest of drawers. Queen Farida's father was raised to the rank of pasha, and appointed Egyptian Ambassador to Persia. Two years later he retired from this post, returned to Egypt, and backed by his son-in-law's influence was elected to a number of industrial boards in Cairo and Alexandria. King Farouk made him a gift of a large villa surrounded by an attractive garden in Alexandria. The Pasha, with his new-found wealth bought himself another villa in Zamalek, a residential district of Cairo.

During the first years of their marriage, Queen Farida's influence over husband was supreme. Strong-willed, autocratic and pleasure loving, she firmly put an end to the Queen Mother's dominion over her son. In consequence, terrible scenes took place between mother and son from which the King emerged unhappy and distraught and he began to make long desert trips to avoid his wife and mother.

Inevitably Queen Farida's predominant influence over the King caused jealousy and discontent among the King's suite. Farouk was a bad judge of men and, for that matter, also of women. His court contained some of the most shameless and unscrupulous rascals in Egypt. Each one of them for personal reasons tried to foment discord between the royal couple by flattery and by pandering to the King's weaknesses, and love of pleasure. Like poisonous weeds overgrowing a garden, every one of them did his utmost to stifle Farouk's better feelings. A contemporary observer has written that it was sad to watch the change coming over the formerly kind and decent young man.

Meanwhile the King watched current affairs in Egypt very closely. Chandos wrote: "The King kept himself well informed on politics and the movement of opinion, and was shrewder and more serious than is usually supposed. I should judge that he was far from sure that we would win and that he kept open some line of retreat to Mussolini and the Axis." It was just this shrewdness, and sympathy for the Axis cause on the part of the King (the palace radio was in touch with Rome, but British Intelligence later recruited the operator, who revised messages in a manner best to serve the Allied cause), that concerned the British early in 1942. At this time his Prime Minister was Ali Maher, who had friends in Berlin and Rome and had been working with the Italians since the days of Fuad. Students in the streets were shouting "We are Rommel's soldiers" and "Long live Ali Maher". Rommel was advancing on Benghazi when Lampson demanded the installation of Nahas, leader of the Wafd and in whom British had faith, as Prime Minister instead of Ali Maher. Farouk dallied, Lampson issued an ultimatum.

A climax, a breaking point was due between these two men whose relations had become increasingly strained. Political tension in Cairo was acute. The British regarded as essential the establishment of a government sympathetic to the Allied cause, under Nahas. Without this, Chandos wrote, "The Ambassador believed . . . there would be a popular outburst and serious riots. He advised the King that we feared for the security of our base in the Delta and pressed him strongly to send for Nahas Pasha. The King flatly refused. I called the Defence Committee together. The Ambassador favoured strong action. It was clear that words would be futile and that a show of force would be necessary if we were to get our way. . . . The abdication and removal of the King might be involved."

General Stone, G.O.C. British troops in Egypt, was asked to make the military arrangements. If the King was to be deposed, someone sensibly asked, what should be done with him? The Navy offered to put him on board ship and cruise in the Red Sea with him until the politicians sorted out the situation. Ceylon was the most likely destination. (Farouk believed that Lampson for some time had been planning to force him to retire to Khartoum.)

The British Ambassador, Miles Wedderburn Lampson, born in 1880, educated at Eton, had entered the Foreign Office in 1903. After he had served in the Far East, particularly in China, his first wife died in Hong Kong and in 1934 he married Jacqueline Aldine Leslie, daughter of the Italian Professor Count Castellani. In the same year he was made High Commissioner for Egypt and the Sudan, replacing Lord Lloyd, a post he held for two years, becoming the first Ambassador in 1936. He was a *charmeur*, a conversationalist who loved to linger and was therefore a good diplomat for the East. Lampson, Toynbee said, "played the part of the good genius in the Anglo-Egyptian drama of 1935–36".

One of those who knew him well and thought well of him wrote: "Lampson's diplomacy was the art of practical adjustment, based on fair dealing, shrewd instinct and tenacity . . . a man of great energy and drive, he demanded much of his subordinates and of the Foreign Office . . . his zest for life was tireless, almost boyish. His clear mind and ready pen worked rapidly at all necessary times, but it was preferably in the midnight hours that the bulk of his 'homework' was done. His actions were preceded by forethought and careful preparation. . . . He was robust, forthright, indomitable, a great figure of the Foreign Office. His massive presence did not belie the strength of his convictions or his personal and political courage; a formidable antagonist and a negotiator whose skill matched his toughness. He disliked appeasers, levellers and petty official-dom and his broad shoulders shrugged off criticism from them." Those who knew him well, but did not particularly like him, have said he was vindictive and a bully to Farouk, and mean. Mangoes from his garden were sold as 'Embassy Mangoes' in the shops, and after a shoot he retained some of the birds shot by guests to sell in Cairo. He liked money and would be seen gambling with Syrians in the Mohamed Ali Club.

He frequently talked about Farouk as "the boy" and treated him as such, condescendingly, which chagrined Farouk greatly. Lampson had not been able to adapt himself to the diminished position of diplomat from High Commissioner. Some of the Embassy staff felt so strongly that Lampson should not have been kept in Egypt that a secret report was sent as a telegram to the Foreign Office outlining their reasons. This was ignored.

Lampson and Nahas worked in close personal co-operation with one another. The Ambassador stood nearly eighteen inches higher than any member of the Egyptian Government and earned himself an adjective once applied to an earlier British Ambassador; overbearing. Lord Chandos dismisses the "popular criticism" of Lampson and defends him "as a jealous guardian of his country's name and obligations, forceful and rigid only about essentials". Alan Moorehead is another of the few who have defended him. In *African Trilogy* he described the Ambassador's job as "a very difficult and delicate mission. The instructions laid on him by the Foreign Office seldom allowed him to go beyond the bounds of ordinary peace-time negotia-tions".

Lampson may or may not have been suitable for Egypt but was certainly most unsuitable for Farouk. It was this man whom the British chose to represent them in Egypt and to deal with a twenty-two-year-old King, forty years his junior. It is little wonder that Lampson was Cromer-like with the boy, treating him with some impatience and lack of appreciation of his intelligence and maturity, and equally understandable that this man was to become the cause of Farouk's hatred for Britain.

At 3 p.m., three hours before the expiry of Lampson's ultimatum to Farouk, the King entered a conference room in Abdin Palace, preceded by Hassanein. Around the table were his uncle, Sherif Sabri, Prime Minister Ali Maher, Nahas, Ahmed Zeiwar, Ismail Sidki, Abdel Fattah Yehia, Ahmed Maher, Bahei Eldin Barakat, Hussein Sirri, Hafiz Ramadan, Hafiz Afifi, Mohamed Mahmoud, Ali Elshamsi, Mohamed Hussein Heikal, Halmi Issar and Mohamed Hassen.

"Our country is facing an hour of danger," Farouk began, "and I am making an appeal to all of you to help me confront it. I feel that in these difficult times we must learn to forget our personal differences. We must work as a single unit, a single opinion, and a single nation. Our country has never made a step forward except when its word has been unanimous, and it has always been harmed when its word was divided. I invited some of you yesterday, and I decided to invite the rest of you today, in order to personally explain to you my point of view. I am asking all of you to help form a coalition government. I think that if each of you will sacrifice something, the nation will gain much. I am trustful that you will accept my advice. In these grave hours, we must forget self and remember only country. When the British Ambassador was here today, I told him that I had already decided to give Nahas Pasha the post of Prime Minister.

"When yesterday's consultations were ended, the British Ambassador met my Chamberlain who informed him that Nahas Pasha refuses to form a coalition government, and he asked that I be informed that it was his desire that Nahas Pasha be given full freedom to select his own cabinet. My Chamberlain communicated to him that the question is being considered by Nahas Pasha and the party leaders, and that they are in the midst of forming a new government. The King has faith in the patriotic sentiments of the leaders and feels that they will surmount all difficulties to his satisfaction. I leave you now to discuss the matter freely, counting upon your patriotism to study the question and to refer to me the opinion of all. In this matter I wish you to know one thing only . . . that I am not afraid of anything, and that I am ready to sacrifice everything in the interest of my country."

Discussion followed and all agreed to form a coalition government, with the single exception of Nahas. Ismail Sidki then proposed a resolution, to be signed by everyone present, of protest at the British ultimatum. It was written there and then and addressed to Sir Miles Lampson: "In answer to a communication you have made to our King, stating that he appoint a certain person selected by you to form the Egyptian cabinet, and in answer to the direct threat of force that accompanied this communication I have the honour as President of the Chamber of Deputies, to inform you, as representative of the government, of my protest at this aggression against the independence of Egypt. It has violated the treaty of friendship existing between us and has placed the relations between our people in great danger. I regret this intervention into our internal affairs, one that has been committed at a time when Great Britain in war is defending the democracy and liberty of nations."

Lampson repeated his demands for a popular government and asked for an answer by 5 p.m. The hour passed. The Ambassador demanded an audience.

Chapter 6

A Devil in the Dawn
(6 p.m. 4th February 1942—18th October 1944)

After dinner at the Embassy on 4th February 1942, the ladies retired, leaving Lyttelton, Minister of State, and Lampson in earnest discussion. Originally planned for 7 p.m. the visit to the palace was delayed until 9 p.m. The principal question to be resolved was whether or not to depose the King, if he complied, as he would by then be three hours past the ultimatum deadline. Lyttelton regarded this as too small an excuse to depose Farouk and Lampson reluctantly agreed.

Shortly before 9 p.m. three cars and an escort left the Embassy as a blind. Immediately after this Lampson and General Stone drove to the palace with an armed escort. General Stone, the only man left alive who was present, has supplied the author with this summary of events during the next hour: "Immediately before the audience took place British troops about a battalion in strength with a section of armoured cars had sealed off all approaches and exits from the palace perimeter.

"The Ambassador, accompanied by myself and our two A.D.C.s, drove to the palace at the appointed time in the Ambassador's car through the outer gateway and up to the front door. I had given orders for a specially selected platoon from the Training School to follow immediately behind our car. It was then to wait in the courtyard outside the front door to be available in case any unpleasantness occurred. All this passed off as arranged without incident.

"The Ambassador and myself were admitted and conducted upstairs to the waiting room from which, after a few minutes, we were taken along the corridor to the King's study where we found him with his Court Chamberlain Hassanein Pasha. We were invited to sit down with him at the table."

Farouk claimed later that he had three Albanian guards hidden behind the curtain of his study door at this moment, each armed with a pistol.

"After a few preliminary words the Ambassador read out his prepared statement which presented the King with the alternatives of Nahas or abdication. At the same time he handed to the King a form of abdication which had previously been drawn up at the Embassy [drafted by Walter Monckton].

"The King took it all in a calm and dignified manner but was obviously a bit shaken on reading the abdication form. It looked for a moment as if he intended to sign it, but Hassanein came round behind him and they had a short consultation which I could not hear. The King then said he agreed to summon Nahas to be Prime Minister and select his own Cabinet and the Ambassador had won his point."

Farouk's own version is that he replied to Lampson: "When I am ready to abdicate, Sir Miles, I shall do so at my pleasure and in the language of my people. I shall not sign this paper. I shall appoint Nahas Pasha as my Prime Minister, but I shall do so only to prevent blood from flowing in the streets of Cairo. But you, Sir Miles, will regret this deed for ever."

"After this tension relaxed, we were offered cigarettes and, after some normal conversation, the meeting came to an end in an apparently friendly atmosphere," added General Stone.

The drama of these events gave rise to the wildest rumours of what had actually taken place. It was said afterwards that when Farouk heard Lampson was on his way to his office he took his revolver from his desk and said, "I'll shoot him as soon as he walks in", and that Pulli dissuaded him from any such action, that telephone lines had been cut, the palace radio seized, and a cordon of tanks surrounded the building. The armed platoon waited outside the front door from where they were in touch with the two armed British A.D.C.s standing outside the King's study. Hassanein's remarks to Farouk when he was about to sign the abdication paper were: "Think what you are doing," at which Farouk asked Lampson for another chance. Other reports claim that Farouk roared with laughter and complained that the declaration had not been typed. This is untrue; however the

King did comment that the paper was 'crumpled and soiled.

Lampson's action was undertaken unbeknown to the Foreign Office. When Farouk agreed to appoint Nahas, the Ambassador looked a little taken aback. It seems he had anticipated he would be able to depose the King; when Hassanein leant over and whispered caution, the course of Farouk's life was altered, as was the history of Egypt.

Nahas had been waiting for his summons but ironically was prevented at first from entering the palace by the cordon of British armoured cars until finally allowed through. Lady Diana Cooper who was staying in the Embassy and witnessed all the moves that evening wrote of the scene when Lampson, Stone and Nahas returned from the palace: "At 11 p.m. I found the Embassy hall a babel of huddled groups—Oliver and Moira Lyttelton, Walter Monckton, Mr. Michael Wright, lots of A.D.C.s, Military Secretaries and unknowns. Wright and Walter see it reminiscent of Munich in not getting an abdication signed, but Oliver and H.E. were 'just certain' they had been right in the present arrangement. H.E. came out of his den, dressed in a pearl-grey *frac*, arm-in-arm with Nahas Pasha, both grinning themselves in two."

Censors cut all reports of this 4th February event but eye-witnesses surmised what had happened. One immediate result was that a pasha team due to play the Royal Artillery at polo the next day did not turn up. There were more serious results. Nasser recalled a letter he wrote to a friend the day after the 4th February event:

"What is to be done, now that the blow has been struck, and we have taken it lying down! Yet I believe the imperialists hold a weak one-trump hand—they are simply bullying."

In the Egyptian Army, Nasser says, the event "wrought a radical change, in both the spirit and disposition of the officers. . . . They were grieved that they had not intervened. . . . But they all thought to themselves that the morrow was close at hand when they would have the opportunity to do so". He admits that "preparations for retaliatory action were eventually attempted, but it was too late".

The wife of a British official who saw Farida next day had to console the Queen, who wept at what had happened and asked, "Why do you treat him like this?" Farouk himself was shocked, stunned and angry. He said that next day he received a personal note from General Stone: "Your Majesty, I regret very much what happened yesterday. I know that you will realize that I am a military man and have had to obey orders", and that Stone had had to insist he accompany Lampson to the palace to avoid British troops being given orders by a civilian. No such note was sent. Strangely, in view of the Wafd's long history of conflict with British influence in Egypt, the change of government was viewed for some time with suspicion by the Allies, and for more than a month the German radio continued to treat the change as a serious setback to the British.

The action taken by Lampson has remained a point of controversy ever since. At the time it secured the government the British wanted but it humiliated the King. Some felt it would have been better for him if he had abdicated: from then on he hated Lampson, a sentiment he expressed in a letter he wrote to a British military war-time friend when he said of Lampson, "I'd hang him if I could!" In time Lampson's action brought down the very Party the British had installed; it was the final inspiration and confirmation of their cause to those forces in Egypt working to rid themselves of Farouk and the British. Lampson, Lyttelton wrote, had "under the exigencies of war and perhaps unwittingly, wrecked the triangle of forces within which the political life of Egypt was evolving".

Sadat, clearly an enemy of Britain and therefore one whose views are to be valued if this is to be a balanced account, reported the cause of the 4th February incident as the student demonstrators who shouted for Rommel and against the British in the streets of Cairo. This, he claimed, gave the British an ideal pretext on which they acted instantly. He analyses its effects as "one of the crucial incidents in contemporary Egyptian history. The King lost face. Virtually a prisoner in his own palace, he played an obscure and insignificant role for the rest of the war.

"Up till now the King had been synonymous with the patriotic idea, and the violation of the Royal Palace was regarded by all patriotic Egyptians as an outrage against Egypt herself. But from now on Farouk changed utterly, and Egypt began to despair of him. He had suffered a severe shock, which was followed by chronic nervous depression.

"Unstable and anxious by temperament, Farouk became the

prey of psychological inhibitions. He suffered from persecution mania. He was irascible and violent. He lived at night and slept during the day. It became gradually obvious that he was a paranoiac. He underwent a physical change at the same time. He became very fat and prematurely aged."

Other interested parties were watching the situation in Egypt closely. Four days after the ultimatum Goebbels wrote in his diary: "The reconstruction of the Egyptian Government has brought no sensational changes. Nahas Pasha declared that he intended to carry out the treaty with England without any reservation . . . I still hope that he may act more favourably for us than we are inclined for the present to assume."

It is to Nahas Pasha's credit that through the following months up to July 1942 he and his Wafdist government remained loyal to the British when their fortunes were very low. The Japs held Hong Kong, Singapore, the Dutch East Indies and Malaya; in Russia the Germans were advancing into the Caucasus; in Libya Tobruk had surrendered and the Panzer Divisions were seventy miles from Alexandria.

The officers of the revolutionary group met again at Zamalek to discuss what action was needed to counteract the 'British insult' of the 4th February incident. "This latest affront to our country gave a new stimulus to the revolutionary movement", they wrote. "Abdel Nasser and Abdel Hakim Amer determined that Egypt must never again suffer such a humiliation. The real revolutionary conspiracy dates back to this time. The movement had now passed from the theoretic to the militant phase. Recruitment was stepped up. Abdel Nasser, during the course of the year, was appointed as an instructor at the Military College where he came into contact with hundreds of cadets and was able to select the best elements for the revolutionary movement. From this time Nasser began asking fellow officers to his home to discover their political feelings, and to enrol them in his own secret organization. The plan of the young Army officers' revolutionary group was to overthrow the Wafd government under Nahas Pasha, reinstate Ali Maher, and join the Axis forces when they arrived. In July 1942 British civilians made preparations to leave Cairo and Alexandria. The British Embassy burned its papers. (A high wind fanned the flames and carried away some of the papers, successfully disseminating information over a wide area of Cairo; a peanut seller was found wrapping his wares in slightly charred Most Secret documents.)

Anwar el Sadat was made spokesman for the Revolutionary Committee but was shortly arrested by the British Counter-Espionage Service after he had made contact with Eppler and Monkaster. These two had arrived in Egypt along the little-used route south of the Siwa Oasis, with £40,000 in false English banknotes printed in Greece, and a radio transmitter. They wore British officers' uniforms, drove a British military vehicle and, when they ran low on petrol, showed their papers at a British military depot which supplied them with fuel. Eppler, alias Hussein Gaafer, returned the salute as he drove away. Once in Cairo they established themselves in considerable luxury in a houseboat on the Nile, living on the next boat to the celebrated dancer Hekmat Fahmy, and transmitted midnight messages to Rommel until caught.

On 11th February 1942, Farouk's twenty-second birthday, crowds in the square in front of Abdin Palace acclaimed the King in demonstrations the like of which had not been seen since his accession. Nahas Pasha broadcast to the nation and spoke of the King's "qualities" and the "benefits bestowed by his rule. . . . The love for his people with which his noble heart is imbued, of his firm will to ameliorate the lot of the nation, of his unshakeable faith in the future of the fatherland!"

The Aga Khan once wrote of Nahas Pasha: "Much of his long-established success as a politician was due to his powers of oratory, to the spell of authority which he could exert over the masses of his fellow-countrymen," he was an "out-and-out monarchist", with a "depth of devotion" for King Farouk. This devotion was accompanied by a strong conviction that the King "would be best served by being constantly reminded of the limitations which hedged his power as a constitutional monarch". "*Le roi règne,*" Nahas would say, "*mais il ne gouverne pas.*"

Farouk, much moved by his birthday demonstrations sent a message to the people: "My dear people—how my heart has rejoiced to see these manifestations of joy and gladness on the part of all of you. . . . Your sentiments stimulate me more than ever to make every effort I can to serve the happiness and glory of my country; now, thanks to your love for me, to your union

round my person, my power is immense. . . . My beloved
people, it is not in the prestige he enjoys on earth that a King
finds his happiness, but in the deep and heartfelt love of his
people. . . . May the All Highest grant that the life of Immortal
Egypt be a life of happiness, of prosperity and peace!"

In the week of party-going after his birthday Farouk met
Princess Fatima Toussoun and became infatuated with her. He
laid on a cinema show for her, drove past her home in his car
in the hope of seeing her, and invited her to dinner at his villa
in Heluan. He went to the extent of declaring to Hassanein that
he wanted to divorce Farida and marry Fatima. It took some
considerable patience and diplomacy on Hassanein's part to
dissuade the King.

After his installation, Nahas, still the bargainer, had written
to Lampson that he had agreed to form a government on the
basis that neither the Anglo-Egyptian Treaty nor Egypt's independence permitted Britain to intervene in her internal affairs
and particularly in matters such as the constitution or resignation of the Cabinet. On 8th April 1942, Ali Maher, whose
influence on Farouk had been ended when he was banished to his
country estate, appeared in the Senate. Nahas quickly had him
imprisoned, adding that he would not tolerate any behaviour
"which might disturb the confidence to which the Allied Power
has a right while she is defending the existence of democracy and
liberty". Two months later Nahas arrested Fifth Columnists
and closed the Royal Automobile Club which had become a nest
bed of pro-Axis elements.

By June the Eighth Army was in retreat, pushed by the Afrika
Korps to within sixty miles of Alexandria. On 1st July, Ciano
reported, "News from Africa is . . . excellent." Mussolini was
in Libya and next day he telegraphed Italy about the future
political government of Egypt. "Rommel is to be the military
commander, and an Italian to be civilian delegate." A sense of
crisis hung over Egypt. Alexandria was quiet, the streets, bars
and hotels had emptied. Many people had left the city, others
stayed on to watch the Germans arrive from the desert. No
doubt some of the women had complied with the confident
German radio exhortation to get out their 'party dresses'. In
Cairo there was action, but not panic. If the Germans and
Italians came it would be the Will of Allah. However there was

a run on the banks, abandoned vehicles crammed the streets, trains to Palestine were packed, the British Embassy threw more papers, codes and maps onto a big bonfire, and Lampson took down his Chinese lanterns which he used to light on dinner-party evenings, clearly marking the edge of the Embassy lawn beside the Nile. Farouk, unenthusiastic at the thought of himself as a Nazi puppet was prepared to leave. In mid-August Rommel boasted that he would be in Cairo within "three or four days".

From 3rd to 11th August Churchill was in Cairo; conferences were held in the British Embassy. It was agreed that Mont-gomery should take command of the Eighth Army—Churchill and Alanbrooke were back in Cairo from 18th to the 23rd August. Alexander and Montgomery were appreciating their new positions of command. Rommel was liable to attack at any moment; 25th or 26th August were considered likely days and Churchill wanted to remain for the attack. He toured the front, bathed in the sea, turning upside down and making the V sign with his legs, and reluctantly left for Gibraltar after dark on the 23rd with a cover of twelve fighters.

The presence of Smuts at the talks was particularly valuable. Chandos wrote of him: "He always seemed to be even more interested in military than in political subjects. His blue eyes sparkled when he surveyed a strategical or a tactical plan. These were clearly subjects upon which he had reflected deeply all through his life and which he held in his grasp. His political vision was, of course, also wide and he ranged over the whole convulsive scene of world politics with a clearness, a simplicity and a penetration which are the stamp of superior intellects." Smuts also met Farouk and commented later to his son, "He was a surprisingly intelligent person."

The centre of the talks was a villa belonging to Chester Beatty, 'Beit el Azraq' (the Blue House), near the Pyramids, a strange mixture of best Arabian and Tottenham Court Road furnishings. This house was surrounded by a grove of Casuarina trees, affording, as Noël Coward put it, "no view at all and a great many mosquitoes". The Blue House became the chief centre of British political activity in the East. The offices of the Minister of State were at 10, Sharia Tolumbat, near G.H.Q., known appropriately as Number Ten. During the talks the road from Cairo to the Pyramids was bordered by heavy lines of extra cable for international communications. A friend of Farouk's told the author this story as an example of the King's strange sense of humour: they were driving on this road together in the same car and the friend remarked on the cables and all the important people in Cairo at that time, to which the King replied, "Yes, you know Stalin would not come because he's frightened of me."

The eyes of the world were on the Western Desert where the struggle for power must sooner or later be resolved. On the next battle hung the destiny of millions. As late as 3rd October 1942, Rommel boasted in Berlin: "Today we stand 100 kilometres from Alexandria and hold the gateway to Egypt, with the full intention of getting there, too." Mussolini flew a white charger out to Libya to be ready for his triumphant ride into Cairo. He had his medals cast for the occasion and guide books to Egypt printed in Italian for the troops. But Rommel knew too well the crippling lack of petrol supplies which restricted his movement. The opportunity for Germany had passed back in July. Keitel later wrote: "One of the biggest occasions we passed by was El Alamein. I would say that, at that climax of the war, we were nearer to victory than any time before or after."

And finally in the full moon of 23rd October, known to veterans of the Eighth Army as a 'Montgomery moon', guns opened fire on Rommel's batteries for twenty minutes, and then altered range to the infantry positions. El Alamein had started. After that first night there was, as F. E. Hughes wrote:

> "a Devil in the dawn—
> Horrific spawn of last night's hideous Moon,
> That hung above the gun's inferno
> And smiled on men who died too soon."

It took twelve days and 13,500 men lost before the 'Hinge of Fate' was turned.

Farouk no longer needed a back door to the Axis. It was obvious where his allegiance should be. In December 1942 he gave £2,000 to both the British and American forces to provide them with comforts for Christmas and the New Year. When the Axis powers were chased out of Egypt he grew a bushy moustache and was continually seen in his R.A.F. Air Marshal's uniform. (When someone made a doll of him in this dress he was delighted and it remained one of his treasured possessions.)

Noël Coward recorded an incident during his stay in Cairo in 1943, when he called for a drink with Sir Miles Lampson at the Auberge des Pyramides. "Our entrance was impressive. Any entrance with Miles is impressive. Everybody bowed and scraped and we were led in state to a table next to the King's. I was so placed that I was able to study him without appearing to stare. I found it almost impossible to believe that he is only twenty-three. He is a big, fine-looking young man with a small beard which I believe once inspired one of his subjects to shout 'God shave the King'." When Farouk rose to leave he came over to speak with Sir Miles and Noël Coward; later they were told the King had settled their bill. Coward commented in his diary on a garden party held two days later: "The King was there in a convivial mood and a white dinner jacket; we had an amicable but highly-strung little conversation. He couldn't possibly have been more courteous or charming but I had the feeling that he was somehow nervous. The local gossip is that he doesn't care for the English very much but I can only say that if this is the case he dissembled it as far as I was concerned with the most exquisite diplomacy."

On 15th November 1943 Farouk was speeding on a highway towards Ismailia. He pulled out to overtake a truck and suddenly saw a car approaching him at speed. This forced him to pull in sharply ahead of the truck, hitting it with the side of his car, losing control and crashing into trees on the edge of the road. The popular story was that when a British serviceman rushed up to the car Farouk opened his eyes and said, "I'm the King of Egypt", the serviceman, believing the balance of the man's mind disturbed, replied, "Yes, mate, and I'm the Emperor of Afghanistan!" A military ambulance rushed him to hospital. At the first diagnosis he was suffering from a mild degree of shock and a crack in the pubic bone of the pelvis, a condition which was not eased when, because the stretcher used to carry the King had been hastily put together, it collapsed, causing the monarch to make contact with the ground with that part of his body least prepared for such a shock at that particular moment. This was a story told by Dr. Andrew Lowdon who treated Farouk. It was subsequently discovered

that he had two fractured ribs without displacement. Sir Ralph
Marnham, then Acting Consultant Surgeon in the Middle East
Forces, Farouk's orthopaedic specialist, Kemi Hussein, and
three of his medical household also attended the King. Unin-
formed sources say that certain important glands had been
crushed beyond redemption. An operation was advised by which
fresh glands should be grafted, and the injured ones removed,
otherwise the lack of glandular secretion would have affected
the brain and deteriorated the reasoning power, and the King
would have become lymphatic and incurably obese. One untrue
report is that the operation being very dangerous, the Egyptian
doctors vetoed it. Another version blamed the British doctors
for Farouk's subsequent condition. It is true that within three
months Farouk was fat, but he had been growing increasingly
corpulent before the operation.

General Stone, G.O.C. British troops, has given the author
the following comments: "He remained in our hospital under
treatment (mainly massage and physiotherapy) for about three
weeks. During his stay he was accommodated in an ordinary
army hut like any normal patient. I used to visit him frequently.
He thoroughly enjoyed being away from Court duties and protocol and being treated by doctors, orderlies and nurses just like
an ordinary army casualty. In fact he was most reluctant to
leave and finally the Prime Minister had to ask me to put in a
word!

"During the course of my conversations with the King he
expressed many good ideas about the development of his
country and about its economic and social problems. One day he
told me that he had appointed Amr Bey, the squash racquets
champion, as Egyptian Ambassador in London and added, 'He
is the sort of young Egyptian I admire. I wish there were more
like him'." General Stone made a very pertinent point on the
reign of Farouk: "One day when I and one or two senior
officers had been invited to a duck shoot by the King, he was
talking about his early days in England and, turning to me, said
with a good deal of feeling: 'How I wish I could have finished
my time at the Shop' [The Royal Military Academy, Wool-
wich]. If he had it might have made a lot of difference in his
character and in the course of subsequent events in Egypt."

Stone also recorded another comment which is important:

"King Farouk was suspected in some quarters of being pro-German. One day when I had an audience with him at the palace he himself brought up the subject. He said, 'Some people say I am pro-German. I assure you that I am not. The only thing I am is pro-Egypt'."

One British officer who visited the King in hospital was Group Captain Patrick Domvile, who took him a small aquarium of fish. By his next visit Farouk had christened each fish with the name of a nurse. The staff loved him; he requested to be regarded as an ordinary patient (despite the fact that a diesel train arrived daily from Cairo with special food) and asked to be treated in the "firm British way". He threw a party and gave presents when he left. A month later Churchill, Eden and Lampson, visited him to congratulate him on his recovery. When he left hospital crowds shouted their welcome, and this touched him: for long afterwards, if advised in the interests of popularity not to make a certain decision, he would say: "But you heard the people cheer me when I left the hospital: that was spontaneous."

During his convalescence Farouk invited ninety men and women of the British and New Zealand Forces to visit the royal estates at Inchass, 35 miles from Cairo, where the twenty-year-old estates included an experimental poultry farm and thousands of acres of citrus orchards. Farouk, whose agents were accused of holding up competitive farmers' goods until the royal produce had been sold on the markets, had more than a mercenary interest in crops and plants and surprised his guests as he took them round the estate, which was rather like Kew Gardens, where much of the research into the plant life and agricultural developments in the Delta were being undertaken, and revealed to them his close interest and wide knowledge of these aspects of his country's economy, which seemed quite exceptional to them against the background of his life and character otherwise.

Sir Miles Lampson became Lord Killearn at this time, which recalls a *faux pas* attributed to Noël Coward who, when dining at the Embassy shortly after the Ambassador's change in title, said to his host, "I hear, sir, you are much more popular than your predecessor Lampson."

A month after the King's car accident Farida gave birth to

another daughter, Fadia. The general disappointment at no son could be felt. When Farouk, who waited outside the room, was told by Lucy Sergeant, the midwife, that the child was a girl he replied, 'Yes, I knew by the cry,' and added that she would be 'loved just the same'."

> They attribute daughters unto God: (far be it from him!) but unto themselves children of the sex which they desire. And when any of them is told the news of the birth of a female, his face becometh black, and he is deeply afflicted: he hideth himself from the people, because of the ill-tidings which have been told him.—*Koran.*

After February 1942 Farouk was naturally anxious to rid himself at the earliest possible opportunity of Nahas. A 'Black Book' containing charges of corruption, compiled by that "keen-witted and spiteful" Copt Makram Ebeid, provided the King with an excellent excuse. It is typical of Farouk that although at this time he was smouldering with indignation and hatred for Nahas, who had been imposed upon him, and for Lampson who had made the imposition, at a party given every Thursday evening by some British friends, and which Farouk invariably attended, when he asked a pretty girl where she lived, and she replied, "Half way between the British Embassy and the residence of Nahas Pasha", Farouk, with his quick wit, replied, "*Mademoiselle, vous vivez dans un très mauvais quartier.*"

The Black Book accused Nahas of having closed down a school in Garden City, Cairo, and rebuilding it as his own private residence; sending a coded message to the Ambassador in London ordering him to buy six white fox furs for his wife, purchasing a car worth twice his annual salary from the Greek millionaire Cozzika, rigging an auction of timber for the State railways; arranging the irrigation of a cousin's lands in order to increase their value; of malpractices concerning passports and visas, and of supplying inside financial information to his wife, who has been compared to Eva Peron, and to her family who used it to make fortunes on the cotton exchange. On 29th March 1942 Makram Ebeid presented his findings, collected in the months following his dismissal as secretary-general of the Wafd (a post he had held for fifteen years) as a petition to Farouk. Thousands of copies of this Black Book were secretly distributed.

Nahas defended himself ably in Parliament, which gave him an overwhelming vote of confidence. Lampson persuaded Farouk not to dismiss Nahas, but the damage had been done and the café gossips of Cairo decided there could be no smoke without fire. Nahas Pasha's image suffered, opinion moved in favour of Farouk whom the radio called "the only defence of the nation and the only hope of the populace . . . in the fight for independence".

Early in 1943 Eden made a speech as Foreign Secretary in which he said that the British Government would encourage economic and political co-operation between Arab States in the Middle East. This has been called the germ of the Arab League, sustained during the war by the formation of the Middle East Supply Centre which was replaced after the war by a diplomatic mission in Cairo, the British Middle East Office. Marlowe names the two principal sponsors of Arab unity as Nahas and Nuri as-Said, Prime Minister of Iraq, both in office as a result of British intervention. Egypt assumed leadership in the move for Arab unity; she was geographically in the centre, wealthier and more advanced than other aspirant member states. After intrigue, misgivings, with some reluctance and unvoiced reservations for the future, the Arab League was born in October 1944 at a conference in Alexandria led by Nahas. One day after the states had signed their membership of the League, Farouk, confident in the public opinion against Nahas engendered by the Black Book campaign, the Wafd's failure to deal satisfactorily with a severe Gambia malaria epidemic in Upper Egypt which killed probably 60,000, and the withdrawal of British support for Nahas, sent the Prime Minister this letter: "As I am anxious to see my country governed by a democratic Ministry working for the fatherland and enforcing the laws of the Constitution in the spirit as well as the letter, giving equality to all Egyptians in rights and duties and bringing to the masses food and clothing, I have decided to dismiss you from office."

Chapter 7

A Time of Inertia
(October 1944—7th May 1945)

An Englishman living in Egypt during the war has given the author the following extract from his diary, written when he was staying at a house at Burg el Arab with friends, in September 1944. King Farouk knew them all.

Coming back after dark from Alamein we found that the King had turned up. He invited himself to dinner, stayed the night, and until the following afternoon. He had the usual hangers-on and as we were 'camping' and had no servants it was something of a trial.

The Mersa Matruh train was stopped to provide us with some delicious water melons. His Majesty had a ravenous appetite that our tins could hardly supply and we got in more food from the village. He ate no bread—presumably because he thinks it fattening—but made up for it in other ways. He breakfasted off: orange juice, melon, rice crispies, scrambled eggs, fish cakes, kidneys, lamb chops, and coffee. He has a big cigar at all hours, but rarely takes alcohol. In the evening (we stayed up until 3 a.m.) he did *sotto voce* ask Pulli to put a little whisky in his coca-cola, but will not accept a drink openly. He had a sheep killed for the villagers, and we heard them until late singing round a great roasting fire. They sent His Majesty the heart and kidneys for breakfast.

He speaks excellent and very fluent English, though with something of a schoolboy vocabulary and slang. He has a very easy small talk and a quick repartee, but, apparently, no conversation. I have never heard him discuss anything serious, though this may be a matter of policy. His laugh is loud, frequent, and over-easily provoked; almost a nervous mannerism. He has a readiness to make *sous entendus* and bawdy jokes of a fairly mild schoolboyish nature. The conversation at Burg became definitely free, and His Majesty delighted to ring the gong in mock censure whenever the convenances were overstepped.

He has absolutely no taste or sensibility, and there is a marked coarseness about him generally. On the other hand he is extremely observant and forgets nothing. In practical matters he is shrewd and knowledgeable. For instance he knew at once why the quail nets along the coast were laid always on the north side of the bushes (the quail come down into the wind; the north wind prevails). Incidentally he told me that he always took a thousand or more quail alive, and kept them on one of his estates so that he could eat quail all the year round. The arrangement was satisfactory he said, though the quail lost weight in captivity.

With his shrewdness goes constant suspicion, probably the result of sad experience. He loves poking into other people's rooms, knowing of their affairs and whereabouts. Seeing R, who had gone upstairs, looking down on the party in the garden from an upper window, he followed her up to see what she was doing. This is characteristic. He also affects a curious omniscience and will never admit that he does not know about something. I was reading Benson's *As We Were*, and he picked it up pretending that he had read it. Again characteristic.

His admiration for America and things American, is paralleled by a dislike and deep distrust of the English. Not unnaturally, after his treatment by Lampson. His dislike of H.E. is projected onto the whole nation. The projection perhaps does not go very deep, and if he could see more English people, young English people, his views might well change. Meanwhile where the English are concerned he is excessively touchy about himself and his country. (This leads him to suspect rudeness where none was intended.)

He dresses badly. Most of the time at Burg having shed his general's uniform, he wore a not very clean white vest and khaki shorts. His energy is amazing and he never goes to bed. The night he kept us up at the palace until 7 a.m. is not apparently exceptional. At Burg we went to bed at 3 a.m. and he was the first up in the morning.

He loves practical jokes of a childish sort. Whips people's cigarettes out of their mouths with his lighter when giving them a light etc. At Burg he asked us why we did not play more 'pranks' on each other.

He seems to do little work. The really serious thing is that his entourage is very third class. The following are always with him: Karim Thabet, a Syrian journalist, who passes for a wit, and has written his life; Commander Rashad, a naval doctor, and ex-heavyweight champion of Egypt, an assuming and very stupid man; Rashad's harmless and colourless wife; and Pulli, his Italian ex-barber, honest with the King, devoted, and actually the best of the bunch. There is also his ex-kennelman, who has graduated into a dinner jacket, not harmful but hardly suitable as a permanent companion. He has in fact no one of any calibre among his close friends. A great pity.

By the time he was twenty-five Farouk had changed in appearance radically from his early days as King. He was now over six feet, heavy, balding, fat-fingered, with bags under his eyes, and heavy lids, but still handsome and outwardly fit despite a weak heart. His moustache had waxed tips, like his father. He shaved off his beard. A thick covering of hair all over his body helped his virile appearance. He swam well and often to keep fit, but his growing corpulence pained him.

He loved to be unconventional and would arrive at friends' villas incognito and unannounced. One Englishman told the author of his first encounter with the King one Saturday afternoon when a large man appeared in the entrance in shorts, grey socks and gym shoes. It was Farouk looking for someone to swim with.

This gaiety, which would induce the King to throw pith pellets at guests during a formal luncheon, was an outward show to hide his inner feelings of disappointment, unhappiness and loneliness. They were also the acts of a young man so strictly brought up that until now he had not had a chance for such childish expression. When the pellets scored a hit he would let out an uncouth, hysterical laugh, to everyone's embarrassment. But he was capable of more genuine humour and kindness. When the Englishman who had first seen him in shorts and socks got married, Farouk had a wedding cake made for him showing a couple in a canopied bed. He was alert and thoughtful. If bored at a villa party he would make a telephone call to the palace, collect together as many people as possible and drive to the palace where the staff had hurriedly laid a feast on trestle tables. This would be followed by interminable hours of films in Technicolor which he mistakenly believed entertained his guests.

For diversion he once dressed up as an Arab sheik and wandered the streets of Cairo at night with two attendants similarly attired. He was charming and not at all pompous. It was typical of him that on one occasion, finding no one at home on one of his impromptu calls on a friend, he spent an hour and a half discussing plants with the under-gardener. Farouk had what has been described as *baladi* humour, wit with a popular touch: with a couple of well-suited remarks the King could immediately put a gardener at his ease.

He preferred the people to the pashas. His ideas of increasing the land holdings of the fellaheen did not endear him to the pasha class. He possibly had more English and American friends at one time than Egyptians. He was proud of his own whiter-skinned Albanian forbears, and called the Sudanese 'blacks'. His charm and tact were such that to a British Ambassador on his first visit to the palace, before the Ambassador had been properly introduced and when he had to register a protest at rioting, Farouk began the discussion by saying, "I realize this must be very embarrassing for you. . . ."

Until 4th February 1942 incident Farouk's behaviour had been exemplary. He now had an inferiority complex to the British. Inner frustration must have made him suffer: he was embittered but unable to show it, except in the intrigues which he arduously pursued with, and against, his politicians. His other channels of expression were irresponsible behaviour which included idle boasts, lies, lack of dignity, the pursuit of women and possessions.

In 1943 Sholto Douglas, head of South East Asia Command, arrived in Cairo and came to realize, in his words, the "state of tension between King Farouk and the British, which, to my way of thinking was both dangerous and unnecessary . . . our Ambassador and the King seemed to loathe the sight and sound of each other. . . . I found our people talking about and treating King Farouk as if he were nothing but a naughty and rather silly boy. . . . It seems to me that it would be much wiser . . . to have him as a friend and an ally rather than play into the hands of our enemies by antagonizing him and giving him cause to work against our vital interests."

To gain Farouk's friendship Douglas invited him to the première of the film *Desert Victory* and laid on a guard of honour for him. "The poor man even admitted to me that he felt the British were taking some notice of him. His pleasure over this was both evident and sincere. . . ." In return Farouk took Douglas on tours of Cairo nightclubs until four or five o'clock in the morning. Apart from his keeping him up late when he had serious problems on his mind, his flippancy, and his fanatical keenness to acquire great wealth, Douglas grew to like Farouk, to the annoyance of less well-informed Allied circles.

Douglas once took advantage of his friendship with the King to explain the great contrast between rich and poor in Egypt and "the unsound state of affairs that existed in his country. . . . I told him that after the war he would find himself in a strong position if he took the right stand . . . but that all would be lost if he did not do something to alleviate the poverty and the misery of the masses of Egypt. Farouk listened carefully, and he expressed his interest in what I was saying, and even a certain sympathy; but there was some gap in our understanding of each other's views that we did not seem able to bridge".

Farouk's embitterment was deepened by the idle, slanderous rumours which originated from Garden City British Intelligence sources that the King was a crypto-fascist and a secret drunkard. He maintained an excellent intelligence service of his own and was never out of touch with these rumours or significant events. When Lord Moyne was murdered in 1944 by members of the Stern gang it was Farouk in person who telephoned a member of the British Intelligence to tell him. Killearn was then informed. Sometime later Farouk telephoned again to say the murderers had been caught. When General Kreipe was kidnapped in Crete and taken clandestinely to Cairo in the war, Farouk sent a congratulatory bottle of champagne to his captors when this knowledge was still top secret.

Farouk enjoyed carrying toffee in his pocket, into which he would dip freely and often in a most unkingly manner. He liked gimmicks and to shock with occasional outrageous behaviour. For instance, at one time Farouk kept a car horn which when sounded let out the screaming howls of a dog run over; at a country reception on a hot day he slipped a piece of ice down down the brassière of a curtsying guest to help her 'cool off'.

His palace of Abdin, built in 1931, could lay six hundred places with gold plate for dinner amid Louis XIV and XV splendour. The menu for one of the King's buffet suppers there read as follows:

Consommé de volaille froid
Tronçon de saumon à la Vénitienne
Soup de mer à l'Orientale
Galantine de faisan d'Ecosse truffée

Agneau de lait à la Bergère
Chaud-froid de pigeons en belle-vue
Aiguillettes de veau à la mode
Poularde de Bresse Lamberty
Yalandji Dolmas
Pâté de gibier à la Mirabeau
Langue de Charolais à la gelée de Porto
Asperges en branches sauce divine
Dinde de Fayoum rôtie froide à la gelée d'or
Salade Gauloise
Baklawa Pyramidal
Charlotte aux fruits
Gâteaux Marguerite
Petits-fours variés
Glaces assorties
Petits pains au caviar
Friandises
Fruits

elegantly printed, with a programme for the evening's entertainment, in blue, red, green and gold, with the royal cipher and crest, and tied with the green ribbon of Egypt.

A stairway from the ground floor of Abdin, from the silver vaults and court offices, led to the top floor reception salons—Red, White, Diplomatic and Suez Canal rooms, the throne room, the King's office and living rooms. Connecting these was the long hall, crowded with heavy sofas and chairs, wall lamps and hung mirrors, French eighteenth century in the Louis XIV style. A private theatre seated four hundred for film previews, plays, concerts, operas, dancers and jugglers, with a gallery in the rear where the Queen sat with her attendants. Farouk occupied one of four large seats in the front row.

In the palace grounds there was a raised swimming pool, marble bandstand, orange groves and an outdoor cinema. In his garages Farouk kept his favourite cars: a jeep, a Ford, a Lincoln Continental, two Packard cabriolets, a Chrysler fluid drive, a Mercedes Benz and four state Rolls-Royces.

He had four A.D.C.s headed by a lieutenant-general, a rear-admiral in command of royal yachts, and a major-domo in command of cooks, stewards, engineers, gardeners, cleaners, doormen, messengers and other staff who were mainly Nubians, dressed in red tarbooshes, highly embroidered monkey jackets, and white gloves.

The palace oppressed him. He had to get out of it. Practically every night found him in L'Auberge des Pyramides. He would not be back until the early hours of the morning and then slept until the afternoon. His idea of democracy was intimacy with every level of person: these sorties gradually lost him the respect of the people. His companions at most parties and night-clubs were the pair who had worked themselves into his confidence, Pulli Bey and later Karim Thabet. Thabet looked odd, evil and repulsive, a hunched man with a short body; a clever and wicked-looking quasimodo. He suffered from eczema on his hands. Thabet was the real courtier, a sycophant who never said a word against Farouk. Pulli was more frank, though kept his remarks to a judicious level of audibility. He was capable at a party of pointing at the fawning group of flatterers with the King and remarking to a fellow guest: "It is a great pity they are surrounding him like that."

Although in the past the King's liking for girls has naturally received more publicity than any other, it is not generally realized that Farouk was almost impotent. He enjoyed female company and needed it but probably took some form of sex stimulants to achieve satisfaction. He kept a silver-handled whip, but one of his mistresses once remarked, "He doesn't bother me very much, you know."

Despite his reputation Farouk was known mostly for his charm and good company. One girl, a singer with E.N.S.A. called Jennifer Leigh, entertaining troops in the Middle East was singing at the Summer Palace in Alexandria one evening in 1944 when the King called to see the cabaret. Afterwards she was invited to sit at his table and found him very easy to talk to. When she asked how she should address him, he told her, "You should be calling me Sire, and it's got nothing to do with a horse." Farouk could spoil his reputation as an excellent wit with these occasional puerile remarks, followed by his loud guffaws. Sobering for a moment he remarked: "You haven't got round to calling me that fat old wog yet."

The King arrived next day to give Miss Leigh lunch and asked her to play the piano for him, to which he sang 'Old Man

River', very flat. He was like a schoolboy, deriving fun from simple pleasures. He went to hear her every night that week, always expecting to hear his favourite Portuguese song 'Tiro-liroliro', and to invite her to his table afterwards for a chat, and their usual repartee. One prank he played happened in the middle of a number when at a signal he arranged for all the house lights to come on suddenly, and was delighted when she did not falter. "Did you like the lights?" he asked her later, with a grin. He asked her to give two command performances in the palace, showered her with flowers, only once told her a vulgar story, and remembered her years afterwards, when he telephoned her in England from Rome to thank her for a gift of records sent to him years before.

He feared for his life and was always personally armed, sitting at the night-club tables with his hand covering a tiny silver pistol, with another revolver little larger than a lighter in his breast pocket. He became increasingly unreliable; his behaviour was unpredictable. Queen Frederika of Greece never forgave him for the approaches he made to her when she was in Egypt during the war. It is claimed he threatened to poison Farida, and that he once drew a pistol and threatened to kill his cousin Prince Wahid Yusri, whom he accused of plotting to overthrow him and of protecting Farida against his outbursts and cruel accounts of his amorous adventures. Farouk even accused Yusri of being the father of his third daughter, Fadia. Farida quietly left Farouk, and moved from Abdin Palace to Koubbeh, taking the three daughters with her.

One night Farouk was returning in his car with a girl friend to Cairo when he was stopped by a makeshift barrier set across the road. He was set upon by robbers who did not recognize their victims but took everything they had and stripped them of their clothes. The robbers then debated whether or not to shoot them, but the man who had suggested this was outvoted and the King was allowed to drive off. As soon as he reached Cairo he went to one of his houses, telephoned the palace for his valet to bring clothes, and then the Chief of Police. Within little time a force of police rushed out of the city to the village, rounded up all the men, razed the huts to the ground and brought all suspects back to gaol. As soon as Farouk knew they were there he dressed in uniform and went down himself to the terror-stricken thieves. A reliable informant has told the author that Farouk asked for the man who had suggested shooting him to step forward. One of the thieves moved forward, Farouk took out his pistol and shot him.

Farouk collected anything from racing camels, clocks and coins, to stamps, matchboxes, razor blade packets and pornographic statues. (British Intelligence in the war, as a matter of course, vetted every telegram the King sent out of Egypt to order coins, etc., from European dealers.) He suffered from kleptomania. There are many examples of how those on whom he paid a visit feared for their treasured possessions; if something caught his eye he would take it home with him occasionally promising and sending a substitute, but as his passion for collecting developed he just commandeered what he wanted.

When the British Embassy put out an appeal during the war for small arms to send back to Britain for the Home Guard, a large stock of every rifle and revolver was collected by Russell Pasha, Chief of Police. Farouk heard of this and informed him he would like to inspect the weapons. Towards the end of the inspection Farouk dismissed Russell Pasha politely, as he was sure he was a busy man. Russell feared the worst: when later the King had left most of the guns had gone, by lorry, with him. Years later when Farouk met the daughter of Russell Pasha he remarked to her, "Many is the grey hair I've put on his head." He managed to accumulate about every type of rifle and submachine gun available and was delighted when the Americans gave him a jeep with a mounted machine gun. To prove his marksmanship to a friend he is reputed once to have taken aim and hit a gardener from the palace window.

His bodyguard competed several times against South African Military teams and were always beaten. "Your people have better match rifles," was Farouk's excuse. Through General Smuts it was arranged that a dozen specially set match rifles be sent from Pretoria. Farouk referred to this several times afterwards with appreciation of South Africa's "sporting spirit".

One of his friends told the author how, after a visit to the Club de Chasse near Cairo, they had all returned to a friend's house with the King to collect their respective cars. Farouk left first, supposedly to return to the palace, but in fact he went to the house of this friend where he arrived a few moments before him and his wife, hid in the garage, and jumped out on them when they drove in. Thabet was with Farouk and while having a drink picked up the wife's stamp album and handed it to Farouk. Her heart sank when the King asked to borrow the album to study her collection of Free French stamps. A week later the album was returned, with gaps where Farouk had selected what he wanted.

Despite his remarks about the British there is no doubt that he enjoyed the company of many service officers, although of course relations with the Embassy were strained. Farouk would not entertain Lampson after 1942. To one Englishman's complaint about the Egyptian flies, which, he protested, settled again immediately one had brushed them off, Farouk replied: "Just like the British here since 1882."

There are many similar accounts during this period of Farouk's reign to this one, told to the author by the widow of an army officer who once had to call on Farouk at his palace on the Sweet Water Canal: "I remember he expected to be there only a few minutes but the King kept him quite a long time and showed him his private museum. I remember asking my husband what sort of man he was and he said: 'I am sorry for him, he is intelligent but a sad man, and disappointed'."

When Farouk dismissed Nahas, Ahmed Maher formed a Saadist government and immediately pronounced an amnesty for all political detainees. This did not include el Sadat, spokesman of the Revolutionary Committee, but within a month, in November 1944, he escaped.

"I escaped," el Sadat recalled, "only to find that Farouk . . . had dashed the high hopes placed in him, and had greeted the Americans with open arms, spending his time hunting, gaming, and drinking with them. It seemed as if he sought in their friendship a solid prop against the day when the British would abandon him.

"For he sensed that the British would desert him, and the idea became a neurotic obsession . . . he always followed the movements of British troops very closely, imagining they were massing to take his throne from him. . . . During these crises, he used to seek refuge in the Castle of Inchass, as if it had some mystic power of sanctuary. He was now a docile and passive

instrument in the hands of the British and was therefore listed
as our Enemy Number One."

Until this time the prime enemy of the Army revolutionary
movement had been the British, but when Farouk paid a visit
to Churchill at the British Embassy in August 1942 the
Egyptian Army officers asked themselves: "How could the
man, in whose person the whole of Egypt had been insulted . . .
so easily forget the indignity which he had suffered. His action
was unworthy of a sovereign, unworthy of the country he represented. But has Farouk ever possessed dignity? Being incapable
of self-respect, how could he respect his throne or his country?
One was forced to the bitter conclusion that what had wounded
Egypt so deeply in the person of its king, had not touched the
king at all."

Lord Mountbatten has given the author the following account
of his visit to Cairo late in 1944: "Our regular Ambassador to
Egypt was away and the Chargé d'Affaires was Mr. Terence
Shone. He came to see me and asked whether I could possibly
spare the time to call on King Farouk. He said that Anglo-
Egyptian relations were rather strained and that no senior
British officer ever took the trouble to see the King or to tell
him what was going on and if the Supreme Allied Commander,
South-East Asia were to do this, this would be of the greatest
help to Anglo-Egyptian relations. I therefore agreed to go.

"I saw the King of Egypt who was extremely affable and
anxious to be pleasant. He reminded me that we had last met
at the Regal Cinema, Marble Arch, in May 1937 at a Ginger
Rogers film and that we had brought him back to Brook House
for a drink.

"I asked him about the political situation and he told me that
if he had not been allowed to get rid of Nahas this time, that in
six months' time there would have been real trouble, as the
country would not any longer stand for corrupt administration.
His Majesty ended by expressing great appreciation that I had
called on him personally and that he wished that more senior
British officers would tell him what was going on in the war.

"Terence Shone told me that it was an excellent thing that
the King had been allowed to change his government, since the
new Prime Minister appeared to be very friendly. If Lampson
had not been away in South Africa on holiday it was considered

that the change of government would not have been allowed to take place as the latter has been backing Nahas and the Wafd to the full up to now. In fact it was clear that the British Ambassador and the King were on extremely bad terms. I hope that my visit helped to smooth things over."

The Yalta Conference decided that only those countries which had declared war on Germany and Japan by 1st March 1945 would qualify for attendance at the San Francisco Conference and become founder members of the United Nations. Hence Ahmed Maher's haste to declare war and secure a place at a peace conference, which Egypt had been denied at Versailles in 1919: Egypt declared war on 24th February 1945, and qualified by one week. The declaration cost Ahmed Maher his life. In crossing between the Chamber of Deputies and the Senate he had to pass through the Pharaonic Hall where there were four young men sitting at a table, and as the Prime Minister approached an assassin got up and fired five shots at him: three bullets hit him in the chest. Farouk's Naval A.D.C. overpowered the assassin, whereupon a crowd which had rushed in on hearing the shots mistakenly assaulted the A.D.C. and the murderers escaped. The assassin, an Axis sympathizer, had been released a few weeks before by Ahmed Maher himself. The loss of Ahmed Maher, an early supporter of Zaghlul, was the loss of one of Egypt's most experienced and respected statesmen.

Though never proved it was widely suspected that the terrorist wing of the Moslem Brotherhood, which by now had infiltrated all other movements, including the clandestine Army officers' group, was responsible for this murder, which proved the forerunner of a series of assassinations and murder attempts. Next on the list was Nahas himself, who survived a plot on 6th December 1945. At a party an hour after the explosion when someone inquired what the noise had been Farouk answered with a laugh: "Someone threw a bomb at Nahas Pasha, but the silly ass missed!" A month later Nahas Pasha's principal intermediary between the Wafd Government and the British Embassy was shot dead.

Murder attempts on British personnel had begun in March 1941. Russell Pasha, who was in Egypt until 1946, described the method of assassination as similar to that which killed Sir Lee Stack in 1924. Otherwise the assassin would be on foot and would shoot at point blank range from the back as the victim walked to the office, or home to lunch. In his car Russell Pasha himself carried a revolver and a "sawn-off twelve-bore shot-gun and also a five-foot quarter-staff with a calf's knuckle-joint shrunk on to the end. . . ."

In the later part of the war, after the scene of action had shifted from the Middle East, Egypt lost all interest in the conflict and devoted more time to national ambitions, and political intrigue. There were serious problems at home, population increase, rent increase, land value increase and an increasing number of political groups which thrived on unrest: the Communists, Ahmed Hussein's Socialist Party, the clandestine Free Officers' movement slowly recruiting its members secretly from among the Army officers, and the Moslem Brotherhood.

In 1943 over 90 per cent of the population of Egypt suffered from ophthalmia, 85 per cent from hookworm, 48 per cent were usually unemployed. The number of millionaires had swelled from 50 before the war to 550. In the Kena and Aswan provinces, 1,250,000 people were reported to be on the starvation line. Two night watchmen who were starving killed a whole family in order to steal their washbasin. The rich grew richer and the poor grew poorer. The price index had risen from 131 in 1939 to 353 in 1944.

El-Barawy summarized the effects of the war which had "helped to intensify and mobilize the new revolutionary energy" as follows: "The change of Egyptian capitalism into a monopolized one that tended to enrich itself at the expense of the masses, and in close connection with foreign interests, feudalism, and the Palace; the gradual alienation of the Wafd leadership from the masses and towards opportunism; the increase of the strength of the working class; the intensification of popular discontent as a consequence of continuous British interference in the internal affairs of the country . . . the sharply increasing cost of living; the human and material losses suffered by . . . participation in the war; the declaration of both the Atlantic and the United Nations Charters which stressed the right of peoples to self-determination; the spread of progressive ideas and theories concerning social justice, especially after the adhesion of Soviet Russia to the Western Allies; and the repression of public liberties as a result of the martial law and press censorship."

On 7th May 1945 Germany surrendered unconditionally. The British were still in Egypt, in debt to the country for £400,000,000. At the time Farouk was concerned with Arab unity, a project with which the British concurred. In February the *Mahroussa* lay at anchor in Yanbu Bay. The hills reverberated with the salvos of saluting guns as the eldest of Ibn Saud's forty sons stepped on board to welcome Farouk and the party went ashore to a temporary town of silk tents. The two Kings reviewed Ibn Saud's bodyguard of Wahhabis with their braided hair and sweeping brown *abaat* gowns. There followed a banquet of roasted sheep and sweetmeats, with poems and songs to entertain the guests after which Ibn Saud accepted the Pan-Arab protocol already signed by Egypt, Syria, Lebanon, Iraq and Transjordan. Next day he invited Farouk to pray in the Mosque of Medina, before the tomb of the Prophet.

The R.A.F. gave Farouk a 180 m.p.h. twin-engined Avro-Anson and invited him to their parties. One officer told the author how he and another officer, both bachelors, were giving a party in Cairo and decided to ask three kings to the celebration, Farouk, Peter of Yugoslavia and George of Greece. All three monarchs attended and the party was going very well. Soon after it was under way, when all guests had had a chance to discover who their fellow guests were, Farouk walked up to his host and said with a twinkle in his eye, "I see you've got a full house." "How is that?" asked the host. "Three kings and two knaves," Farouk replied.

Perhaps the most astute remark credited to Farouk is the one he made when the news came that Lord Killearn was to leave Egypt. He said: "I only really ever had one thing against that man; he would never acknowledge that I am the power behind the throne."

The Free Officers' Society still plotted. "There was", wrote El Sadat, "a time of inertia and depression, when the idea of a revolution seemed very far off. . . ."

Chapter 8

The Tiger of Faluja
(May 1945—January 1949)

After the war Egypt emerged as the richest and strongest of the Middle East countries. With the increase in industrialization labour forces grew in size and strength of their organization. One of the most remarkable facts of the last fifty years was the way Egypt, after World War II, suddenly developed the idea of being the leader of the 'Arab' world. Until the end of World War I or thereabouts, Egyptians were hostile to, and contemptuous of Arabs. Their patriotism was purely Egyptian. Their culture, their structure of society, their ethnic origins were all quite different from Arab countries east of Suez. In the Arab Revolt in World War I, and the subsequent struggles between the wars, the Syrian rebellion against the French, Zionism, nationalism in Iraq, Ibn Saud and the Wahhabis and other passionate and fanatical movements which swept the Arab world, Egypt seemed no more interested than Italy or Spain. Egypt had, of course, been half Europeanized since Mahomed Ali, whereas the other Arab countries had been inside the Ottoman Empire in an entirely different world. It was only at the end of World War II that Egypt suddenly blossomed out as an 'Arab' country. Her politicians suddenly glimpsed an imperial future by replacing the British Empire.

King Abdulla thought himself a noble Arab and had not much time for these Egyptian assumptions of superiority . . . an element of rivalry between the two Kings arose. King Abdulla on paying a visit to Egypt gave a very poor description of Farouk, who he said, as related by General Glubb, was "so ill-mannered and stood with both hands in his pockets".

This visit took place in January 1946. Farouk welcomed Ibn Saud with full ceremony. The two Kings drove together in an open coach between the crowds, Farouk was noticeably fatter, his sword belt slanting across his large stomach, though he appeared as alert as ever, looking inquisitively into the crowds and searching the faces. On 12th January Ibn Saud gave a dinner for Farouk and next afternoon they were at Heliopolis for the races together. Three days later the two Kings issued this joint statement: "We associate ourselves with all Moslem Arabs in their belief that Palestine is an Arab country, and that it is the right of its people and the right of Moslem Arabs everywhere to preserve it as an Arab land. All the efforts by the Arab Kings, heads of Governments, and peoples in support of the Palestinian Arabs were made to maintain the principles of justice. We confirm the constitution of the Arab League, which is that each Arab country has the right to decide its own future and enjoy independence. . . ." At noon everyone lunched in the Manasterli Palace, new headquarters of the Arab League.

After the war Farouk had gathered round him two groups, one largely foreign and corrupt, another of Egyptians who genuinely believed in Egypt's need for a throne . . . Mortada el Maraghi, son of the influential Sheik of Al Azhar, Abdel Fattah Amr, who became Egyptian Ambassador in London, and Hassan Youssef, who became Deputy Chief of the Royal Cabinet. But Farouk failed his supporters. Tom Little explained: "His hatred of the British (only partially modified by the astute tact of the new British Ambassador, Sir Ronald Campbell), his hatred of the Wafd, his love of pleasure and the society of bad people, made his behaviour incalculable. . . . Perhaps the basic trouble was that Farouk was intelligent enough to be cynical about the political life of the country and lacked the intellectual and moral stamina to be interested in its improvement."

But this stamina was not lacking elsewhere in Egypt. The dynamism of nationalism moved from the political parties to movements such as the Moslem Brotherhood, the communist groups, the trade unions and in the Army movement. Nationalism to all these groups meant a fight for the same goal with two synonymous objectives; riddance of the British occupation manifested by their troops, and overthrow of the Egyptian ruling class, symbolized by the King. In the Brotherhood oaths were taken at night, on a revolver and the Koran, quickly increasing membership. Recruits were formed into cells of plotting. Several cells made a section. Within each section factories were started behind shops and in sheds to produce bottle bombs and revolvers. With strength the movement became more open. "On 8th September 1945 El Banna told his brethren 'that if conditions remained as they were and there were no immediate reforms, revolution would inevitably ensue'." (Little.)

On 12th November 1945 Farouk's speech at the opening of Parliament, the first since the end of the war, made it clear which way he was thinking: "Today Egypt is more resolved than ever to see an end to all restrictions to independence by the withdrawal of all foreign troops and to reaffirm the unity of the Nile Valley. . . ." A month later Prime Minister Nokrashi in vain requested Britain to open negotiations for revisions to the 1936 Treaty. The British Foreign Office acted in an arrogant and callous manner. They were tardy in realizing that the sun was setting on the Empire, and that independence for African countries would begin in the north-eastern corner of that continent.

Student riots in the Fuad I University, and labour disturbances in January 1946 led to Nokrashi's resignation as Prime Minister. Ismail Sidki Pasha, seventy-one and ill, took over. On 18th February large crowds gathered in Abdin Palace square demanding evacuation of British troops from Egypt and freedom for the Sudan. Students distributed leaflets condemning 'British Imperialism' and another crowd outside the British barracks at Kasr-el-Nil yelled "A bas l'Angleterre"—"Down with Bevin the Criminal".

In the rioting in Cairo students tried to burn down the Victory Club while members of the Mohamed Ali Club opposite stood on their balcony and shouted encouragement. In March demonstrators committed outrages against British military and civilian personnel and property. For the first time the Soviet Embassy committed itself in a statement expressing sympathy for the National Committee of Workers and Students. Farouk referred to the student demonstrations as a "healthy demonstration of the people's ambition to realize its just claims". The British, however, were not the only victims of these riots. In the Abbas Bridge demonstrations in February, students shouted for

Farouk's abdication and tore his poster portrait from the walls.

Despite his age Sidki was the one man who could handle the intricate political situation. Farouk later said of him, "Sidki was a statesman, he travelled first class; second class carriages were empty, all other politicians were third class."

Sidki worked to resolve the dangerous situation. He raided the Wafd and Kotla party offices, shut down eleven quasi-communist organizations, and arrested leading officials of the Moslem Brotherhood. He attacked all extremist movements except the Army's secret society, of which he presumably knew nothing. In October 1946 he signed an agreement with Bevin that British forces would be withdrawn from Cairo, Alexandria and the Delta by 31st March 1947 and from Egypt by September 1949, but this agreement fell down over the Sudan question.

In April 1946 preliminary negotiations for revisions to the Anglo-Egyptian Treaty were begun. Britain's Ambassador Sir Ronald Campbell was received by King Farouk and Sidki Pasha on the 4th and two weeks later preliminary meetings were held before formal negotiations. Farouk received a British delegation, led by Lord Stansgate, to tea. Sidki was very pleased to meet Lord Stansgate and during the visit said, "I could sense the same good spirit in Lord Stansgate as he displayed when, as Mr. Wedgwood Benn, he defended the Egyptian cause . . . just after World War I, when few other Britons spoke favourably on behalf of my country. Thus Wedgwood Benn's name is always remembered as a ray of hope in Egypt."

On 6th May Attlee read to the House an announcement which had already been made in Cairo: "It is the considered policy of His Majesty's Government in the United Kingdom to consolidate their alliance with Egypt. . . . The Government of the United Kingdom have proposed the withdrawal of the British naval, military and air forces from Egyptian territory. . . ."

Churchill immediately condemned the procedure taken by the Government. Bevin defended it, pointing out the development of the United Nations Organization "in which all countries, great and small, feel that they have a new status".

Withdrawal began on Thursday, 4th July, when Lieutenant-General Sir Charles Allfrey, British G.O.C., handed to Ferik

Attallah Pasha, Egyptian Chief of Staff, a silver replica of the key to the Citadel which had first passed to the British when handed to Sir Charles Watson on 14th September 1882, after the victory over Arabi at Tel el Kebir.

Treaty negotiations moved slowly for weeks. In June they were at a standstill when Lord Montgomery arrived in Egypt with a clear brief from Bevin to 'ginger-up' the evacuation of the Delta cities and so demonstrate British sincerity to the Egyptians. Montgomery discussed the situation with the Ambassador, and the C.-in-C. Middle East, Sir Bernard Paget, and also talked with Farouk and Sidki. "To the two latter", Montgomery wrote, "I spoke very plainly. . . . I rubbed into the King and Sidki that both sides must approach the problem in an atmosphere of mutual confidence . . ." but "The King didn't seem interested . . . he kept on saying that what Egypt was suffering from was forty years of British misrule! So I did not waste any more time on him. Sidki displayed much more understanding."

In October Sidki talked with Bevin in London but Egypt and Britain could not agree on the interpretation of the Sudan Protocol: Sidki's statement that "Britain has accepted the unity of Egypt and the Sudan under the Egyptian crown" was held to conflict with Attlee's statement made two days later in Parliament that "no change in the existing status and administration of the Sudan is contemplated". It was plain that no agreement could be reached on the Sudan question, either by the British, their administration in the Sudan itself, or the Egyptians. Sidki resigned on 8th December 1946. His successor Nokrashi broke off negotiations with Britain in January 1947 and put the case for evacuation of British troops from, and unity of, the Nile Valley before the United Nations, but no agreement could be reached by the U.N. Security Council.

Meanwhile Egypt's problems were added to in 1947 by the greatest cholera epidemic since 1902 "when a pilgrim returning from Mecca poured a bottle of holy Zemzem water into the wells of Mousha in Assiut, with the idea of spreading its blessed properties, and so reduced the population of his country by 35,000 within six months". (P. Hughes.) The problem of British occupation still persisted. Owing to the cholera epidemic the Opening of Parliament ceremony in November 1947 was curtailed. The Speech from the Throne opened with familiar post-war words, a reaffirmation of the Egyptian will to achieve complete independence, unabridged sovereignty, unity of the Nile Valley, and the "evacuation of both parts of the Valley, Egypt and Sudan by foreign troops".

Lack of solution and the tardiness in endeavouring to find one inspired plotters and gave them time to realize their plans for violence. On 7th May 1948 the British Ministry of Information and the British Food Office in Cairo were bombed. In October that year Egypt was held spellbound by reports in the press of bomb plots planned by a society led by a member of the Egyptian Pasha class. These plans had been uncovered and the gang brought to trial to face accusation of "criminal complicity in the murder of certain Egyptian personalities and members of the British forces in Egypt. . . ." Egypt struggled to throw off the unwanted British yoke. London called her "ungrateful": she replied "Perfide Albion" and counted the number of times Egypt had been promised independence, beginning with Gladstone.

In the years immediately after World War II Farouk took the opportunity each summer to get away from Egypt for his first holidays abroad since he had come to the throne. He needed a retreat and chose the Kazira villa in the mountains of Cyprus between Kakopetria and Troödos. Here he had seclusion and no restriction. His plane or yacht were ready to move for an excursionary trip, to Mersin in Turkey (where he once arrived unexpectedly and representatives had to be flown to meet him) or for short cruises in the Mediterranean. In the villa he kept a suitcase full of money for gambling sessions. He went out in a dark suit, dark glasses with a gardenia or carnation in his buttonhole, to watch beauty parades and threw parties afterwards for low caste but good looking Cypriot, Lebanese and Greek girls, parties dancing on the patio round a fire in the centre, and surrounded by a glass screen of many colours. The parties were late and licentious. He became an escapist: funny mirrors in the villa distorted the reality of the image, purple hearts kept in his shaving cabinet gave him abnormal sustenance, hashish through a hookah drugged him; he tried Zivania gin, whisky and brandy, which he would never have been seen drinking in Cairo or Alexandria where his only departure from strict Moslem ruling that his friends admitted was the occasional bottle of champagne. He liked to watch the boys in the open latrines when they left school. He learnt all the Greek swearwords he could. But he was not a bad man, he merely wanted to try everything. He was mature, nearly thirty years of age, but still childish. Every morning he would spread the bed with newspapers and let his pet rabbit play on them. The rabbit was called Farouk because other female rabbits were brought to be mated with it.

And he loved to eat. A whole venison would disappear in four helpings. Pigeons, partridge, quail and chicken were his favourite birds. He liked the blood mixed with egg and lemon as gravy. He liked goose eggs, caviare was flown in and fish came daily from the coast. For five months each year he was away from it all, with his servants, his parrot, his rabbit and the girls.

At this time a diversion arose which Egypt could ill afford to take but to which she was committed because of her implication with the Arab League.

From 1923 to 1948, Palestine had been governed by Britain under a League of Nations mandate. It was understood by the British that Palestine should become a home for the Jews without encroaching on the Arab population. Zionists, however, claimed that the whole of Palestine was their proper home. The League of Arab States, founded under British aegis, was united in practically only one cause, opposition to Zionism. On 15th May 1948 when the mandate ended, British troops were withdrawn. On the same day the Jewish State of Israel was formed and the Palestine Arabs united with the Arab armies of Egypt, Syria, Lebanon and Jordan. When the Nokrashi cabinet met in secret session to consider military action in Palestine, it was decided that no war should be contemplated as the Egyptian Army was unprepared. Nokrashi changed his view; at Farouk's insistence (some Egyptians have even claimed that Farouk ordered the advance of troops without informing his Prime Minister) the Arabs invaded Palestine and were expected, with their forty to one majority, to win easily.

At this point Nasser was in something of a dilemma. If the Arabs won the Egyptian Army would return home victorious and Farouk would receive full credit for sending them to war.

This would be a severe hindrance to the plotters for revolution who relied on a growing nationalist feeling against the King. Before the war began Nasser had even considered resigning from the army and with others had offered his services to the Grand Mufti of Jerusalem as 'civilian Volunteers'. This was declined as it was not supported by the Egyptian Government.

As the Egyptian Army was sent on its way to fight in Palestine the last straw was loaded onto the camel's back. Nasser wrote: "We have been duped—pushed into a battle for which we were unprepared. Vile ambitions, insidious intrigues and inordinate lusts are toying with our destinies. . . ." The Palestine campaign saw the final dedication of the young officers in their revolutionary plans. "We were fighting in Palestine, but all our thoughts were concentrated on Egypt. . . . It was in Palestine that the cells of the Free Officers gathered together in trenches and at outposts in deep deliberation. . . ."

As the Egyptian Army advanced it attacked small settlements, and surrounded worthless objectives, forcing them to fight back and wasting its own ammunition. Coastal batteries were not allowed to fire on Israeli naval patrols without first referring to Army H.Q. in Cairo. The high command of the Egyptian Army was abysmal. When ammunition ran out buyers were sent to scour Europe for additional supplies. They found them; at a price. Everyone wanted to sell arms to the Egyptians. A Turkish and a Greek pirate became main suppliers; a German promised a U-boat and half a Nazi crew; an Englishman tried to sell some old Mulberry harbour; the Italians salvaged shells from a sunken wreck and sold them those. They charged what price they liked. One food deal kept the army well supplied, day after day, with asparagus. Undoubtedly King Farouk was in league with the buyers and received his own percentage on the deals, but no one can argue that he was purposely treacherous in supplying his own men with rifles which blew up in their faces. There was an army committee which was meant to examine all arms.

The Israelis fought back superbly. Only the British trained Arab Legion ('Glubb's girls', with their long ringlets) fought with effect. The Legion advanced on Tel Aviv but was held back by the defenders. King Abdullah of Jordan was bent on seizing Jerusalem. The Israelis then soundly defeated the

Egyptian Army (a makeshift Israeli gunboat sank the *Emir Farouk*, flagship of the Egyptian Navy) and drove it back into the Gaza Strip where Nasser gained the title 'the tiger of Faluja' after his desperate defensive in the Faluja Pocket. He recognized the lack of leadership and efficient command as the real reason why the Egyptian Army was defeated in this war. It was not until later that the Army learnt of Farouk's finger in the arms deal pie.

Soon after the end of the Palestine war, the Moslem Brotherhood were accused of plotting to overthrow the government and Crown. Farouk had been concerned about the Moslem Brotherhood since the early 1940s when he must have come across some of their publications calling for 'Moslem Rule'. He had been sufficiently roused to form a special information service which reported weekly to him the latest of El Banna's movements. El Banna sensed the King's hostility and attempted to convey his Brotherhood's moral and religious aims to Farouk, through the doctor Youssef Rashad. But Farouk was sceptical and Prime Minister Nokrashi ordered the dissolution of the movement, confiscation of its property, and arrest of its members. Hassan el Banna immediately requested Karim Thabet to impress again on the King the Brotherhood's objectives as solely religious and to stress that he could help Farouk fight communism, which the King despised. But Farouk remained unmoved and showed Thabet calendars recently discovered by the police on which the Royal portrait had been replaced by that of El Banna.

In December 1938 Prime Minister Nokrashi was assassinated in the lift in his own Ministry of Interior, by a terrorist disguised as a police officer. Abdel Hadi took over and began bravely by arresting Brotherhood members and crowding them into camps. At this time, because of the connections between some army officers and Hassan el Banna, Hadi must have come close to discovering the Army movement. On 13th February 1949 El Banna was himself shot in the back as he entered the Young Men's Moslem Association. The assassin, wearing an overcoat and scarf over his *galabiya*, escaped. Pulli told Major Sansom, security officer to the British Embassy, that the murder had been planned in the palace, but unbeknown to the King. Medical assistance may have been deliberately withheld from El Banna who had almost bled to death by the time he reached hospital. Farouk was blamed: an uneasy atmosphere hung over the country. Again to quote Tom Little: "Egypt consisted of a hated king, a hated government and a sullen docile people permeated by groups plotting rebellion in secret."

Farouk now commanded no respect, from Egyptian or foreigner, in his country which thirteen years before had worshipped the very ground he walked on. One evening in 1945 he attended a party given by the American Military Attaché appropriately dressed in his uniform of Air Marshal of the Egyptian Air Force. On leaving he was unable to find his hat. The Attaché was extremely concerned. Someone said they had seen a certain American Major playing with the hat, and as he lived in the same building and had consumed much whisky that evening it seemed reasonable to suppose that he had taken the King's hat home with him. The Attaché wanted to call his Embassy and have the flat searched immediately but Farouk took command and suggested knocking on the Major's door and frightening him by letting him know they suspected him. The drunken Major slammed the door in their faces. Farouk, who had drunk nothing more than Coca-Cola all evening, observed: "Now he knows we know he has my hat, he will attempt to get rid of it. I want no fuss; let's await events in the garden." Two minutes later a window opened and out came the King's hat. This story, told to the author separately by two persons who were at the party, is recorded to show the undignified treatment, indeed the open insults Farouk now had to bear from Americans and from the British. It also illustrates the outward calm with which he bore these insults, turning them into a joke.

At home in his palace office he used a small mahogany desk. The walls were panelled and the floors highly polished parquet, strewn with Persian rugs. His bathroom had walls of white alabaster, an Italian marble floor in the middle of which there was a sunken pool, old Moorish style. One wall was covered in a mosaic showing two naked girls bending over a fountain. There was a special room for massage, one for pedicure and manicure, closets to keep towels warm and for clothes.

His character did not change. He liked animals, particularly a pet Alsatian named Loretto. He still reacted against those who, he suspected, used their intelligence or better education against him. He was a good speaker, his subjects loved his annual New Year speech which he always began with the words "My beloved people". Futility pleased him; he would think little of taking part of a coffee set and not returning it, so spoiling the owner's possession. He was known to attend a British party once, not as an open guest, but hidden behind a hedge in the garden from where he could keep an eye on the behaviour of the guests uninhibited by his presence. He once arrived at a diplomatic reception in shorts and poured a jug of cold water over the Swedish Ambassador from the third floor of the R.A.C., Cairo, as he felt the Ambassador was retiring too early. This encouraged everyone else to stay until dawn.

For Shem el Nassim the King gave a party for his friends. The guests, including English, Americans, French, Jews, Egyptians and Copts, would arrive before 10 a.m. for breakfast in a large tent. It was traditional that everyone ate a spring onion and when the palace photographer arrived he would be bombarded with onions. Everyone swam in the pool, and had drinks afterwards. At one of these parties a cousin of the King, attracted by one of the girls, attempted to enter the ladies' changing room. When Farouk heard of it he exiled the cousin to the top diving board where he remained for the day without food or drink.

At one informal reception when the King was entertaining American and English friends he sat on the floor studying books on a shelf and when a friend came up to him Farouk crossed his legs, folded his arms and said, "Oriental Potentate—What!" He had a principle never to give a photograph of himself to a friend. Once, however, after a friend had pestered him and persisted in asking, Farouk replied, "All right", and produced a new £100 note from his pocket, gave it to him and said, "Here is my latest picture". He still boasted, and once claimed to the British Ambassador that he had been present (possibly true) at the interrogation by torture of two Israelis who had been caught attempting to poison an Egyptian water supply during the Palestine war. There was a strand of cruelty in his character.

On 17th May 1945 Farouk signed the marriage contract of his sister Princess Faiza at her wedding with Mohamed Rauf at the Abdin Palace. A month later Farouk's aunt, Princess

Nimetullah, died at Marg, her country house eleven miles east of Cairo. Farouk remembered the happy times when she visited his father at Koubbeh, fifteen years before. He had always remained very fond of her. He went to Marg to pay his last respects, and also awaited the funeral procession at the mosque.

After five years of marriage to the Shah of Persia, Fawzia returned to Egypt to recuperate from a severe attack of malaria. She did not go back to the Shah, who blamed Farouk for preventing her. It is a measure of Farouk's fear of his mother that when waiting for Nazli to come and see him when she had been informed that Fawzia was leaving Persia, the King was perspiring with anxiety and agitation.

When Fawzia unpacked, Farouk commandeered the Persian crown jewels for his collection. It is even claimed that when the Shah's father was to be buried in Egypt, Farouk removed the decorations and sword from the dead man's possessions and despite protests never gave them back. There are also unreliable but entertaining stories of how Farouk was once invited to a party in a house at Heluan which he immediately liked and said so in a loud voice. When the owner did not take the hint and offer the place to Farouk, the King took out a revolver and shot pieces off the chandelier. Next day he commandeered the house. Once when Prince Seif el-Islam, son of the Emir of the Yemen, visited him for lunch, Farouk suggested for comfort at the dining table he remove his sword and jewelled scabbard. After lunch the sword could not be found; it had joined the Farouk collection.

An American friend once showed Farouk a new type of razor he had bought. The King could not resist gadgets (he kept an agent in the U.S.A. to supply him with the latest types) and after examining it pocketed it with a "thanks, old chap" and a hearty laugh. The friend was very annoyed until the next day Pulli turned up with an envelope full of gold coins with instructions that they should be made into a bracelet for the American's daughter.

Farouk continued to add to his collections. Koubbeh Palace contained the paintings, sculpture and stamps. Ras el Tin had the most valuable objects, on the Mediterranean coast with a private pier which could be most useful if a quick escape from Egypt became imperative. Amongst his possessions he kept erotica, pornographic photographs, mechanical sex devices and sex pharmaceuticals.

At night he continued the round of night clubs, every one of which kept a table permanently reserved for him. L'Auberge des Pyramides, where Camelia, Lillian Cohen played and through which he sold brandy from his own cellar, the Scarabee with Annie Berrier and the Helmia Palace nightclub with Samia Gamal, were his favourites. His yachts, the *Fakhr-al-Behar* and the *Mahroussa* were permanently in readiness for fun or earnest departure. The Royal Automobile Club on Kasr el Nil in Cairo was his favourite gambling house. One night there at poker he is said to have been called when holding three kings. His opponent had a full house but Farouk insisted he had won: "I am the fourth King", he explained. More seriously he once confided to ex-King Zog of Albania: "In ten years there will only be five Kings left in the world, the King of England and the Kings of Clubs, Diamonds, Hearts and Spades."

On 19th February 1946 a car crash with a British military lorry in Cairo killed Ahmed Hassanein, Farouk's tutor in England and mentor for ten years, a man who had become powerful in Egypt as the liaison between crown and government. His untimely death must be regarded as another tragedy in Farouk's life, for without this leader of his faithful civil servants with whom he worked well during the day, the King was more inclined towards the alternative palace clique of Thabet, Pulli, and others. Now there was no serious counterpart to the wasteful side of Farouk's life of barren hours in nightclubs. It gradually absorbed his attention. Queen Nazli, who it is believed had undergone a morganatic marriage with Hassanein, left for Europe, taking Fathia with her. She did not return. Eventually, possibly at Thabet's instigation, Farouk was to banish his mother, confiscate her money and property and declare her mentally unbalanced. This treatment turned many against the King: he never saw his mother again.

His entourage still included the volatile Karim Thabet, as press secretary par excellence, who exercised his lively imagination and well-developed sense of how to say whatever the listener wanted to hear; a valet who read reports to the King in his bath and took notes in reply: Elias Andraus, a Levantine who acted as economic adviser to the King, handling investment of the considerable royal income; and a man called Edmond Gahlan listed in *Who's Who in Egypt* in 1948 as "Businessman, general purveyor to the Royal Palaces".

Farouk was not the first of his dynasty to be influenced by his servants: his ancestor the Khedive Tewfik was so under the sway of his valet, Frederique, that the Khedive became known to those who understood just how effective this influence was, as Mademoiselle Frederique.

On 6th May 1947, the anniversary of Farouk's assumption of the throne, the Metro Theatre was dynamited. One morning in that year, after a night at L'Auberge des Pyramides he called unexpectedly on his brother-in-law and sister, walked into their bedroom and told them that he felt all was lost and nothing could save him. A year later Farouk was jeered at for the first time as he left a cinema. He was then twenty-eight.

In November 1948 this communiqué was issued by the palace chamberlain: "The will of Allah, our supreme God, has decreed that the sacred ties between two noble spouses be loosened, and he has turned the heart of His Majesty, King Farouk, and that of Her Majesty, Queen Farida, to this act. . . ." And so Farouk lost what remaining respect the country held for him when he divorced Farida, the beautiful and competent wife who had loved him and suffered his treatment of her and his behaviour with other women until she could stand it no longer. She admitted however that the fault did not rest entirely with Farouk, and he was to love his first wife to the end. It was Farida who insisted on a divorce several years before it was granted. She shut herself up in the palace, leaving it only at night in a small car, bearing an ordinary number, which she drove herself. She refused to see or to speak with her husband and avoided her duties as a queen as much as possible. It is reported that Farouk had tears in his eyes when he finally signed the deed of divorce. He was only nineteen when he married, and was doubtless unfaithful after the first three years of their marriage. But no other woman, certainly not his second wife, was ever able to take Farida's place in his affections.

By the time he was divorced Farouk had had children by other women. The pashas of Egypt were beginning to despair of him themselves: if he fell they would fall also.

At the beginning of 1949 "The pressure of overpopulation, the increased cost of living, the influence of foreign ideas, and the humiliation of the Palestine war . . . combined to complete the disillusionment and disgust of public opinion. For the first time Egyptian domestic politics became more than a matter of rivalries and disputes between various political factions. The spectators were swarming on to the pitch" (John Marlowe).

Neguib, who had fought in the Palestine campaign and once was taken for dead when shot in the lung, eventually to be chosen as the figurehead of the revolt, wrote of the scandal concerning the buying of arms for the Egyptian Army in the war: "I was unaware of the fact that the King himself was involved in the arms racket until the spring of 1950. . . . We succeeded in forcing Nahas to authorize an investigation of the Ministry of War. The investigation resulted in the indictment of thirteen persons, including Prince Abbas Halim, a cousin of the King." Antonio Pulli was named by Neguib as an accomplice, as was Edmond Gahlan, whom he called "the King's strawman in the arms racket". Cheque books were found, Neguib claimed, which showed payments made by Gahlan to Farouk through the Cairo Branch of the Banque Belge et Internationale.

By as early as 1947 the clandestine Army movement had enrolled over one thousand officer members. Now it began to swell into a corps committed to mutiny. Nasser "instituted a revolutionary administrative system, which he divided into five sections: economic affairs, combat personnel, security, terrorism and propaganda" (Anwar el Sadat). Nasser is a clever man. He did not presume to think that he would be able to control the entire movement which was now under way, being carried to its goal by its own momentum. He therefore formed a secret society within a secret movement: only this small clique knew the plans for revolution. Farouk was within three years of his downfall.

In April 1950 an article appeared in *The Islamic Review* ardently in favour of the Wafd who had just been returned to power. It spoke with the energy of a party which had been resting for a while and was now returned, determined for its own part in the coming struggle. The Palestine campaign, it said, "had fateful and catastrophic effects not only on Egypt, but on the whole of the Arab and Islamic world. With a Jewish State now established in the Holy Land, and surviving as a monumental reminder of the defeat of the Arab and Islamic world, the integrity and international prestige of the Arabs and Muslims has become a mockery in the eyes of the world". On the Sudan question it accused Britain of having "taken full advantage of the weak status of the late Egyptian Governments, of 'devious means', 'façades' and 'imperialist activities' ".

On Farouk it said: ". . . the King and his advisers came to realize that dissatisfaction amongst the people had assumed an alarming phase. . . . The political unrest in the country and the activities of seditious organizations . . . were indicative of the eminence of a ruthless and bloody revolution. . . ."

Chapter 9

Creeping Discontent
(February 1949—25th January 1952)

King Farouk began his last three years with a strange act. A General who had once served with the Imperial German Army and had been second in command in the Western Desert, was brought into Egypt clandestinely. His task was to rebuild the Egyptian Army with the instruction of ex-Wehrmacht Officers. Ex-S.S. Officers also offered their services to Egypt. One of the General's first requests of Farouk was to ask for the reports on the failures in the Palestine Campaign, which had not been published. The General's arrival was known to the King, the Secretary-General of the Arab League and one or two others: the British discovered his presence perhaps two months later.

The Wafd were confirmed in power by the January 1950 elections and their last two years of corrupt rule began.

Early in 1950 there was a flurry of British visits to Egypt. Foreign Secretary Ernest Bevin went for talks. (This day, 28th January incidentally, was one of the coldest ever recorded in Cairo, with hoarfrost on the road to the Pyramids). The Commander-in-Chief of the Mediterranean Fleet, Admiral Sir Arthur Power, returning with part of the fleet through the Suez Canal, came to luncheon with the King. The Duke of Edinburgh was first lieutenant of the destroyer *Chequers* which was with the flagship, and was also at the lunch. On 12th March, the centenary of Mohamed Ali's death, the Duke and Duchess of Gloucester visited Farouk and the Duke made the King an honorary Major-General in the British Army. In June the King received Field-Marshal Sir William Slim. These were all attempts to establish better relations with the King, and there were reports that he might visit Britain again after the thirteen years which had elapsed since he was last there.

Another visitor to Egypt in January 1950 was the Vice-Admiral commanding the First Cruiser Squadron of the Mediterranean Fleet, the Earl Mountbatten of Burma, who in a note to the author described this visit which was contrary to regulations as British ships were not supposed to visit Egypt because Anglo-Egyptian relations were very poor Mountbatten obtained permission from his Commander-in-Chief (Admiral Sir Arthur Power), and the Ambassador (Sir Ronald Campbell) obtained clearance from the Egyptian authorities. Mountbatten arrived in his flag ship, the *Liverpool*, and was in Alexandria from 17th January, originally until the 21st but finally until the 22nd.

The Ambassador invited him to stay at the British Embassy in Cairo. He had arranged a special audience with King Farouk in full dress to be treated as a very formal occasion. Mountbatten expected to be ten minutes with the King but in fact was kept for over an hour talking, quite alone. Towards the end of their conversation Farouk said he would like to return the visit on board the flagship and asked when this would be convenient. When told that this would not be possible because Mountbatten had to leave on the following day for a meeting with the Commanders-in-Chief of the Middle East in the Canal Zone, the King appeared very crestfallen and asked whether there was no possibility of his coming to pay a personal visit.

The British did not wish to appear enthusiastic in inviting a monarch with whom the world believed they were on very poor terms. However, the British Ambassador saw the value of such a meeting and at his request Mountbatten decided to defer his departure and duly sent a letter to King Farouk, informing him of this and inviting him to luncheon on the flagship *Liverpool* on the Sunday. The King accepted with alacrity.

On 22nd January Alexandria was in gala dress on account of the King's visit. All ships in harbour were dressed. The Egyptian ships and the *Liverpool* were dressed overall. On the arrival of the royal train all ships in harbour, including the *Liverpool*, fired a twenty-one-gun royal salute. A guard of honour of Royal Marines and a band paraded to receive the

King on the quarter deck and then a heavy shower of rain came down. This meant that the awnings had to be sloped to enable the rain to run off them. It also meant that the two ranks for the Guard of Honour had to be moved very close together as there was much less room. When the King came on board, with his great bulk he found difficulty in moving down between the lines of the Guard of Honour and had to shuffle sideways. When he arrived in Mountbatten's cabin he jokingly complained that there hadn't been room to pass between the ranks of the Guard of Honour. Instead of giving a conventional explanation Mountbatten said that in future he would arrange that the Naval Attaché would move between the ranks of the Guard of Honour before the King (because the Attaché was the only person on board bigger than the King himself). The King laughed loudly at this joke.

Lord Mountbatten recounted that before lunch he saw one of Farouk's A.D.C.s pick up one of the Admiral's matchboxes, hold it up for the King to see, the King nodded his head and the A.D.C. slipped the matchbox into his pocket. The Admiral then said to the King, "Are you by any chance a collector of matchbox lids, Sir?" Farouk asked "Why?" and Mountbatten replied, "Because your A.D.C. has just taken one of my matchboxes with your consent." Farouk laughed heartily and admitted that he was a matchbox lid collector. Mountbatten then offered him one of which there were only two specimens in the world and Farouk got very excited. The ship's paymaster, Commander Covey Crump, was a collector of matchbox lids and gave the King one of his own matchbox lids marked 'Covey's Crumptious Matches'. Farouk promised to send a matchbox or two in return.

The King left after staying quite a long while after lunch in high good humour. Reporters and photographers were surprised to see his showing such pleasure at being on board a British ship at a time when relations were so strained. A month later a crate arrived addressed to Lord Mountbatten on board the *Liverpool* from the King of Egypt containing six gross of special matchboxes with the Egyptian royal arms on them. There were enough to give a dozen to every officer and man in the ship.

To celebrate his appointment as honorary General in the

British Army Farouk invited members of the British forces to visit his country estate. Chief guests were the three heads of services, General Crocker, Air Chief Marshal Baker and Rear-Admiral Campbell. After lunch they were given a personally conducted tour of his stud farm and driven around somewhat perilously in his new red M.G. sports car. On that afternoon his guests found Farouk an uninhibited, slightly shy host with good manners, exhibiting a sense of history and broad reading. He later showed them round the house and grounds and the swimming pool where rumour had it his *houris* performed by floodlight. He conveyed the impression to his guests that he bemoaned his fate and how happy he could have been if he could have pushed all his politicians under water.

On 10th May 1950 Farouk's sister Fathia married a Copt commoner, Riad Ghali. Queen Nazli, despite the King's efforts to dissuade her, had agreed to this marriage, openly embarrassing the King and severing for ever any ties between mother and son. Farouk issued a royal rescript depriving Fathia of her title as Princess and his mother her title of Queen and confiscating all their property. "Call me Madam" is reputedly Fathia's reply.

When Sir Ronald Campbell left Egypt in May 1950 after his four years as Ambassador during which he had worked with tenacity, despite active opposition, to maintain Anglo-Egyptian relations, Farouk broke precedent by personally attending an informal farewell tea party given in Koubbeh Palace. At the beginning of his period of office in 1946 Sir Ronald Campbell's only instructions had been to establish good relations with King Farouk. Amr Pasha, Farouk's young pro-British counsellor, did his best to help foment a close relationship between the British Ambassador and the King, but Farouk did little to follow up these promptings. He may have suspected a concerted plan by the British to influence him towards more serious personal conduct and a more active interest in state affairs, and with this he may have feared he would be in for a course of moral lectures from Amr who was well aware of the King's poor personal behaviour and *fainéantisme* in foreign affairs.

The British Ambassador was granted formal audiences with the King. On one or two occasions the King made semi-secret calls at the British Embassy, and went duck shooting with the

Ambassador. It cannot have been easy for him, the monarch of a country seeking emancipation from British tutelage, to decide to expose himself to the criticism that he singled out the representative of the 'oppressing' country for marks of confidential friendship. Had it not been for a possible fear of exposing himself to 'pie-jaws' and to criticism for showing friendship towards a country which had humiliated Egypt, Farouk may have encouraged more open friendship with the Ambassador in the hope that he might gain the good opinion of King George, who had made a considerable impression on him as a youth. Farouk would have liked to have been regarded and accepted as a member of a select club of respected monarchs. As time went by, however, and he continued his unpraiseworthy way of life, he realized clearly, but rather sadly, that he could never hope to see his wish fulfilled. He was fond of saying that he did not expect to last as King of Egypt. He also seemed to be progessively abandoning his initial wishes to be the first Egyptian King, a native sovereign in sympathy with and loved by his people. His efforts in any such worthwhile aim were spasmodic and ineffectual. He lacked *esprit de suite*. He was progressively resigning himself to the whims of his private life. This was the easy way out for a man who, not by way of hyperbole, once described himself as "totally uneducated".

To deal with a man like this was very difficult. If his mind was untrained it was shrewd, intelligent and quick. He was very quick with counter-argument; it was necessary for a diplomat to think well beforehand to avoid exposing himself to what one Ambassador described as "a point-scoring wise-cracking repartee". Farouk had a ready memory for scoring points in conversation. He would sometimes argue seriously and philosophically to meet arguments put to him but this did not usually last for long. He enjoyed banter and was always ready with apposite jokes. He responded to courtesy, ordinary deference and friendliness. He could be affable, and show a good deal of dignity and demeanour when he felt inclined. When Sir Ronald Campbell left Egypt Sir Ralph Stevenson became British Ambassador.

King Farouk grew bigger, to over twenty stone; glandular trouble brought on obesity, to the King's despair but to the cartoonists' delight. With his size grew the wildness of the rumours about him, the orgies and sexual exhibitions laid on in the palace, and about the impetuous, indulgent and practical-joking aspects of his character. In 1949 he reversed the decision of the judges at L'Auberge des Pyramides Miss Egypt Beauty Contest. He liked to whistle and imitate street hawkers. Once he flew over delta villages dropping celluloid balls to the fellaheen who were urged to exchange these for sweets at royal depots. No one knew what he would try next, he lived for fun. His associations with women seldom lasted long, though some developed into affairs, as one with the wife of a young military doctor. His jokes did not lack originality, as during an operation on Pulli he ordered him, as he had recently become a Moslem, to be circumcized as well while under the anaesthetic. When the victim woke to this discovery the King's guffaws of almost asinine laughter were heard long afterwards.

He continued to eat well and to consume vast quantities of liquid. Those who have seen him eat say he really did enjoy his meals. Breakfast could be five eggs, porridge, beans and cocoa. Oysters were flown in regularly from Copenhagen. Though heavy in body he has been described in Arabic as *khafif*, light-weight in mind. His bulk necessitated special chairs to be built for him: at Gezira they had three, one in the garden, in the restaurant, and on the balcony overlooking the swimming pool, although the King only visited there two or three times in years.

One man who knew him described Farouk's schizophrenia as geared to the sun; when the sun went down the King became a different man. One can almost imagine the King tearing off his uniform at the end of the day, ready for the night out. An observer wrote of Farouk at the Scarabée: "Fat, balding and slow moving, he sits for hours hunched over a table in the smoky gloom, surrounded by his courtiers and bodyguards, peering sleepily through his dark glasses at Annie Bernier as she leans back against the piano . . . from time to time a waiter refills his glass with Coca-Cola. . . . His eyes are hidden, his thick lips seldom smile and his body hardly moves. One wonders what he could have been thinking through all those hours, night after night. He was a ship with no anchor and no harbour, floating aimlessly, drifting."

He was drifting. One night a cousin and another relative of the King went gambling at the Automobile Club. When they arrived they noticed the King at one of the tables, to their dismay, because protocol demanded that no one should leave before Farouk, and they knew he was in the habit of staying at the tables until dawn. It was near breakfast time when only the King was left playing, all other players were sitting out, quietly and uncomfortably dozing in their chairs waiting for the monarch to go home, when his cousin finally lost her patience and, abandoning etiquette, went up to Farouk and pleaded, "Majesty, please, why don't you go home?" He looked at her, tired, and rather sadly replied, "Home? What is that? You have a home to go to, I do not."

The vast palaces of Montazah, Ras el Tin and Abdin (which Farouk once called "that hot-box") were not homes. He had little family life. Ministers walked backwards out of his office when leaving him. He had his retreats of Inchass and a seventeen-room garçonnière as part of the Moassat Hospital in Alexandria, but his main social intercourse was found in the villas of friends where he could act informally.

Farouk never forgot 4th February 1942. He spoke to each new British Ambassador of that evening when Lampson came to the palace. The King, in a ridiculous confidential manner, expected the Ambassador to believe he had had a loaded pistol in the drawer of his desk, adding that it had been touch and go whether or not he would have shot Lampson as he walked in. One foreign Ambassador to Egypt told the author how the King had once claimed to him that the British had tried to shoot him three times.

His wit never failed him. On a visit to the British Cathedral in Cairo, to which he had presented silver grilles, the King was taken round by the Bishop who showed him a book on the Cathedral stall telling how the Jews left Egypt, named 'The Route of the Exodus'. "Have you got another, showing how they returned?" asked Farouk.

From 10th August to 19th October 1950 the King was on holiday in France, Spain and Italy, travelling incognito (with seven Cadillacs and outriders, and a private plane) as Fuad Pasha Masri, Fuad the Egyptian. By now he was nearly bald. He still appeared proud and dignified, with powerful shoulders and a strong handshake, but all the freshness in his face had disappeared. He looked more serious, almost sinister. On his arrival at the Hotel du Golf, Deauville, from Marseilles he exclaimed in mock surprise at the crowd gathered to see him, "Why, I'm incognito!" and took twenty-five rooms at the hotel, two of which were occupied by Annie Berrier, and Samia Gamal, Egypt's national dancer. In the evenings he entertained or played baccarat and chemin de fer at the Casino with the Aga and Begum Khan, Aly Khan and Rita Hayworth, the Maharaja of Rajpipla, and Prince Ibn Saud. Police held back the press. All eyes watched the big red 1,000,000 franc counters being placed as the King played several tables at once, using runners to place his bets.

Annie Berrier was singing at the Ambassador in Deauville. She had a new number called 'Song of the Nile', and Farouk gave a tremendous party at the Casino to help launch it. They lunched at the William the Conqueror restaurant, Dives sur Mer. When the whim took them everyone went off to San Sebastian. At times the King would not allow photographers near him. For others he posed as he left the Casino, in baggy black silk trousers, white tuxedo, lined cloak, dark glasses taken off for the photographers, and an expressionless face.

As the weeks of playboy living dragged on, the excesses of whole floors in luxury hotels, and thousands of pounds on a card, made Egypt the comic turn of the world. The French invented a new word from Farouk's name for extravagance. The family were beginning to despair of Farouk: "My nephew is throwing it all away", Mohamed Ali complained.

More important was the growing impatience in Egypt which expressed itself in varying ways when Farouk returned. "To have as their symbol this ludicrous falstaffian spendthrift was a wound to all Egyptians," wrote Desmond Stewart. An Army major drove an explosive-laden jeep into Abdin Palace in an abortive attempt to blow up the King. On 17th October 1950 Egyptian Opposition parties delivered a petition to Abdin Palace in Cairo warning the King that the patience of the people was at an end and a national revolt was likely. The petition, signed by Saadists, Liberals, Nationalists, Kotlists and some Independent leaders, stated:

> Egypt today is passing through a stage which may be considered the most critical in the country's history. It is regrettable that, whenever the country looks towards the palace, obstacles are put

in the way for no apparent reason. Circumstances have placed in the palace certain officials who do not deserve that honour. These ill advise, and mishandle matters. Some of them have even come under the suspicion—now being investigated—that they are implicated in the arms scandal affecting our valiant army.

The belief prevails that justice will be incapable of touching these officials. . . .

The World Press describes us as a public that bears injustice silently, and says we do not know that we are being maltreated and driven like animals. Allah knows that our breasts are boiling with anger, and that only a little hope restrains us. . . .

The country remembers the happy days when your Majesty was the honest good shepherd. All the hopes of the country were concentrated on your Majesty.

The petition continued, declaring its right as the opposition to point out the situation brought about by the corrupt Wafd and concluded by calling for the dismissal of all those who have wronged the country, lowered Egypt's prestige, and utterly failed to give her freedom, unity and progress.

Nahas described the petition as redundant, devoid of truth, and unworthy of a reply. To draw attention away from his own problems, in his October speech to celebrate Hejira, the New Year, Nahas began once again to cry for freedom from foreign occupation and to praise Farouk as 'Protector of the faith and a generous benefactor".

For his part Farouk felt total disillusionment. He had by now realized that the various political parties consisted of nothing more than self-seeking men. As king he allowed himself to adopt a fatal attitude: apathy.

Meanwhile underground, early in 1950, Nasser had been made chairman of the executive committee of el Dobbat el Ahrar, the Free Officers' Society. His colleagues were Abdul Amer, Kamal Hussein, Hassan Ibrahim, Salah Salem, Abdul Rauf, Gamal Salem, Khaled Mohieddin, Abdul el-Bahdadi, and Anwar el Sadat. For three years after the Palestine armistice Nasser perfected his secret military organization. His code name was 'Zaghlul'; a telephone call from Zaghlul convened meetings, the first of which was held at Faluja where Nasser had fought in the Palestine war. Nasser later wrote of his planning during those years.

"I thought of the assassination of many whom I considered

to be obstacles obstructing the way to the future development of the mother country. . . .

"I even thought of assassinating the ex-King [Farouk] and some of his confederates—those evil geniuses who played havoc with our rights and liberties. . . .

"We possessed terrible and terrifying secrets. We had secret symbols and signs. We moved under cover of darkness and stored stacks of pistols and bombs. . . ." He described one night when he had organized an attempt on a man's life and how when the shots were fired at the victim and the cars roared away, with Nasser driving one, "the sound of cries and lamentations—the wailings of a woman, the screams of a terrified child and continuous cries for help" pursued and afflicted him long after he was out of earshot. The sounds haunted him all night, and when he learnt that the intended victim had survived he vowed not to attempt any more assassinations.

Within a month of his return from holiday in Europe Farouk's Opening of Parliament speech was read by Nahas. It crystallized the cry for independence: "Since the cessation of hostilities, the people of the Valley of the Nile, Egyptian and Sudanese, have made constant pleas for the union that would satisfy their national aspirations. This has been impeded by the Treaty of 1936, one that is in contradiction with the principles of the U.N. My Government maintains that this Treaty has lost its validity, and it is inevitable that we ask that it is abolished, and that we arrive at an understanding between Egypt and England based on new principles. These principles are the total and complete evacuation of British troops, and the unity of Egypt and the Sudan under the Egyptian crown. My government awaits the receipt of an immediate confirmation of the acceptance of these points of view."

The speech was marked by riots in Cairo, correctly interpreted by the *New York Times* next day: "The violence that accompanied yesterday's opening session of Parliament is indicative of a precarious internal situation. The Wafd Government has been a great disappointment to those who hoped for social progress and economic reconstruction in Egypt after the fiasco of the Palestinian War. There has been no less inefficiency and corruption than usual: . . . the activities of King Farouk have brought him world-wide criticism; economic distress, already acute, has been increasing steadily. . . .

"Outsiders will find it difficult to believe that the present agitation . . . is not a tactic to divert popular feeling from grave internal abuses and neglect."

The British reply in part to the Egyptian demands was as follows: "The Defence of the Middle East is of interest not only to Great Britain, but to other countries in the Atlantic Alliance and to Egypt. The British Government cannot approve of any move that will leave the Middle East without adequate defence. As for the Sudan, it has been the theatre of great progress, political, social and economic, in these last years. It would be painful to disturb this progress. The attitude of the British Government has not changed nor will it change, and it reaffirms in this case that she will respect the will of the Sudanese and that at the opportune moment, they will be permitted to decide freely what they wish for their future."

On 11th February Farouk, who later recalled that he had been for years "a lonely man in my heart", announced his engagement to Narriman Sadek. She was sixteen, he thirty. She was the daughter of a civil servant, and was betrothed to Zaki Hachem, an economic aide to the U.N. secretariat. Responsible for the introduction was Ahmed Neguib Bey, the King's jeweller, who had arranged for Farouk to be concealed in his shop in Rue Abdel Khalek Saroit and watching when Narriman's father brought her in on the pretext of buying some trinket. When Farouk had seen her the betrothal to Hachem was called off but it was some weeks before palace circles were convinced that Farouk was seriously considering marriage with Narriman. As his visits to her became more frequent he ordered a high wall to be built round her garden, so that he could not be seen from the street when he called.

He sent her to Rome to learn French and to be instructed in music, conversation and general knowledge before announcing the engagement, which was a splendid example of Karim Thabet's prose: "Rendering praise to God, His Majesty's Cabinet is happy to announce to the noble Egyptian people the good news of the betrothal of their King, who has given them his heart and his love.

"On this blessed day when the country celebrates with gladness and joy the glorious anniversary of the royal birth, there took place by the grace of God the betrothal of our well-beloved Sovereign with the Descendant of an illustrious and noble family, Mlle Narriman Sadek, daughter of Hussein Fahmy Sadek Bey.

"In announcing the news of this happy betrothal of the great Farouk, His Majesty's Cabinet thanks Divine Providence for its beneficence, and prays that it may surround His Majesty with its high solicitude, secure his happiness and felicity, and make of this blessed betrothal a source of happy omen for beloved Egypt and for the august royal family."

On 6th May Farouk married Narriman. 2,500 people gathered in the square outside Koubbeh Palace, surrounded by lancers and foot guards. On the announcement bugles sounded, and cannon began the 101-gun salute. Farouk then gave a reception, attended only by male guests. Narriman formally entered the city in the evening, under a triumphal arch surmounted with a pink neon heart, and arrived at Koubbeh in a motorcade of Rolls-Royce, five motorcycles, three jeeps, two red Cadillacs and eleven other cars. Receptions, garden parties, parades and fireworks lasted for days.

The wedding took place in the Ismail room, Abdin Palace. Farouk later went through the wedding presents, culled all those of gold and melted them down into bricks. This insight into his attitude to money, which, because of the wealth he had, many people have wrongly assumed to be irresponsible, is also shown by the precise entries on expenditure in the account books in his office at Abdin Palace.

In June Farouk and Narriman arrived in the *Mahroussa* with two warships, for their honeymoon on Capri, and booked all 150 rooms at the Caesar Augustus Hotel. Thirteen weeks later they were still honeymooning, in thirty-two rooms of the Carlton Hotel, Cannes. The King sometimes did not rise until 4 p.m., when he and Narriman could be seen, dressed identically in grey flannel slacks, yachting jackets and white caps. In the evening croupiers called him 'the locomotive', for his persistent energy in gambling. Twice a week a private plane arrived from Egypt with mail and State papers. Two agents of the Moslem Brotherhood were reported to be trailing Farouk on the

Riviera. Even after his second marriage Farouk continued to see other girls. One young singer was installed in Shepheard's Hotel at his expense. As his friend Gracie Fields put it, "Love was his sickness."

Between 1950 and 1952 the old Fascist Greenshirt Party of Ahmed Hussein, known as the Socialist Party, carried on a virulent newspaper campaign, openly attacking the King and the royal family. The party, wrote C. Issawi, published photographs "showing the most appalling conditions prevailing in the country, under headings such as: 'This is your fate, Egyptian citizen, under capitalism.' Its leading slogan was 'Revolution'."

The newspaper *Akhbar el-Yom* carried on a campaign against the King, thinly veiled in its intentions. This campaign began with a reprint, on the anniversary of Farouk's assumption of the throne, of the fifteen-year-old statement which he had then made, beginning with the words: "I shall have the interest of the country at heart before all other matters." Then the editor, Ali Amin, published two consecutive life-story articles, ostensibly on the Duke of Windsor and ex-King Michael of Rumania but obviously referring directly to Farouk, with such headlines as: "King Must Leave, Prime Minister says". In June a Cairo paper published a portrait of Farouk with no name underneath but merely the question "Who is this?" The text ran along these lines: "Is he intelligent? Is he an idiot? One does not know, for he has intelligence but acts like a madman. His appearance is one of innocence, but then one of a criminal. . . . He has furious eyes like a tiger but he acts like a mouse. . . . He lives and yet one would believe him dead. He is at the same time in heaven and in hell. He has everything but has lost all. His possessions do not interest him any more. His only interest lies in what he has not got. He wants everything." Nowhere did the article mention the King by name.

The intention and message of it all was more than obvious. Egypt was not only at loggerheads with Britain, she was now openly fighting the King. A defamatory press campaign such as this has a telling effect, as it did on Farouk. When the Aga Khan met Farouk on his last visit to Europe before the King's abdication he recorded these comments:

"I was immediately aware of a great change in him. He was enveloped in a mood of depressed fatalism, an atmosphere of

'I cannot do what I wish—very well, let them do what they want'."

He was now resigned to leaving Egypt. Since 1947 he had gambled to win money and had indulged in all manner of deals, one of which involved the sale of war scrap from the Western Desert. Once the palace issued a notice that the King would accept only presents made of gold for his birthday (with as little decoration as possible, was almost implied). Farouk then melted them down on a special machine kept in the cellar. One of his brothers-in-law remembers distinctly the day Farouk claimed with satisfaction, "I am now as rich as the Nizam of Hydera-bad." He had been salting his money away for years, in Italy, the U.S.A., and carried by private plane to Swiss Banks by his aides. In October 1951 he told Narriman to prepare to leave.

Those with an axe to grind were playing on the growing troubles in Egypt. In September 1951 *The Times* quoted a Western diplomat's view of increasing communist influence in Egypt: "Communism started raising its head . . . towards the end of February or the early part of March. Then Communist Front papers started to reappear . . . they are anti-monarchy, anti-government, anti-British, anti-American, anti-everything. They are taking the vast, creeping discontent in this country, and surely binding it into a movement."

Wafd corruption had reached such a state that Farouk was about to use this as an excuse to dismiss Nahas when the Prime Minister forestalled him by announcing Egypt's unilateral abrogation of the 1936 Anglo-Egyptian Treaty. The Wafd Minister of the Interior, Fuad Serag ed-Din, harassed the 80,000 British troops in the Canal Zone with guerrilla attacks and sabotage. Egyptians cut off fresh food supplies and withdrew the Zone's labour force which had to be replaced by African troops.

A year of fruitless negotiations between Egypt and Britain ended in a situation in which the British Ambassador sat with his 'finger on the button'. Eden said of October 1951: "The position I had to face in Egypt was more forbidding than any-thing . . . in Persia. [The British had recently evacuated and lost the Abadan refinery.] In Egypt the outlook was much darker; almost everything seemed rotten in the State. Food prices were rising sharply and income tax had been increased upon all but those best able to pay. 'Liberation Squads' were occupied extorting subscriptions . . . intimidation was rife."

Egypt wanted Farouk to be declared King of the Sudan but Great Britain could not agree to this, although urged by the United States. By November left-wing elements were calling for a complete boycott of the British; forbidding the sale of Egyptian cotton to England, and demanding Government arms for the people to make a more serious resistance against the British. At the height of the Anglo-Egyptian dispute Farouk made moves which confirmed his imperialist and capitalist outlook to the revolutionary element in Egypt. He appointed pro-British Hafiz Afifi as head of the Royal Cabinet; he recalled Abdel Fattah Amr, Ambassador in London and an avowed anglophile, to become his political adviser; placed his economic adviser, Elias Andraus, on the board of the Bank Misr; and made his own candidate, General Heidar, Commander-in-Chief of the Army.

Neguib described Heidar, whose nickname was 'The Jailer' as a "former prison director whom the King had exceptionally promoted to the rank of Lieutenant-General in order to make him Commander-in-Chief. The highest rank he had held in the regular Army was that of a second lieutenant". From Heidar Neguib learnt that Farouk regarded him as an enemy; Neguib was concerned that Farouk may have understood his connection with the Free Officers, and not until later did he discover that Farouk's displeasure was founded on Neguib's lack of co-operation in supplying soldiers detached from the Frontier Corps as guards and servants for the palace. Neguib's indignation was further roused by Farouk's exploits at Ras el Hekma, on the Mediterranean coast between Alexandria and Mersa Matruh, where the "King had built himself a summer palace with stolen materials on stolen land with the use of stolen labour". Neguib wrote, "I . . . was described by the King at the time as a 'Don Quixote who was riding for a fall'."

The young enthusiastic element within the Army relied on Farouk to get rid of the incompetent higher command which had been responsible for the Palestine fiasco, but the palace maintained Heidar in his post. Neguib tried many times to speak directly with Farouk to explain the officers' grievances, but the King was surrounded by a moat of impenetrable schemers with other sympathies. Neguib was relieved of his position as Chief of the Frontier Administration and his job given to a favourite of Farouk's, Major-General Hussein Sirri Amer. (Some time later when Amer was driving home one night his car was riddled by fourteen machine-gun bullets, but he escaped.)

El Sadat reported in 1951 that "The King was informed by his agents of the undercurrent of agitation in the Army, and he was well aware that something was afoot. We heard that he had referred to the Free Officers in veiled terms to the Chief of Staff, Ferik Heidar Pasha. Our Committee met in Cairo, and fixed the *coup d'état* for March 1952. Gamal Abdel Nasser was re-elected president. But events were proceeding at a dizzy speed, and the great day was postponed for the last time". Although El Sadat writes "March 1952" here Neguib wrote later that until the Officers' Club election in January 1952 "the Free Officers had assumed it would not be possible for us to revolt before the year 1955".

The Free Officer cells grew in number. A cell was composed of five members each of whom had to form a fresh cell, and pay monthly subscriptions. For security reasons members of newly-recruited cells knew only the leader of their parent cell. This created a situation wherein no one could be sure who belonged to what. El Sadat showed the intricacy of this weave when he reported that another movement, led by Captain Moustapha Sedky, attempted to join forces with Nasser: "He [Sedky] believed that our aims were Utopian, and that it was better to try to gain the King's confidence and set him on the right path. This was manifestly absurd, for the root of the trouble lay with the King, and the compromise suggested would have meant a betrayal of our revolutionary ideals."

El Sadat also claimed how a Free Officer joined the Sedky movement to discover that "the group which had planned to convert the King, had soon been converted by him, and became his iron guard. Farouk very cleverly pretended to espouse their cause, corrupting them with gifts and favours—notably, orgiastic evenings with champagne, caviare and pretty women. The Sedky group yielded to such persuasive arguments, and became one of the chief instruments of the King's intrigues".

By the close of the year the three-cornered struggle intensified. The King and the British had each tried to win the support of the Wafd but were now impelled to join forces against it. Attacks on British troops in the Canal Zone were variously led or supported by the Moslem Brothers, Wafd Youth, Communists, Socialists, and even the Egyptian auxiliary police.

The Free Officers were bold enough to distribute a circular, "The Army Say 'NO' to Farouk" just before elections were due at the Officers' Club in Cairo on 6th January 1952 when all of the King's candidates led by General Hussein Sirri Amer were defeated and all of the Free Officers' candidates were elected. Of the 334 votes that were cast for president—276 were cast for Neguib. Farouk declared the election null and void. Events now began to happen with speed. The destiny of Egypt was flowing like the Nile in flood when it boils out of the sluices at Aswan.

Mawawi Bey, who had commanded the Egyptian forces in Palestine, was now leader of the Phalangist liberation movement against the British. On 12th and 15th January 1952 his 'National Liberation Army' launched its first major attacks from the villages of Tel el Kebir and El Hammada. The British 1st Guards Brigade occupied the area and arrested all guerrilla suspects, among them the Inspector General of the Egyptian Police administration.

At 6.20 a.m. on 16th January a Crown Prince, Ahmed Fuad, was born to Narriman, a month premature. King Farouk announced the birth and prayed God that "it would be the prelude to the happiness and well being of the nation and a good omen to the country", and that "God would remove the country's present embarrassment and bring it to all success". Just three days later the country's "embarrassment" reached its height when Egyptian commandos made an open attack on the garrison at Tel el Kebir. The British Commander-in-Chief, General Erskine, sent an ultimatum to the Egyptians at 7 a.m. on 25th January demanding surrender within two hours. The commander of the Egyptian police sought instructions from Serag ed-Din in Cairo, strong man of the Wafd, who saw an opportunity, not for a military victory, which was impossible against the British odds of arms and men, but for political capital to be made from the defeat which would follow if he ordered his men to fight. He gave the order to resist. By 11 a.m. approximately sixty Egyptians were dead. The British lost three men.

It is possible that Serag ed-Din had in turn telephoned **Farouk** for his endorsement of the proposal to resist and that the King, not wishing to appear in collaboration with the British, agreed. Six months later it was announced that Farouk had donated £3,000 to help the Liberation Army at this time. The short amount of time which General Erskine allowed the Egyptians to make up their minds has also been called unjust, inferring that a longer delay would have enabled diplomacy in Cairo to prevent lives being lost. After the battle the British Foreign Office issued a statement claiming: "There is abundant evidence to show that these Egyptian police have both connived at and taken an active part in numerous other attacks on the British forces culminating in their aggressive attitude during the recent drive to clear up terrorist organizations and army dumps in Ismailia. In the circumstances General Erskine has had no alternative but to request the disarmament of the auxiliary police. . . ."

In the afternoon the news of the Egyptian police martyrdom reached Cairo. The Wafd Youth gathered at 7 p.m. A Council of Ministers met in the night to decide on diplomatic action against the British, and the British Consulate advised all its subjects to act with care and stay at home next day, Saturday, 26th January 1952.

Chapter 10

Black Saturday
(26th January 1952—11 p.m. 22nd July 1952)

The words of Neguib himself adequately describe Black Saturday, as the day became known. "On the morning of 26th January, as if by pre-arrangement, mobs began to gather all over Cairo. Resolute action on the part of the Government or the Palace would probably have prevented the holocaust that followed. No action of any sort was taken. Before long the mobs were attacking and setting fire to numerous foreign and luxury establishments. Before the Army was permitted to re-establish order, seventeen foreigners (including nine Britons and one Canadian) and fifty-odd Egyptians had been killed. A British club, a Jewish school, an office of the Moslem Brotherhood, four hotels, four nightclubs, seven department stores, seventeen cafés and restaurants, eighteen cinemas, and seventy other commercial establishments had been destroyed."

As it happened that day Farouk was giving a banquet at Abdin for the Army to celebrate the birth of his son. Neguib attended, and wrote later, "Farouk and Heidar had seemed pre-occupied throughout the banquet, but neither had even so much as mentioned the riots. Their frequent whispered conferences with various couriers, however, indicated that they were aware of what was happening."

Action on the 26th fell into four categories, the first passive, the strike by the police; the rest active, student gatherings to hear inflammatory speeches, incendiary squads moving systematically into the city, to be followed by wild mobs glorying in collective crime, and managing to take a few personal reprisals undetected in the general holocaust.

Incendiaries levered open shop shutters or cut through them with acetylene equipment before lobbing molotov cocktails inside. At the Turf Club the Canadian Trade Commissioner, and other Britons who tried to escape were forced back into the burning building by the mob who then "pulled the bodies, blackened and swollen with the heat, into the street". At 2.30 p.m. the arsonists attacked the most famous and historic hotel in Egypt, Shepheard's. "Two singers from the Italian Opera Company", related J. & S. Lacouture, "fled in their underclothes, clutching boxes of jewels in their hands, while one unfortunate girl threw herself in a panic from the fourth floor into the street below." Other famous places burnt were Groppi's and the shops Cicurel and Chemla in Via Fuad. At Mena House near the Pyramids the staff fought off the mob, aided by the dragomans and camel men who would lose their livelihood if the hotel was burned. One Barclays Bank official left for lunch in his car and in driving along a street more crowded than usual his chauffeur knocked a man down. The official sat forward and cried out for the chauffeur to stop but he kept going with the explanation, "It's not a good day to stop, sir." Within hours Barclays Bank and other British offices were smoking ruins. There was some evidence that these main targets were the objects of the mob's displeasure and that the British as individuals were left unmolested.

The day wore on. Cairo burned. No one moved to stop it. Farouk was at the luncheon. Nahas was in a Turkish bath and having a pedicure. Serag ed-Din was either completing a real estate deal or moving a piece of new furniture he had just bought. Another minister was speculating on the cotton market. Everyone played a waiting game. The Government did not move. The Army could not move without permission. The Police would not move (indeed they unbuttoned their tunics and joined in). The British would not move, neither would the Americans, although it is believed that their Ambassador, Jefferson Caffery, was about to deploy his Embassy marines. Farouk did not move, although at 4 p.m. he heard a rumour that British troops from the Canal Zone were within thirty miles of Cairo.

After lunch Sir Ralph Stevenson, who calculated that it was a matter of time before Farouk acted, ordered his car out. He intended paying a visit to Jefferson Caffery whose Embassy was opposite. The British Embassy was defended by roof-top guns, and the Ambassador took an armed guard with him in the car, but as the car was about to leave the garden gate a burst of machine-gun fire came swinging down the street. "More better inside, Excellency," observed the driver. "More better indeed," agreed Sir Ralph, and he returned to contact Caffery by telephone instead.

Sir Anthony Eden later wrote of that Saturday afternoon in London: "While Cairo blazed, messages began to come through from the Embassy to the Foreign Office and on the teleprinter from our military headquarters in the Canal Zone to the War Office. A plan had been worked out under which our forces would intervene in Cairo and Alexandria to protect the lives and property of British subjects. . . .

"The belief that we had the forces and the conviction that we were prepared to use them were powerful arguments in prodding the Egyptian Army to quell the riots." The Egyptian Army finally moved in late in the afternoon, when the organized arsonists had done their worst, destroying almost 400 buildings and the homes, or means of livelihood for 12,000 people.

Who was guilty? Farouk, the Wafd, the British, the Moslem Brotherhood, the Russian Communists, or the Nazi Socialists; all were blamed by one or another. It is now generally recognized that the last three, in that order respectively of importance, were to blame It was their men who filled the wire cages in Cairo courts in the weeks of trials which followed.

On Sunday at 11 p.m Farouk sent a courier with armed escort to Nahas Pasha's house with a note of his dismissal, and Ali Maher Pasha formed a Cabinet of Independents with himself as prime minister and military governor. Farouk proclaimed martial law. In Cairo a curfew was imposed from 6 p.m. to 6 a.m. A deathly pall of smoke and quiet hung over Cairo after that night and Sunday. Curfew warnings were broadcast at intervals of two minutes, and no passes were issued. At six o'clock life in Cairo came to a standstill. The quiet was punctuated by occasional volleys fired in the heart of the city, the clatter of Egyptian bren carriers patrolling the streets, and the clicking of the heels of soldiers mounting guard at all key buildings and street corners. The Army had orders to shoot at sight.

Early in 1952 after the burning of Cairo foreign newspaper correspondents were still unaware of the true situation in Egypt. Farouk's removal of Nahas and annulment of the Wafd's power was described by correspondents with praise for Farouk: "The King rose above events—even dominated them—in a way that no other Egyptian could have done. He demonstrated that although he has been ridiculed abroad and called unpopular at home, he still knows how to use his power in a crisis . . . with the all-important aid of a loyal army he stopped in one night a deterioration of public order that was beginning to look very much like a revolution." Within a few months it was. In fact on 10th February the Free Officers' Executive Committee met. Revolution was fixed for March, to be subsequently postponed.

Ali Maher lasted only four weeks. Ahmed Neguib el Hilali became Prime Minister, to be ousted by Farouk in favour of Sirri Amer, who lasted seventeen days. The curfew in Cairo was not lifted until May and in this month Farouk again learnt of the Army members who were plotting against him, he believed the plotters to be supported by a secret politburo of the Moslem Brotherhood supplied with money by the Russians. The plotters were known to the British and American Embassies.

At this time when the British would not recognize the title of King of the Sudan for Farouk, the King was granted the title of 'El Sayed', signifying his direct descent from the Prophet. Thus he joined the five other Moslem kings with similar claims: Ibn Saud, Talal, Faisal, Imam Sayf al-Islam Ahmad of Yemen, and Idriss of Libya. Karim Thabet encouraged Farouk to make this claim, for which Thabet was described by Neguib as "the most hated of all the King's cronies . . . because he was a cynic who had made Egyptian Moslems look ridiculous. . . . Farouk, as everyone knew, was a descendant of Albanians and Circassians on his father's side and of Turks and French on his mother's side. . . . If there was any Arabic blood in Farouk's veins, it was so diluted that it couldn't possibly have been traced back to Mohammed, and it was a sacrilege for anyone to have tried to do so."

Martial law still existed in June, Hilali had promised to lift it by the October elections, but did not get a chance. He fell from office on 30th June when he tried to expose corruption in the

Wafd. It was widely believed at the time that Farouk had been bribed to dismiss Hilali by those who wanted the government's investigations into their finances halted. The fact that the American Ambassador in Egypt had had talks with Karim Thabet, and Abboud Pasha, a man of immense wealth whom Hilali was pressing for unpaid taxes, shortly before Hilali fell from office, had been widely misinterpreted in Egypt. To use Sir Anthony Eden's words, "More plainly, Britain resented American interference in Egyptian politics, and in the question of Farouk's title as King of the Sudan."

After Hilali it "proved difficult to form another government. There was a general sense of impending disaster, particularly among the politicians in Alexandria, where the Government was in summer residence. Many of them believed that the King was at this time mentally unstable and that it was useless to attempt to govern" (Little). In the last few months of his reign, what Neguib termed the King's 'Kitchen Cabinet' ruled in the palace under Farouk. These included the well known Pulli and Thabet, Mohamed Hassan el Suleimani, the King's valet; Edmund Gahlan; Elias Andraus; Mohamed Hilmi Hussein, a driver mechanic; Abd el Aziz, butler; Hassan Akef, pilot; Dr. Yussef Rashad; Dr. Hafiz Afifi; and Mohamed Neguib Salem, a treasurer.

Lacouture summarized the situation: "Even in Farouk's immediate circle, princes and dignitaries openly criticized everything he did, his divorce, his remarriage with a middle-class woman. . . . Even the birth of an heir did not melt this ill will. . . . In the palace a seedy clique of Levantine procurers and Nubian valets organized the King's entertainment, brought down governments and made army appointments. . . . There was no longer a man in Cairo who, if he had a handsome wife, was not afraid to take her anywhere where she might meet Farouk: it might prove fatal to oppose the whims of a crowned Gargantua, who seemed to thrive on scandals, trying to kill himself with excesses, a man who had lost every illusion he ever held. One day in July he sent a note to a woman friend, a singer, which was signed F.F.—'Farouk foutu'."

The month of July, the last Farouk was to see in power, opened with sweltering heat in Cairo. Everyone who was anyone was taking the sea air at Alexandria; all but a few. Significant events happened almost daily from now on. On the 2nd Hussein Sirri became Prime Minister and successfully stopped the political gyrations which had kept Cairo dizzy for five days. Leading industrialist Sirri, who had been called upon before to lead his country at a critical time, announced his Cabinet Ministers. One name stood out among the list, Karim Thabet, as Minister of State. In confirming Sirri's appointment Farouk wrote exhorting him to work for the "national demands of evacuation and unity, the restoration of democratic life, and the introduction of progressive reforms".

One of the Free Officers, Colonel Okasha, described later in an article in *El-Tahrir* an event which took place a week after Sirri took office, on the 10th: "Gamal [Nasser] and Khaled [Muhieddin] came to my house and asked me, as they often did, to play Rimsky-Korsakov's Scheherezade. Soon the symphony began to exert its charm. Gamal listened attentively, with dreamy eyes. At the last note, he stood up, lifted the needle off the record and said abruptly: 'We shall strike at the beginning of next month'."

On the same day, the King, through his butler, had sent a pencil note to Afifi, Chief of the Royal Cabinet. It was handed in turn to Sirri. It read: "Heidar [then C.-in-C. Armed Forces] must be removed within five days unless he dissolves the executive committee of the Officers' Club and removes the twelve officers who have been conspiring against His Majesty the King." On the 15th Farouk suspended the Officers' Club committee.

On 18th July the Free Officers, against Nasser's judgment, drew up a list of 'traitors' for liquidation. Meanwhile, as Karim Thabet revealed in his memoirs, published by the Egyptian daily *Al-Misry* in October 1952, Farouk drew up secret proposals in the evening of this same day, the 18th. These involved the imprisonment of Neguib, and, through a senior police officer, a series of assassinations of Free Officers whose murder Farouk demanded within a month. On the 19th Sirri asked Farouk to appoint Neguib Minister of War, probably as a test. The King passed the test; he would not agree to the appointment: the officers were certain then that he understood their plans. Neguib himself stated the situation precisely when he wrote, "Everyone seemed to assume by then, without actually

knowing what was going on, that I was not only the President
of the Officers' Club but also the leader of 'the twelve officers'
whom Farouk had been waiting for Heidar to arrest."

On 20th July Hussein Sirri telephoned Ras el Tin and
Montazah and eventually reached the King in the Royal Automobile Club. He warned Farouk that only two steps were open
to him; to satisfy the people and the Army by making Neguib
Minister of War, or to arrest him and the other Free Officers.
He told the King that revolt was imminent. The King asked for
the names of those responsible, Sirri gave them. "Moarsin!"
(Those pimps!) was Farouk's reply, and he hung up. Sirri
resigned.

Okasha wrote: "On 20th July I was lunching at my home
when the telephone rang with the sound peculiar to long-
distance calls. It was Ahmed Abul Fath [his brother-in-law]
who, phoning from Alexandria, told me that Husain Sirri was
going to resign; that the King was going to impose General
Sirri Amir on the next cabinet as Minister for War, and that
this appointment would be followed at once by the arrest of
fourteen of us. I immediately went to see Gamal, whose house,
as usual, was full of officers, and I let him know what had
happened." Nasser and Abdel Hakim Amer had been to
Neguib's house that day to warn him to be ready to put the
coup into action, but, as there were two friends present, had to
disguise the real reason for their visit, and so delayed the date
of revolution. The Free Officers went into conference and
plotted the overthrow for 5th August. Neguib wrote: "Our
first objective would be to seize power and appoint a Prime
Minister. . . . Our second . . . to allay the fears of the British,
the Americans, and other foreigners. . . . Our third . . . to get
rid of the King. . . . We resolved to do everything possible to
avoid bloodshed, but not to shrink from it if necessary to attain
our ends. A score of picked officers were alerted to expect
telephone calls at their homes at 2100 every night until further
notice." Neguib wrote this much later. It is more true to
say that the *coup* was planned to stabilize the political situation.
Few of the participants thought at the time that their action
would lead to the expulsion of the King. Neguib himself was
selected as leader only when another General had declined.

On the night of 20th July Farouk astonished everyone by

reappointing Hilali (the fifth Egyptian Government in six months) who in turn insisted that the King's thirty-year-old brother-in-law and cousin, Ismail Sherin, second husband of Princess Fawzia, should be appointed as Minister of War.

El Sadat wrote: "22nd July 1952. We had been waiting for this day for ten years. . . . Now the Executive Committee issued battle orders. We adopted the slogan. Resolution and Boldness. The password was Nasr [Victory]. Zero hour was midnight."

On the 22nd Karim Thabet was reported to be preparing to leave the country on holiday the next day. Nahas and Serag ed-Din had recently left for Europe.

At 4 p.m. on 22nd July Hilali took office officially and presented his Ministers to the King in the summer palace in Alexandria. "At five o'clock, having dismissed the Ministers, Farouk took his late afternoon bath. Two hundred kilometres away, in a little house at Manshiyat el Bakri, a suburb on the east of Cairo, were eight young men in their shirt sleeves. One of them haltingly read a note of six typewritten papers . . . the plan for the military rising . . ." (J. & S. Lacouture). At 7 p.m. a member of the American Embassy knew of the imminent revolution from a young newspaperman in touch with the Free Officers. He delayed telling his Ambassador who was in Alexandria. At 9 p.m. Farouk ordered the arrest of the Free Officers, two of whom called to see him at Montazah that evening to betray their cause and confirm their loyalty to the throne, but too late. A meeting was called of all senior Army staff for 11 p.m.

Chapter 11

Revolution
(Midnight 22nd July 1952—6 p.m. 26th July 1952)

The *coup d'état* was a military exercise, not entirely pre-planned but formulated as circumstances demanded in the following days. The Free Officers were uncertain themselves of developments and how they would cope with them; it was their determination which enabled them to carry off a *coup* which, in retrospect, seems surprisingly simple. The story is perhaps best told in military diary form.

22nd July. *2400* hours. Armoured cars and tanks took over key points.

23rd July. *0130.* The broadcasting offices, station, telephone exchange and the airports had been seized. Alexandria was suspicious of events in Cairo. The Prime Minister telephoned the Officers' Club and demanded to know what was happening. He made contact after G.H.Q. senior officers had been arrested, and spoke to a member of the new regime who assured him that all was well. This satisfied the Prime Minister.

Captain Ahmed Kamel, commanding Farouk's guard at Ras el Tin Palace received a call from Cairo reporting unusual troop movements. Kamel telephoned the valet Hassan who spoke to Farouk. The King gave no orders.

0300. The Free Officers gathered again at G.H.Q. It was all over.

0330. In Alexandria conflicting reports were reaching the palace. El Hilali called on Farouk; a report had come that

British troops were mobilizing in the Canal Zone, preparing to advance on Cairo. El Hilali ordered the police not to obstruct the foreign troops.

0400. The American Embassy was informed that the *coup d'état* had been successful.

0430. A small yacht which had been out for a night's sea fishing made into Alexandria harbour. On board were relatives and friends of the King, including Princess Faiza and her husband Bulent Rauf, Robert Simpson, personal Secretary to the American Ambassador, and Adel Sabet, a cousin. As they passed the naval warships in the harbour they noticed activity on board, and the ships getting up steam. "What a life in the Navy, to be up so early," were their thoughts. What struck them as more strange was that most of the lights at Montazah were on. (The Egyptian Navy remained loyal and sent a warship to anchor off Montazah.)

0500. In his book El Sadat claims that Neguib was first informed of the *coup* at this time, but this seems unlikely as in his own book Neguib speaks of his moves in aid of the *coup*, throughout the night.

0600. Mr. John Hamilton, Counsellor at the British Embassy was told of the *coup*.

0700. Two proclamations to the people were broadcast in Neguib's name stating that the Army meant nothing more than to remove the corrupt men from the King's entourage and adding that "the Army will undertake responsibility for law and order in co-operation with the policy and I want to assure our brother foreigners of the safety of their lives and property, for which the Army considers itself responsible".

Farouk sent Narriman's uncle, Mustafa Zadek, by private plane to Cairo to ask Neguib what was going on.

0800. John Hamilton had informed the Foreign Office in London by this time. Eden wrote: "From 8 a.m. onwards the King was frequently on the telephone to the United States Ambassador. He repeated, each time more clearly, that only foreign intervention could save him and his dynasty. He did not ask explicitly for British military action, but the implication was obvious. I had frequently indicated to our Embassy that British forces would not intervene to keep King Farouk on his throne."

1200. Zadek telephoned Farouk with an assurance that Neguib had few demands to make. The Free Officers asked sixty-eight-year-old Ali Maher to be President of the Council.

1600. Prime Minister Hilali handed his resignation to the King.

2300. John Hamilton saw Neguib and delivered Eden's message to him. Hamilton and Neguib had known each other in the Sudan and as Neguib took down the message from the Foreign Secretary that Britain would not intervene to support the King, Neguib looked up and said, "You know, this reminds me of taking down dictation at Gordon College."

24th July. Ali Maher requested an audience with the King. Captain Kamel of Farouk's staff drove to St. Stephen's Hotel in Alexandria to collect Ali Maher and bring him to the palace, without escort. Maher brought the revolutionists' demands in a four-page letter written and signed by Neguib. They were that the King dismiss Thabet, Pulli, Andraus, Hassan, Hussein, Akef, Rashad, and Nasr immediately.

In the afternoon the Army claimed to have intercepted messages sent out by Farouk on the Montazah Palace radio asking help from General Slim at British G.H.Q. in the Canal Zone. Eden consulted Truman through Acheson. The President of the United States was against foreign intervention.

Throughout the day Alexandria and Cairo were rife with rumours. Neguib broadcast for a second time in the evening: "It gives me great pleasure to address you again, despite the heavy burdens that I have assumed in the present delicate circumstances. I am talking to you personally in order to dispel the malicious rumours being spread by your enemies. . . . The movement has no personal aims. . . . It's only purpose is to introduce reforms and to purge the Army and the Government of evil-doers and thus restore respect for the Constitution."

2100. Ali Maher returned to Cairo to tell Neguib, "His Majesty has deigned to approve such of the Army's requests as it has so far been possible to submit to him." Farouk had requested that Pulli and Hassan be allowed to stay with him. The first two objectives of the *coup* had been achieved. The third was now put in motion.

In the evening Farouk called the family together and told them to pack. His disillusionment was now total. Most of his courtiers, including Thabet whom he had promoted and maintained, were leaving him, like rats from a sinking ship. He sent another message to U.S. Ambassador Caffery asking for help. By night Commander Gamel Salem and his brother Major Salah Salem reported that they had control of forces in Sinai; Mohieddin controlled Alexandria.

25th July. In the early hours Farouk, himself at the wheel of a Mercedes, drove Narriman, Fuad and his English nurse Ann Chermside, from Montazah to Ras el Tin, to be nearer his yacht. The A.D.C. Hassan Akef travelled beside Farouk, holding a submachine-gun. Another car with his three daughters and their French governess Simone Tabouret was close behind.

0300. Kamel brought Admiral Galal Alhuba, Commander of the port of Alexandria, to Farouk in Montazah and on finding everyone gone drove quickly to Ras el Tin where all was confusion. Farouk wanted to leave at once but Alhuba explained he had orders from the Army not to move.

The King was now desperately seeking help. He sent his pilot Akef to Almaza airfield to prepare one of his thirteen planes, a C47, for escape, but the Army barred his way. He sent messages to the Americans, but his pride prevented him from calling again on the British. Farouk finally called the captain of his yacht, and Wahid Shawki, commander of the Coast Guards, to help him. His plan was to sail that night but this was impossible as the *Mahroussa* had recently been overhauled and installed with new batteries which were on shore for charging.

To have collected the workmen and crew together at night to prepare the *Mahroussa* would have caused too much activity and noise.

0600. Twenty-six tanks and armoured cars, a field artillery battery and a battalion of motorized infantry were sent to surround Montazah and Ras el Tin. In Cairo Abdin and Koubbeh were also invested. Ras el Tin had about 800 defenders, including the Sudanese guard. Farouk ordered all downstairs windows to be barricaded and machine-guns fixed along the corridors.

0700. The King and his family were wakened with the news that several hundred troops were approaching from the railway line. Farouk watched them from the balcony, though his later claims that he personally came under heavy Bren gunfire and himself returned the fire, are unlikely. The Neguibists came in via the stables where they slew Princess Ferial's Arab pony with a bayonet thrust.

0800. Three Lancaster bombers of the Egyptian Air Force buzzed the palace. The royal guard opened machine-gun fire on the surrounding troops. Farouk could see armoured cars outside and artillery facing him from the beaches. Telephone lines from the palace were cut but Farouk had always kept two secret telephone lines from the palace, which had remained undetected, and he now telephoned Ali Maher and Jefferson Caffery again for help. The Navy signalled from the harbour requesting permission to do battle with the insurgents in the harbour forts but Farouk refused to let them. The King's chief A.D.C., a Sudanese named Negoumi, negotiated a cease fire with the Neguibists. Meanwhile Caffery's Naval Attaché drove to see Neguib at Mustafa Pasha Barracks for an assurance of the King's safety. Those members of the Free Officer movement in Alexandria began to debate what should be done with the King. There were three possibilities open to them: to execute him without trial; to hold him in gaol for trial; or to exile him. There was an active element of opinion which demanded his execution. When Aziz el Masri, once the King's tutor, was asked his thoughts he replied, "A head only interests me after it has fallen." Nasser was against execution.

2300. Gamal Salem flew from Alexandria to the Cairo officers for their opinion.

26th July. 0200. The debate to determine Farouk's fate finished.

0430. Salem returned with the following note from Nasser: "The Liberation Movement should get rid of Farouk as quickly as possible in order to deal with what is more important—namely, the need to purge the country of the corruption that Farouk will leave behind him. We must pave the way towards a new era in which the people will enjoy their sovereign rights and live in dignity. Justice is one of our objectives. We cannot execute Farouk without a trial. [This could have made him a martyr.] Neither can we afford to keep him in jail and pre-occupy ourselves with the rights and wrongs of his case at the risk of neglecting the other purposes of the revolution. Let us spare Farouk and send him into exile. History will sentence him to death." The decision not to execute Farouk had been made with a majority of one, as there had been a majority of one in the debate on what to do with Louis XVI, but then it had been for the guillotine.

0900. El Sadat handed Neguib the Army's ultimatum to Farouk who in turn passed it to Prime Minister Ali Maher. Sadat wrote: "When Ali Maher finished reading it, he was as pale as death. I broke the silence by remarking that it was partly his fault that it had come to this, for he had been responsible for Farouk's political education. Ali Maher reported in a voice charged with emotion: 'Yes, it is true. I often advised him, but he would never listen. He deserved this end.' "

1015. Ali Maher called to deliver the ultimatum to Farouk.

1042. Farouk later recalled that this was the precise time at which he read the words of the ultimatum: "In view of your . . . misrule, your violations of the Constitution, your contempt for the will of the nation, which has gone so far that no citizen can any longer feel his life, property or dignity to be safe . . . and because under your protection traitors and swindlers are allowed to amass scandalous fortunes by wasting public monies while the people are dying of privation and hunger; and since these abuses were aggravated during the war in Palestine which gave rise to an abominable traffic in arms and munitions . . . the Army, which represents the strength of the people, has ordered me to demand that your Majesty abdicate in favour of the heir to the throne, His Highness Ahmed Fuad, on this day, Saturday, 26th July 1952, and that you leave the country on the same day before six o'clock. In the event of a rejection of this ultimatum, you will be held responsible for the consequences."

(*Signed*) Mohamed Neguib.
Commander-in-Chief of the Armed Forces.

1100. The First Secretary of the American Embassy, a one-eyed man named Joseph Sparks, informed Neguib that the U.S. Government considered the *coup d'état* as an internal matter of direct concern to Egyptians only. At this time Robert Simpson Caffery's tall personal secretary, demanded access to the King and was finally allowed through the cordon. Ali Maher later told Neguib that Simpson appeared in the corridor outside the reception room where he was speaking to Farouk.

"Come in, come in," called Farouk. "I've never been so glad to see anyone in my life. We haven't much time. I have just two things to tell your Ambassador. Ask him if he will do what he can to save my life—if he does, will he come to say good-bye? They're making me abdicate at twelve and leave the country at six."

1130. The American Ambassador came to assure Farouk of his own personal safety. When Farouk's personal staff learnt what was happening they asked him to let them resist. Negoumi, in charge of the royal guard that day, wanted permission to fight off the officers when they arrived and the King's faithful Albanian bodyguard, some of whom he had recruited from King Zog, pleaded with him to let them shoot down the officers. They had been trained for such an eventuality and were exasperated when they were deprived of the final test of their loyalty.

1230. Suliman Hafiz arrived with the abdication document

which read: "Whereas we have always sought the happiness and welfare of our People and sincerely wish to spare them the difficulties which have arisen in this critical time.

"We therefore submit to the will of the people.

"We have decided to abdicate the Throne in favour of Our Heir, Prince Ahmed Fuad, and in the present Rescript do give our orders to this end to His Excellency Ali Maher Pasha, Prime Minister, that he may act accordingly."

The following account, quoted by R. Badrawi in *The Military Coup*, is taken from a letter addressed to Ali Maher from Suliman Hafiz who stood by the King while he read the abdication document, and then asked the King to sign it. "He cast a brief glance over the text and asked me what the Act was based on. I replied that provision had been made for it in the preamble to the Constitution. He appeared calm, but judging from his slight coughs and the shuffling of his feet he was terribly nervous and trying to control himself. He read the document twice, then begged me to add to the phrase 'the will of the people' a reference to 'Our Will'. I pointed out to him that the text was drafted in the form of a royal rescript. He asked me whether that meant that the royal will was understood? I said that it was. He signed and said: 'I hope that in view of the circumstances you will excuse this signature. I had better sign it again.' He did."

The King spent his last six hours in Egypt packing. He again pleaded for Pulli and Hassan to be allowed to stay with him and asked permission to take his stamps and coins with him. He also requested to be allowed to return to Egypt as a private citizen, to which he received the placating reply, "Why not. The Duke of Windsor sometimes returns to England." Meanwhile he named the three-man Regency to rule until his son came of age. The Army were occupied with more immediate problems; they were frightened that the British might intervene at the last moment, and had sent troops to guard the approach road from the Canal Zone. They were also concerned that Ali Maher might be playing a double game, and secretly supporting Farouk, and that the Navy or Coast Guard might blow up the *Mahroussa* before she could take the King away. Farouk's last desperate gamble, offering to let Neguib form a government, and to make him a Field Marshal, had no effect.

1700. Princess Faiza insisted on going to say goodbye to her brother. She and her husband Bulent Rauf were in her house in the Mustafa Pasha district five kilometres from Alexandria Their friend Adel Sabet approached Ali Maher who in turn spoke to the Free Officers and it was arranged that they be allowed into Ras el Tin. An official of the Arab League, Saad Negm, accompanied them on the drive.

1730. All the family had collected in the Grand Salon of Ras el Tin Palace. Farouk, eighteen-year-old Narriman and their six-month-old son and his nurse; his daughters, clutching their pets, Princess Fawzia and Ismail Sherin; Princess Faiza and Bulent Rauf.

1740. Ali Maher, Jefferson Caffery and Robert Simpson arrived. The King spoke to Jefferson Caffery: "Many bad things will be said about me when I go. I want you to realize one thing, that is my children are coming with me of their own free will." At this Farouk called his children over and asked them if they wanted to go with him. They replied "Yes". From the windows could be seen whisky crates waiting to be loaded onto the launch: they were full of gold ingots. The King said goodbye to Ali Maher and shook hands with Jefferson Caffery.

1745. Farouk walked into the courtyard. The palace guard and the Sudanese formed a last guard of honour. A band played the national anthem while his flag was lowered, folded and handed to him.

1755. Farouk, his family and 204 pieces of luggage left the jetty to the servants' wails of lament which followed them out to the *Mahroussa* where she was waiting to sail.

1800. Ex-King Farouk, wearing the white uniform of Admiral of the Fleet as a final gesture of respect to his Navy, climbed aboard the *Mahroussa*, followed by the new King of Egypt held in his nurse's arms. At the same moment an Army jeep carrying General Neguib, Ahmed Shawki, Husain el Shafi and Gamal Salem was desperately trying to reach the harbour, delayed by the crowd, and by its driver who took the wrong turning and ended up on the other side of the palace. Neguib finally had to board the *Mahroussa* by Jacob's ladder. Later Neguib wrote:

Faruk was waiting for us on the bridge. I saluted him and he returned my salute. A long and embarrassing pause ensued. Neither of us knew what to say. We were both gripped by a mixture of emotions that brought us close to tears.

"*Effendim*," I said at last, addressing him politely as a private citizen rather than a king. "You remember that I was the only Egyptian officer who submitted his resignation in 1942."

"Yes, I remember," said Faruk.

"I was ashamed of the humiliation to which the King of Egypt had been subjected."

"I know."

"We were loyal to the throne in 1942, but many things have changed since then."

"Yes, I know. Many things have changed."

"It was you, *effendim*, who forced us to do what we have done."

Faruk's reply will puzzle me for the rest of my life.

"I know," he said. "You've done what I always intended to do myself."

I was so surprised that I could think of nothing more to say. I saluted and the others did likewise. Faruk returned our salutes and we all shook hands.

"I'm sorry not to have received you at the quay," he said, "but you ordered me to be out of Egypt by 1800. I kept my word."

We nodded and prepared to leave the bridge. But Faruk had not yet finished.

"I hope you'll take good care of the Army," he said. "My grandfather, you know, created it."

"The Egyptian Army", I said, "is in good hands."

"Your task will be difficult. It isn't easy, you know, to govern Egypt."

Such were Faruk's last words. I felt sorry for him as we disembarked. Faruk, I knew, would fail as an exile even as he had failed as a king. But he was such an unhappy man in every way that I would take no pleasure in his destruction, necessary though it was.

Another report claims that Farouk commented to Neguib:

"*Vous m'avez plumé pour votre déjeuner,*
j'allais vous accommoder pour mon souper."

Farouk's version of the interview claimed that in the few

seconds' privacy which the two had together before the other officers clambered aboard after their leader, Neguib blurted out: "Sir, I am not responsible for this. We had hoped to achieve only good by this *coup*, but it got out of hand—the effects have been too far-reaching. I hope you will understand. . . . There are others—fanatical ones—I was not called upon—I implore that you do not hold me responsible."

Farouk said later that at best these seemed to be the words of a man who was overwhelmed, almost of a man who was being pushed too hard from behind.

Before leaving the yacht, in an inconspicuous place, Neguib bent to kiss the King's hand. The *Mahroussa* sailed to a twenty-one-gun salute, and with the stars and crescent flying.

The *coup d'état* or rather the *coup de palais*, which is what it was, cost two men killed and seven wounded. Nasser wrote: "It is not true that 23rd July Revolution broke out due to the results of the Palestine offensive. Nor did it break out because of the defective arms. . . . Farther from the truth still, is the assertion that it broke out following the crisis of the Army Officers' Club election . . . all above causes were incidental.

"Perhaps their greatest effect was to spur us to a swifter pace on the road to revolution, but we nevertheless were already advancing with striding steps on that road."

It seems clear that the Americans, trading on the general dislike of the British, had ingratiated themselves with the Army and in a way had abetted the *coup* by showing their toleration of the Free Officer movement. One Cairo resident told the author that she had seen a senior official of the American Embassy sitting next to an Army officer whom she later realized was Nasser, in the Rivoli Cinema as early as December 1951.

A book published in 1962, *Central Intelligence Agency*, claims to give *the inside story* of the American C.I.A.'s moves in Egypt. It states that the "C.I.A. assisted in the ousting of King Farouk" and that the "C.I.A. was well aware of Nasser and his behind-the-scenes manœuvrings". Of January 1952 the book's author claims, "It was probably at this time that the United States and Great Britain decided Farouk would have to go. That is, both C.I.A. and British Intelligence began casting about for somebody to take over. . . .

"C.I.A. agents and British Intelligence agents were close to these young reformers [Free Officers] at the time and correctly gauged their strength." The book further claims that the C.I.A. "gave the word" for the *coup d'état*.

It also seems clear that, right until the last moment, Farouk still believed he could put off the revolt and keep his throne. This is the final example of his poor judgment of men, and the final result of his mistrust of everyone and lack of determination to make decisions: had he acted in February 1952 he might still have saved himself. By July there was not a man in Egypt prepared to help him; no patriot prepared to sacrifice his opinion, his will or himself for his King.

Chapter 12

Exile
(27th July 1952—2.08 a.m. 18th March 1965)

"To me", the Aga Khan wrote of Farouk, "there will always
. . . be something enigmatic in the sad yet remarkable man's
character. There are many baffling contradictions about him,
yet at the back of them all there is great charm and a genuine
and compelling simplicity. His father died when he was still a
boy, his mother went abroad almost immediately. In England
he lived to all intents and purposes a prisoner in a vast country
house . . . he had no proper schooling, never went to a University. . . . He has, I think always felt hampered by the lack of
education which both his station and his talents merited. This
may well have developed in him an inferiority complex. . . .

"Nobody bothered to teach him that a man's chief capital is
time."

The Aga Khan listed Farouk's good qualities as piety;
courtesy, kindness especially to the poor, to humble fellahin and
servants; and his patriotism and pride in his country.

"Each of us, it is said, is composed of many diverse and
conflicting elements; seldom in one human being has the
mingling been more complex and more contradictory than in
this ill-starred yet amiable and talented king."

The Aga Khan compared the fall of Farouk to that of Ahmed
Shah, last of the Kajar dynasty in Iran. Each of them "had
embraced a profound and defeatist resignation and had lost
faith in his power to fulfil his duties and serve his people".

Many people had comments to make on Farouk's fall; few
had any sympathy for him. Neguib said of him: "His ears were
as of stone, his eyes as of ice, he scorned warnings and called

their authors children." Salah el Salem, one of the Free Officers, said later, "We never thought it would be that easy." Neither the British nor the Americans helped him. The Pasha class blamed Farouk, and felt he had no right to leave them and Egypt: morally he had betrayed his mission. His tutor commented: "*Capax imperii nisi imperasset.*" A calendar hanging on a wall in Port Said carried this symbolic caption: "He came to this country without an enemy—he left without a friend."

His departure on the *Mahroussa* recalled the day the Khedive Ismail (with three hundred women) sailed to exile. The ease with which an Egyptian alters his allegiance was admirably illustrated the day that Khedive sailed, and is quoted by Madame Tugay whose aunt, as a little girl, was present. "Egyptian dignitaries filled saloons and covered the deck, weeping copiously and loudly proclaiming their unswerving loyalty to so kind a master. Nothing, they declared, could ever induce them to serve another. At the signal for departure they went ashore, forming a black, frock-coated throng on the quay. A moment later, before the astonished gaze of the girl watching from the ship, they quietly disappeared. In the distance . . . she saw them hurrying and pushing their way to the waiting carriages, to be the first to pay homage to the new ruler!"

After Farouk's expulsion Egyptian papers indulged in vitriolic summaries of the former King's faults, a man who, according to *Al-Akhbar*, had "instigated treachery, injustice, greediness and corruption . . . who used the influence of monarchy as a whip to flog the backs of the liberals and to tear the faces of the disdainful, who imposed misery and slavery . . ." "To Farouk Egypt was a private estate, the Egyptians the means of satiating his appetites" (*El-Baraway*). His faults were further listed: flagrant interference in political and judicial appointments, unrestricted granting of honours and titles; attempts to muzzle the press; responsibility for the 4th February ultimatum; responsibility for the Palestine war; apathy in seeking a solution to the Sudan problem; the failure of Egypt's policy on the Arab States; his personal way of life; and his instigation of assassinations.

The whisky crates, full of gold ingots (which Farouk claimed held whisky and champagne packed by his faithful old wine steward Ahmed Ali), on the dockside on the day of abdication were loaded on board the *Mahroussa*. It is said the Army heard of this after the yacht had sailed and sent a cable ordering her return. This was ignored. After five hours at sea the *Mahroussa*, destined for Naples, drastically altered course in an attempt to throw off pursuit by the torpedo boat reported following them from Alexandria. Farouk believed the Moslem Brotherhood were chasing him to murder him. One can but estimate the size of the operation, and the number of persons involved in moving the ex-King and his possessions. Scores of cables poured into the *Mahroussa* requesting interviews with Farouk on his arrival. There is little doubt that he had many friends working for his cause in Italy; within little time the fortune taken from Egypt (supplemented by a few gold accessories lifted from the *Mahroussa* as she crossed the Mediterranean) was absorbed into Farouk's funds abroad.

On hearing of the *coup* Nahas broke off his holiday in Switzerland and boarded an aeroplane for the first time in his life (aged seventy-three) and hastened to Neguib's side. But this move failed; the days of the Wafd had also ended. When the *Mahroussa* docked in Naples on 29th July the Royal Standard was lowered, the flag of the Egyptian Navy run up, and the crew paraded to bid farewell; two sailors jumped ship. The Egyptian Ambassador to Italy met Farouk and his family, who took forty rooms at the Eden Paradise Hotel, Capri, and for two days stayed barricaded inside. Farouk played games and asked his daughters riddles while reporters thronged the streets and gardens outside and photographers waited in the foyer, on the stairs and trained telescopic lenses on the family from neighbouring rooftops.

On the third day of exile, on the terrace of the hotel, Farouk held a press conference and addressed three hundred reporters from a hammock: "I hope you will forgive me if I do not speak as freely as you would like me to. While I am no longer king, I still have several grave responsibilities, and one of them is towards the Italian Government, which has courteously given me hospitality here. I want to carefully avoid saying anything that might possibly embarrass them.

"I repeat I am no longer king, but I do have with me the King of Egypt and I owe him a responsibility. So you can see that with all the problems that have fallen on my shoulders, I would like not to add to them by any unguarded remark. So far as the present government in Egypt is concerned, I wish them all the luck in the world, because they have need of it. Governing a country in these days of world crisis is no easy matter. When I became king at sixteen years of age, I was hopeful that I could improve the position of my country in its relations with other nations of the world, and my love for Egypt and for the people of my country even though I am in exile is as great today as it was then.

"Because I can no longer return to Egypt, I must seek a new home and as yet I do not know where to look, nor have I even begun to think about it. I've read in the papers that I am on my way to America, England, Switzerland, and to the South of France. [He collected newspaper cuttings concerning his destination, and the possible whereabouts of his fortune.] Those of you who have written this know more about it than I do. The only thing I am sure of is that I would like to stay here in Capri because I have to think of the well-being of my four children. Whatever has happened surely has not been their fault, but it has upset them, especially the girls who are old enough to understand. Right now the subjects of my new kingdom are the children. We'll swim, take bathes, and walk tranquilly with all of you, if you will let us. I can only ask you to accept us without too much noise."

Wild, if quiet, rumours went about concerning the size of fortune Farouk had managed to take out of Egypt. However, one Italian weekly magazine reported that he had no more than £600 stuffed in his pocket at the last moment by a faithful secretary, and was now seeking a job. Farouk himself conceded that "by the standards of the very poor I am still to be envied". He permitted the first formal newsreel pictures of himself and family, sitting next to an impassive Narriman, he adjusted his glasses and held Fuad on his right knee, looking gruff, gently patting Fuad who looked up at his father, blissfully unaware of events.

The ex-King was now known as Prince Farouk Fuad of Egypt and the Queen as Princess Narriman. He and the family could be seen each day at the Villa Canzone del Mare, which belonged to Gracie Fields, in swimming shorts, tennis shoes, sun hat and gold-rimmed sunglasses. The little girls played with the Alsatian puppies and swam in the pool. On 7th August he announced that "for the time being" he would stay on Capri. He cut down the number of his rooms to twenty-seven with fifteen bathrooms, a private dining-room and lift. In the evenings he and Narriman mixed in the crowded Capri main square, Farouk holding a cigar, and dressed in shabby light trousers with his shirt outside.

By autumn he was settling into exile. The hullabaloo had quietened and the hard reality met Farouk and Narriman. They moved to a villa in Frascati, south of Rome. By October Narriman was reported to be consulting a divorce lawyer in Lausanne; she was planning to leave her husband.

Farouk wrote his memoirs for British Sunday papers, an entertaining mixture of isolated astute comments and evidence of his fertile imagination which allowed him to see himself in situations in his life which were pure wishful thinking: springing out of bed as reveille sounded at 'the Shop' (the Royal Military Academy, Woolwich), dashing into a cold shower and pulling on the skin-tight uniform trousers before he could dry properly, in order to be on parade on time; fighting with his Army in the Palestine front line; and surviving on one meal a day of bread, oil and cheese when sailing on the *Mahroussa* to exile.

In January 1953 Farouk and Narriman took a suite at Pontresina in Engadine for the winter sports; meanwhile in Egypt, to celebrate their first six months in power, the Army held a Liberation Rally, sang the liberation hymn and unfurled the liberation flag of red, white and black bars which, Neguib wrote, "signified the new blood of the future, the purity of our ideals, and the black corruption of the past". In February Farouk cancelled his birthday reception and sent the amount he was to have spent on it, £800, to the relief fund for Victims of European floods, as a gesture of 'human solidarity'.

Narriman published her ghost-written memoirs full of such stuff as "His shoulders fascinated me, and his arms and his powerful wrists covered with dark, virile hair. . . . And I found love such as I would never have dared to hope for". But the glamour wore thin for her. In March Farouk's mother-in-law visited them in their thirty-room villa. She left for Switzerland with her daughter, and her poodle Jou Jou, but without Fuad. Narriman asked alimony of £5,000 a month. Farouk's lawyer announced to the press that the ex-King was "awaiting every new development with full faith in the justice of God" and that he "bows to His will with absolute sincerity". A few hours later Farouk met a blonde in the Boîte Pigalle. Narriman had left him to return to Egypt, without her son or her jewels, at nineteen back to a villa in Heliopolis where she had started.

In April Farouk was at the Hotel Majestic on the Riviera, looking gay again in a double-breasted suit and wide hat; the smiling crowds waited to film him. Eight weeks later Ahmed Fuad II was officially deposed, on 18th June. Thus ended the world's oldest kingdom, and the Mohamed Ali Dynasty. The supreme Military Tribunal suggested that Prince Farouk be tried in his absence for his responsibility for defective arms in the Palestine war. Some arms, they claimed, had never been sent to the front, but remained in a Cairo Depot. Farouk was accused of implication in the murder of Hassan el Banna of the Moslem Brotherhood. All property belonging to the heirs of Mohamed Ali was confiscated and nearly four hundred members of the Royal family lost all their possessions.

The Tribunal hanged four found guilty of treasonable activities on behalf of the British, condemned but did not sentence Nahas, deprived Madame Nahas of 322 acres of farmland. Dr. Ahmed Nakib of the Moassat hospital and Mohamed Hilmi Hussein of Farouk's staff were sentenced to fifteen years in prison. (Hilmi the chauffeur had become an honorary Brigadier and had amassed a small fortune between 1944 and 1952,) Sirri Amer, captured while trying to escape to Libya in a stolen car, was sentenced to life imprisonment. Karim Thabet was put in irons in Turah prison and sentenced for life. He spent some time writing a vitriolic account of his services with the ex-King. Serag ed-Din was given fifteen years. (These sentences were later lightened.)

Antonio Pulli's house was searched. He then told the Army everything, denounced Farouk and was allowed to go free. He is still in Egypt. Pietro della Valle had remained faithful to Farouk, and with the two Albanian guards Shaker and Yacob went with him into exile. In November there was another movement in Cairo to brand Farouk as a 'criminal' and not a political refugee, but it was doubted that the Italians would extradite him.

By the end of 1953 plans had been made by the Army to sell the palace collections which Farouk had amassed in addition to the collections he had inherited from his father. This penchant for acquisition was a result of his inferiority complex. For years the world had speculated on the nature and size of the Farouk collections; they were now revealed for the first time when newsmen were allowed into Koubbeh Palace. One wrote afterwards that he had seen "the world's biggest and most expensive accumulation of junk. It threw a pitiless light on the character of the man who had lived there. . . . Farouk's tastes sometimes seemed curiously childish, like those of a schoolboy who has never grown up beyond the French postcard stage. Above all the palace gave the impression that someone had feverishly and indiscriminately crammed possessions into the vast rooms, to ward off loneliness, or perhaps despair".

The reporters toured through the palace and stared at the hoard. In a gaming room a cabinet was full of roulette wheels, dice, and packs of cards with *Esquire*-type girls on the back. On a keyboard hung keys to apartments in Cairo, each clearly labelled with the girl's name. In the vaults six safes contained medals, coins and stamps. On his study desk, beside the nude statuettes, lay boxes of tricks, including pocket radiation counters inscribed 'Measure Nuclear Energy Yourself' and a penknife bristling with all manner of blades. In his bedroom were glamour girl photographs, Kodachrome nudes with pocket viewers, pictures of Narriman and a pile of U.S. comics. There were six telephones and two radios beside the bed. In the dressing-room were one hundred suits, fifty walking sticks, seventy-five pairs of binoculars, a thousand ties, some with the initial F five inches high. Between the first and second floors there was a windowless room, a sort of treasury with boxes of rubies, diamonds, emeralds, and platinum brooches.

The Army had also confiscated all his land, which amounted to 28,000 acres when he left. After months of negotiation it was decided that Sotheby's of London should auction most of his possessions. It was their responsibility to catalogue all categories, to appoint an auctioneer, and to conduct the auctions. This called for not simply an enormous amount of work in a hot climate but inestimable patience in dealing with the Army who at best were completely ignorant and highly suspicious of the

foreigners handling what were now Egyptian national possessions. For months the fate of Farouk's antiquities was in the
balance: to send his Egyptian pieces to the National Museum
in Cairo would be like adding a drop to the ocean, whereas if
sold there were enough magnificent pieces to enhance museums
around the world. However, they were not sold and remained
in Egypt.

In addition to antiquities the collections included a fine private
library containing many interesting and rare books on Egypt,
and a collection of old illuminated Korans; a unique collection
of the development of the playing card from ancient to modern
times, including cards used by all the kings of France, by Chinese
emperors, the cards used in the first casino in Monaco, and
cards from the Mississippi gambling boats; a collection of
essences and rare plant distillations, perfumes as taken by the
Phoenicians to the Ancient Britons, and medieval perfumes of
Italy and France and the Orient (of course assumed by the
revolutionists to be Farouk's philtres); pornography; stamps;
coins and medals; silver, silver-gilt and gold; objects of vertu,
watches, jewellery; glass, French paper weights and Gallé
glass. There were worthless hordes of razor-blade packets and,
amassed by Farouk the phillumenist, hundreds of matchbox
tops. "The Palace Collections of Egypt", Sotheby's wrote, "to
be sold by auction in Cairo in February and March of 1954
constitute the most extensive and remarkable collections of
their kind ever to be offered for public sale. The occasion
inevitably suggests comparison with the sales of the Whitehall
collections under the Commonwealth or of the contents of
Versailles in 1793."

One of Sotheby's staff, John Synge, spent months paving the
way for the sales. Peter Wilson, the chairman, flew out to
make arrangements. The team of specialists included world
experts in their fields, coin dealers Fred and Albert Baldwin,
stamp dealer Cyril Harmer, Fabergé expert Kenneth Snowman;
Tim Clarke of Sotheby's on objects of vertu and silver, and
Eyles of Garrards on precious stones. Between them they had
to cope with Colonel Mahmoud Younis and Major Gaafir who
acted as liaison with the Egyptian Army; with unique specimens
in the collections which even world experts could not have seen
before; with oddities, such as a Pepsi-Cola bottle mounted in

gold; with ignorant methods which had been used to test and catalogue the objects, such as scratching to check the metal, and markings in ink; all sufficient to exasperate an expert. The final hindrance was the insistence by the Army that they should fix the reserves for all lots because they were afraid of being cheated, with the result that reserves were fixed so high that nearly half the lots remained unsold. A Jewish jeweller from Alexandria recommended an auctioneer to Sotheby's one day over tea at Groppi's. His name was M. George Lee: as well as being a good auctioneer he spoke about eight languages. The Government appointed him auctioneer at the sales, an interesting commission for this established dealer who had bought much for Farouk in the past, and who once had reported the King to the police for pocketing one of his ivory statuettes.

During the weeks of preparation for the sales one of Sotheby's staff kept a diary, from which the following are extracts:

> Major Gaafir takes us on a tour of the palace, and we see something of the fabulous collections made by Farouk. His own apartments, which form the west wing, immediately over the museum, comprise some half dozen bed and dressing-rooms, with two bathrooms in mauve and green alabaster; also a kitchen. In these rooms are deep, fitted cupboards, and they contain collections of wirelesses, pipes, medicine samples, (including two dozen bottles of arsenic), postcards, walking sticks, razors, ashtrays, pornography, and ties; also a shelf of large fishing flies in the form of plastic nudes. The furniture is ugly, and in no way remarkable; the pictures are painted by his daughters, and a signed portrait of Hitler hangs in his dressing-room.
>
> These apartments are divided from the Queen's by the length of the palace—this length being occupied by various personal staff rooms, a large hall with various types of pianola, electric organ, and musical machines; a gymnasium fitted with all kinds of slimming devices, a chemical laboratory; and a dentist's surgery.
>
> The Queen's apartments have an air of comfort and intimacy, quite lacking in those of the King. The furniture is all reproduction French, but the silk walls, the carpets, and the tapestry chairs make many of the rooms attractive. As we walk round we come across various committees making lists of the Queen's clothes (mostly by Dior), her shoes, hats, and countless unopened boxes of powder, scent, bath salts etc.
>
> Among these rooms is that of Farouk's mother, Queen Nazli. It seems that she was kept as a slave by her husband, and that when he died she began to enjoy a romantic existence which earlier repressions made wild and extragavant. The furniture and walls of

her bedroom are veneered throughout in looking glass; this includes the head and foot of her large bed.

The ground floor, similarly divided between the King and Queen by a great carpeted hall, is made up of reception and dining-rooms; also Farouk's office, with a bronze fist on his desk inscribed "I will do" in Arabic. Major Gaafir pointed out, "But he wouldn't", opened his mouth and let himself laugh.

In one room is a showcase of pornographic books, each opened at a sufficiently exciting page. They are mostly modern and French, but some are eighteenth and nineteenth century, so may be valuable. Around the walls are pinned various erotic postcards, and a series of 'filthy pictures' made into playing cards. On a table by the door is a magnifying projector, and two boxes of slides. The wall cases contain various 'positions' in bronze.

The second room is decorated entirely by the water colour and chalk drawings of 'F. Fabiano', who has cleverly illustrated every variety of normal sexual intercourse that one can imagine. The wall cases contain such an assortment of erotica as includes amber phalluses, bronze love scenes, pornographic cocktail glasses, and corkscrews in every sexual shape that the craftsman could devise.

Of the remaining rooms in the museum one is given to Farouk's collection of antiquities, the others to an exhibition of nudes— 300 paintings, 50 studio photographs ('Ruth', 'Curves', 'Danish Beauty', 'Outlines' etc.) and countless studies in china, marble, bronze, copper, alabaster, and ivory; also cheap plastic nudes with jokes like "Is that Fanny Browne?" written across them; and drinking mugs in the shape of torsos.

Committees from the Customs Office, from the Ministry of Finance, and the Assay Office are at present making detailed inventories of the palace contents. They work in the museum, weighing, testing, and valuing each object, their leader is a large and noisy eunuch, whom they call Abdullah; another is Kaniny, and a third, Farouk. They seem anxious to help us, but we are allowed to touch nothing until it has been through the inventory process. It seems that in the museum alone there are some 4,000 objects. With the overtime question settled, we can work till four o'clock in the afternoon, bringing with us from the flat a picnic lunch. Major Gaafir has given us the King's balcony to use as our own—so we shall enjoy royal comfort for at least a part of each day. Leading from this balcony is Farouk's bedroom; in it is a cupboard full of penny dreadfuls, modern pornography, letters from Narriman *"a déposer aux pieds de Sa Majesté"*, books on Portuguese politics, many photographs of himself in Capri, lists of girls (with their addresses and telephone numbers) from every capital in Western Europe—and a series of photographs showing how elephants copulate!

Sat. 4th April. We asked Younis how, in the catalogues, we should refer to the ex-King and Queen. His reply was straight-forward: "They are nothing now, call them just 'Farouk' and 'Narriman'."

I'm interested by the ruthlessness of revolution; the inability of its officers to see the past in any sort of historical perspective. The vulgar disrespect with which Farouk and his possessions are treated slightly shocks me; the laughter at his private letters; the jokes about his bedroom; the way you are shown his bathroom and lavatory—now made filthy by workmen.

Wed. 15th April. Our last day at Koubbeh. We are preparing to leave at 4 o'clock when a message comes to the museum, would we please wait for a few minutes "as something is going to happen".

We wait till 4.30 and nothing happens. I go out into the museum corridor and meet Major G; he looks a little serious and a little excited. He whispers to me: "The King is here; the Govern-ment has brought him secretly into the country." Before I have time to think there comes down the corridor a cortège of officers and civilians led by Farouk. He is dressed as an Admiral of the Fleet, and wears dark glasses. For a moment I have no doubt it is him. He walks straight past me, his hands behind his back, looking neither right nor left, into the room where the others are waiting. I watch their reaction of utter bewilderment and confusion. The King moves on into a further room—and then a burst of laughter, uncontrolled, hopeless peals of laughter.

It was a carefully planned joke—the best I have ever had played on me. 'Faruk' is an actor called Arqero—a double of the King.

In his private files at Ras el Tin Farouk had kept a dossier during his reign of no fewer than sixteen men, Austrians, Italians, French and mid-Orientals who had been arrested at one time or another for impersonating the King in order to swindle jewellers, hoteliers and susceptible ladies.

Finally the catalogues were finished and the full extent of the Farouk collections could be realized. The stamps were the first to be sold, the largest collection in the world, requiring four days for auction. On studying the catalogues one moves into the fascinating world of the specialist, each with his own language, as in the stamp catalogue:

The early essays and proofs are in themselves a wonderful group. Blocks, multiples and varieties of the first issue are exceptional with a fantastic multiple of twelve—the only known block—of the 5-piastre rose on a large part original front. The following issues from 1867 to 1875 are very strongly represented . . . the later issues are practically complete and are enhanced by artists' original sketches and designs, essays and proofs. From 1925 when the

Survey of Egypt took over the production of all Egyptian stamps it became the practice to send to the palace two complete sheets of all stamps; also sheets of Proofs on carton paper overprinted on reverse 'Cancelled' in English or Arabic, in addition to colour trials, die proofs. Of certain issues special Royal Printings of imperforate miniature sheets of nine stamps were made, whilst there are many important varieties including imperforate sheets, others with double and inverted overprints.

There were tête-bêche pairs, rare Reunions, British Guiana 'Cottonreels', Hawaiian 'Missionaries', Mauritius primitives, stamp rugs, forgeries, entires, covers, obliterations . . . stamps of every colour: dull purple, rose-lake, pale yellow on pelure paper, 'vermillion vif', black, bistre, carmine-brown, orange, yellow-buff, blue on blue paper. . . .

Farouk's coin collection took three months to catalogue and eleven days to sell and consisted mainly of nineteenth- and twentieth-century issues, with the largest collection of American coins outside the U.S. Treasury. Some older pieces included four bars discovered wrapped in newspaper in a corner; they proved to be fourth-century A.D. Roman gold ingots. The 2,798 lots included coins from a hundred countries, 8,500 coins and medals in gold, and 164 specimens in platinum. Many of the coins had come from other large private collections, others from less authentic sources, such as the 20-dollar double eagle which had disappeared from the museum of the Philadelphia Mint years before. The U.S. Government claimed it, but then it mysteriously disappeared again.

In studying the catalogue one again enters the world of the specialist, a numismatist's paradise of doubloons and dobras, stuivers, scudi, perpera and zlotys; a Tibet temple money brick, a Leeds half guinea, a Britannia groat, Byzantine tremisses, Minh Mang cash, Selim III sequins, a Catherine I square ten kopek; Changchow ration dollars and Shensi candareens . . . heavy flans and bevelled eges; half eagles and split ticals. . . .

Farouk loved objects that could be held in the hand. Kenneth Snowman, expert on Fabergé, wrote that the King "fell a natural victim to the insidious charm of Carl Fabergé's work. . . . Those sleek objects made in St. Petersburg for the delectation of the doomed Romanovs were exercises in perfectionism; there is an unmistakable note of desperation about their meticulous finish and patiently expressed detail that was bound to arouse sympathy in the bosom of an oriental monarch growing increasingly unsure of his sovereignty". The collections of automata and Fabergé at Luton Hoo, and that belonging to Queen Mary compare with the Farouk collection. He had collected every type of luxury article; Louis XV, Louis XVI and Georgian scent flacons, enamelled or gold, or of coloured golds or encrusted with jewels; étuis to hold toilet implements or needles, in bloodstone or agate with gold cagework mounts, or in gold and silver; gold enamelled knives; piqué counter cases; gold patch boxes, and a magnificent Louis XVI *brûle-parfum* of agate with solid gold mounts; a great series of snuff-boxes including several made at Dresden by the celebrated Johann Christian Neuber, French boxes of mother-o'-pearl with Chinese scenes, and two sumptuous boxes encrusted with diamonds, made to the order of Frederick the Great.

The variety of watches was astounding. There were French and English gold and silver watches; *montres fantaisie* in the form of shells, flowers and butterflies which delighted the Parisian ladies of the First Empire; watches made in London and Geneva for export to Turkey; singing bird boxes; and harps, seals and snuff boxes concealing watches and musical movements. From England there was a superb George II architectural table-clock by James Cox, from Switzerland a whole series of exquisite musical automata, on which moving scenes played to the accompaniment of music. Pre-eminent in this section was the famous 'Magician Box', where the spectator's questions were answered by a mechanical wizard.

There were boxes made in Switzerland richly encrusted with diamonds and ordered for presentation by the Sultans of Turkey and Khedives of Egypt, and several gold telescopes, charmingly enamelled and with diamond sprays. The Near East was represented by many sumptuous Turkish jewelled coffee-cup holders, known as zarfs, by a superb jewelled rattle surmounted by the Turkish crown in diamonds and emeralds, and by a celebrated Persian gold and enamel dish. The delicate craftsmanship of the workmasters of Carl Fabergé could be seen in many characteristic products; paper knives, walking sticks, bell pushes, seals, cigarette-cases, writing-table sets, and above all, in a famous Imperial Easter Egg, made as a gift from the Czar Nicholas II to his wife Alexandra Feodorovna, the outer egg of which, of pale mauve matt enamel latticed with diamond ribbons, opened to reveal a white gold swan floating on an aquamarine lake. And many heavy and valuable objects in 18-carat gold, notably a magnificent diamond and gold coffee-set of a large circular tray and twenty-four zarfs.

When Snowman arrived to catalogue the objects of vertu he found the Army guards using the Fabergé Easter egg as a football (in the sale it made £6,400 and another Easter egg in red enamel with diamonds fetched £4,200). The soldiers in charge of the collections had so used the automatic erotica that they were "without exception bereft of movement, paralysed by sheer over-work and exhaustion".

The majority of the silver was of Egyptian, Turkish, French and English origin with examples of German, Dutch, Italian, Norwegian, Russian, Persian and Chinese silver or gold. Outstanding in the collection was the Chinese gold coffee set and the gold tea set by Ahmed Neguib, Farouk's jeweller, General Kléber's toilet set, and a dressing set apparently presented by the Empress Eugénie to the Khedive Ismail. A large quantity of massive English and French plate was included in the sale including a remarkable series of French candelabra illustrating the fable of La Fontaine and weighing more than 6,600 ounces. There were silver sweetmeat dishes, a tarboosh stand, incense burners, ewers, inkpots, mustard pots, meat dishes, dressing sets, jewel caskets, writing sets, hanging lamps, finger bowls, fruit bowls, candelabra, cigar boxes, trays, tankards, tureens, lobster forks, game skewers and vegetable dishes, a scented water vase, cruet frames, mugs, sugar sifters, asparagus servers, sauce ladles, olive spoons, ice spoons, tea spoons, basting spoons, jam spoons, grape scissors, and a dinner service which had been purchased in London for £27,000 only three years before.

The silver and glass had been kept in a series of large rooms on the ground floor of Abdin Palace, thousands of pieces stacked on shelves. Other cupboards were full of art nouveau Gallé glass in various colours, decorated with flowers, fruit and some with landscapes. Farouk had been a legend in the paperweight market; when he stopped collecting the market was seriously affected. He had amassed about five hundred weights including rare snake and overlay weights.

Before the sales took place Farouk's legal representatives

issued a warning that action would be taken against any pur-
chaser of Farouk's property, but this did not prove a hindrance
and on the appointed day in February 1954 a military band,
according to an observer, struck up with a "limited repertoire
of waltzes and tangos, all served with unmistakably Islamic
flavour". The stretch of lawn at Koubbeh Palace, gay with
marquees and tables, sheltered by large coloured sunshades
presented a festive appearance "not far removed from the
Members Enclosure at Wimbledon or a gouache by Raoul
Dufy". While hungry kites hovered and wheeled above the
"sprawling yellow sports pavilion" of Koubbeh, the prospective
buyers crossed the lawns and entered the palace along crême de
menthe carpets to the sale room with its rostrum draped in
the red, white and black Egyptian flag. For days dealers, col-
lectors and celebrities had been arriving from all over the
world. Viewing had been hampered by the fact that the Army,
ever suspicious, had driven nails into the showcases, successfully
preventing the inspection of any pieces until the services were
obtained of one overworked Abdul Hamid and his pincers. The
rostrum was surrounded by bayonets. The military, Snowman
wrote, had as much "idea of how to run an auction sale of art
objects as the Gordon Highlanders would have of taking over
the management of the Stock Exchange". President Neguib
viewed the lots just before the sale, after which some gold
doubloons were withdrawn.

Just before the auctioneer Lee was about to invite the first bid
in French, Arabic and English, for the opening lot of stamps,
a spokesman for the Egyptian government stood up and
announced that anyone who during the sale bid £5,000 or over
would be granted access to the pornographic collection. This
provided a lively start.

The auction went on for weeks, only interrupted by breaks
for coffee, or angry arguments over the splitting of lots, and
entertaining outbursts by an eccentric dealer who announced
her retirement from the room and on her return loudly condemned the Egyptian Army for its deficiency of what she
considered to be normal facilities required by a group of people
gathered in one place. Rings were operating in the dealers.
Lee tactfully and successfully broke one of the rings by sending
for a screen from the Queen's apartments and having it placed

directly across the line of vision between two dealers who had been signalling to one another during the bidding. There was tax on all purchases. Many buyers qualified for what became known as their 'pornographic peep', including the Aga Khan who was wheeled off to the rooms, each protected by steel grilles and electric ray alarms and outside which hung the notice: "The Secret Museum—Farouk was a man of sensuous, often vulgar taste; we have taken his collections of pornography from his chambers; they may be seen inside."

In the middle of the sale Neguib was deposed and resigned, and Nasser finally achieved the position he had been working towards for many years.

In exile Farouk quietened and was satisfied looking after his money. It was announced that Narriman would marry Dr. Adham el Nakib, son of a friend of Farouk who conducted a clinic at Moassat Hospital in Alexandria. Farouk continued to live in his apartment in Rome with the Albanian guards and a staff of forty, and could be identified occasionally in the streets, driving a maroon Mercedes. One night at the Belvedere delle Rose he met eighteen-year-old Irma Capece Minutolo when she failed to win a beauty contest; she accompanied him for years. He bought an apartment on Via Guido Baldo del Monti, and rented one for Irma in the same street. With her he was seen in the Excelsior and at the Fonte dei Papi bar on the Tiber and occasionally paid visits to poor families, of the many which wrote begging letters to him, to leave food baskets with them. He and Irma visited his children in Lausanne.

Farouk still maintained a serious interest in the affairs of Egypt and in July 1955 made a statement in Paris denouncing the new government which, he said, had plunged the country into "an unprecedented regime of terror and almost inextricable economic difficulties". He thought the solution of Egypt's problems lay in the restoration of the monarchy "in some form" (Prince Mahmoud Namouk, cousin of Farouk, had been sentenced to fifteen years' imprisonment for plotting against Nasser) and claimed he could have crushed the 1952 *coup* with police and military forces, but chose to leave to avoid bloodshed. After three years the revolution had become "a tyrannic dictatorship, the 'free' officers little despots; Egypt, a police state, and the Egyptians a captive people". "Egypt", he continued, "has now become a troublemaker . . . in an attempt to regain Western support, the military rulers have had to resort naively to diplomatic blackmail, playing simultaneously an anti-communist, a neutralist, and pro-Russian game."

Even his detractors, he concluded, would honestly concede that Egypt under the monarchy was a country where, though parliamentary life was imperfect, there were democratic freedoms and "at least everyone felt free and secure", where people were entitled to a fair trial "and a prisoner not subjected to Nazi-like tortures . . . where there was economic prosperity, work and bread for all, despite the many social inequalities and discriminations". Now this country had been reduced by a handful of incompetent and greedy individuals to one of fear and despair.

There were rumours of Egyptian agents being sent to Italy to assassinate Farouk. Fifteen months later, soon after the Suez crisis Farouk sent a confidential message to Sir Anthony Eden, M. Coty and President Eisenhower. He stated again that he had left Egypt to avoid civil war, and continued:

> We have never ceased to follow developments in our country with the greatest attention and we have never forgotten Egypt's supreme interests. Although unwilling to discuss and judge the policy of our country since our departure, we must, alas, realize that we have foreseen and predicted the grievous developments shown by the recent events.
>
> With the greatest compassion are we considering the dangerous march of our country and choose this moment to raise our voice and to ask you, knowing the deep humanity of your country and yourself, to try by all possible means to devise a peaceful solution of the problems which now divide your Government from the Egyptian people, who cannot be held responsible for the mistakes of their leaders.
>
> We invoke God, praying that the voice of reason and of heart should prevail, and that our beloved people and the whole of mankind should be spared the horrors of conflict which, we are sure, can still be averted.
>
> Farouk of Egypt

This was perhaps the last evidence of his serious interest in Egypt. From 1956 his life became a social round of the international circuit, Geneva, Cannes, Rome; he was granted the citizenship of Monaco. His only business, apart from protecting his money interests, was petty libel actions, one against an Italian chocolate manufacturer who named his product 'Farouk', and another against Elsa Maxwell for libel in her book in which she quoted a telegram she once sent to Farouk, refusing a social invitation, saying that she did not keep company with "clowns, monkeys, profligates, and evil-doers". He won both actions.

His health was deteriorating. His heart was very weak. He weighed twenty stone, and his left eye lid was turning inside out. He became a pathetic, sad man with little but his children to live for, and except for Fuad and about seven he had had by other women, they were almost adults. There are incidents of Farouk telephoning old friends he had met in the war after years had passed, to ask how they were. On his birthday he never failed to write to his midwife, Lucy Sergeant, in Worthing, Sussex. He remembered birthdays and Christmas, with the help of his private secretary Lucien Gallas. But in conversation he was forgetful and would tell the same stories over again, weeping if he met persons with whom he had once had a good time.

Of the women he had really loved, or who had been very good friends to him, they were now scattered between Paris, Beirut, and Rio de Janeiro, most of them married. Of his old staff Karim Thabet died, Pulli was in Cairo. Mohamed Hussein had escaped to Khartoum where he opened a hotel, his doctor Youssef Rashad began a fishing business on the Red Sea, his pilot left Egypt and his Naval A.D.C. Akef went to Kuwait. His mother Nazli lived in Beverly Hills, California and his first wife Farida had moved to the outskirts of Beirut after the *coup d'état*.

Farida later commented on her separation from Farouk. "The truth . . . is that I wished to have my freedom from King Farouk as much, I suppose, as he wished for his freedom from me. The King knew I wanted a divorce and he told me bluntly that he would give me one on condition that I never remarried. I agreed to this condition. Life was intolerable as it was and I would have agreed to anything to be free. All I had asked from my husband was affection, but this was denied to me. I would not ask my ex-husband for anything. One has some dignity and my former husband knew that the very small allowance I was

made was quite insufficient to maintain me after he had dismissed me. . . .

"I managed to follow the careers of my daughters through an
occasional news report and from letters received from friends."

Farida reverted to her former name, Safinaz Zulficar, and to
her hobbies of cutting and sewing her own wardrobe, and paint-
ing portraits of her daughters from photographs. Several times
she attempted to see Farouk again, and once was in the room
next to where he was gambling in Monte Carlo but he sent a
message saying there was nothing to discuss.

"I did not hate King Farouk. What was there to hate? Only
pity is in my heart, pity but no hate."

Of his sisters, Fawzia married an economist in Alexandria;
Faiza married a Turk, Faika married an Egyptian, Fathia married
an Egyptian Copt. Of his daughters Ferial married a Swiss
hotelier, Fadia married a Russian geologist.

For ten years Farouk lived in Rome in the Via Archimede,
Parioli and in the Villa Dusmet at Grotta Ferata, and grew old
before his time. The family lived at Cully, and at Lutry, near
the lake at Lausanne. He watched and envied the people round
him who led what, by his standard, were normal lives, based on
a normal childhood and education. It would not be surprising if
Farouk had resented his harsh upbringing which allowed him
no time with children his own age. The greatest tragedy of all
was his father's untimely death: Farouk had adored his father
and admired him increasingly throughout his reign in Egypt
as he realized how strong his father must have been. He put on
even more weight, his kidneys were weak and his blood pressure
high. He retired more and more frequently to Switzerland for
heart treatment: from 1963 onwards he realized he might die at
any moment. He became more generous, and more religious,
and met a new girl friend, Sonia Romanoff.

On 16th March 1965 Sonia Romanoff visited Farouk's flat and
listened while he "reminisced about the old days—something
very rare for him. 'When I left Egypt there wasn't a friend who
defended me. Those to whom I was kindest spoke the worst
evil, and it will be no different when I leave here, . . . we have
an old peasant proverb in Egypt: "When the bull falls a
thousand knives appear" '." Only two weeks before this he had
left a heart clinic in Switzerland.

Twenty-four hours later at 10 p.m. on 17th March Farouk drove from his home to nearby Via Chelini 9, and stopped in to see Irma at her apartment (from the account by M. Stern, a reporter in Rome). He switched on the television set, sat back in the chair, watched, and listened to Irma at the same time. In the place of honour near the television set was a photograph of the two of them taken in Switzerland a few years before. The frame was in the form of a cheque drawn on the Bank of Happiness and its amount, written in by the ex-King, was for 365 days. It was signed Farouk.

"An hour later Farouk rose heavily from his seat, said good-bye, and left. He drove to the house of Annamaria Gatti, his date for the evening."

He drove his white Fiat 2300 to 8 la Viale Ostiense, collected Annamaria and drove out to a roadside inn called 'Île de France'. At midnight they began dinner; a dozen oysters, washed down with Evian mineral water, leg of lamb, fried potatoes, beans, a bottle of ginger soda. Desert was Monte Bianco followed by two small bottles of Coca-Cola and two oranges.

He lit a Havana cigar and began to pull contentedly when suddenly the cigar dropped from his mouth, his eyes stared and his head fell back. Known for his jokes, this behaviour did not at first convince Annamaria Gatti that anything was wrong, but within seconds she realized and her scream brought the waiter and manager.

"Farouk was unconscious and breathing with difficulty. With considerable effort they stretched him across two tables. When this was done, the waiter opened his jacket and massaged his chest. The director was already on the telephone calling for help.

"A Red Cross ambulance arrived a few minutes later and Dr. Nicola Massa hurried to the unconscious ex-King. . . . Farouk's pulse was weak and his breathing laboured. The doctor filled a syringe with camphor solution and injected it, then called the stretcher bearers.

"Farouk was driven swiftly to the hospital of San Camillo where he was immediately placed in an oxygen tent. While several doctors hovered about, he grew rapidly weaker. Ten minutes later, at 2.08 a.m. on 18th March 1965, exactly thirty-five days past his forty-fifth birthday, Farouk was dead."

"All pure things become corrupt;
  All things go to decay,
  The wayfaring of youth toward death
  Is death: Pain is the way.
  On every head only grey hairs should grow
  To warn us whither we must go.
  And thou who hopest still some good conclusion,
  Thou drowned man tossed in oceans of illusion,
  Tell me this: Where are they who hurried on
  Before us? Foot and footprint lost and gone!
  Mercy for all my many trespasses!
  Thou Best of all who know what Mercy is!"

                                    By Radi, the last real Caliph
                    (quoted in *Muhammad's People* by E. Schroeder)

Narriman and her mother came from Egypt to pay their
respects. Ferial, Fawzia and Fuad came from Lausanne for the
funeral. Farida came from Beirut. Other friends included the
Prince and Princess of Hesse. The doors to the morgue were
flanked by palm fronds while around the entrance stood a bank
of wreaths too large to take inside. Large banner ribbons
named the donors: "SAR la Princesse Fevkie Fouad", "M.
Taher Pacha", "Umberto" and "Khany Hussein Pacha".

The walnut coffin, draped with the stars, crown and crescent
of Royal Egypt, was carried out of the morgue by more than
six coffin bearers. The leading pall bearer wore white gloves,
and steadied a corner of the coffin. The crowd of mourners fell
in behind. His son, thirteen-year-old Ahmed Fuad, followed close
behind, dark, downcast, with tousled hair. The women followed, his daughters, wife, and a mistress, heavily veiled and
dressed in black. The men were in lounge suits; some wore dark
glasses. The faithful Albanian bodyguards still searched the
crowd for possible disturbances, as they had done habitually for
years. The coffin was pushed into the back of a glass-sided
motor hearse and the three or four hundred friends and those
drawn from curiosity followed off after the hearse as it made
its way slowly down the road, flanked by a couple of carabinieri,
their white gloves and bandoliers showing against the dark
crowd. This, Farouk's last procession, a wandering group behind the single vehicle, was a far cry from the pomp and

applause of those processions he had seen as young King of Egypt.

Farouk's will requested burial in Egypt, a country he had never ceased to love, or, if this proved impossible, in any Moslem country. Permission to bury him in. the United Arab Republic. was sought by Ismail Sherin, Farouk's brother-in-law, from President Nasser and accordingly two days later a Comet of United Arab Airlines took off from Fumicino Airport with the body, escorted by his sister Faika. The plane was delayed in Athens and arrived at Cairo at 11 p.m. Sherin and his wife met the plane and drove the body to the King's ancestor Ibrahim Pasha's tomb. With few of his family present, some Egyptian officials standing by as readings were made from the Koran, the body wrapped in a single sheet, turned towards Mecca and placed in the prepared tomb, in simple Moslem fashion Farouk was laid to rest in the dead of night at about 2 a.m., almost at the exact time that he had died.

Epilogue

"When the inevitable day of judgement shall suddenly come
. . . it will abase some, and exalt others. When the earth shall
be shaken with a violent shock; and the mountains shall be
dashed in pieces, and shall become as dust scattered abroad;
and ye shall be separated into three distinct classes; the companions of the right hand (how happy shall the companions of
the right hand be!), and the companions of the left hand (how
miserable shall the companions of the left hand be!) and those
who have preceded others in the faith, shall precede them to
paradise. These are they who shall approach near unto God:
they shall dwell in gardens of delight. . . . Reposing on couches
adorned with gold and precious stones; sitting opposite to one
another thereon. Youths which shall continue in their bloom
for ever, shall go round about to attend them, with goblets, and
beakers, and a cup of flowing wine; their heads shall not ache by
drinking the same, neither shall their reason be disturbed: and
with fruits of the sorts which they shall choose, and the flesh of
birds of the kind which they shall desire. And there shall accompany them fair damsels having large black eyes, resembling
pearls hidden in their shells; as a reward for that which they
shall have wrought. They shall not hear therein any vain dis-
course, or any charge of sin; but only the salutation, Peace!
Peace! And the companions of the right hand . . . shall have
their abode among lote-trees free from thorns, and trees of
mauz loaded regularly with their produce from top to bottom;
under an extended shade, near a flowing water, and amidst
fruits in abundance, which shall not fail, nor shall be forbidden

to be gathered: and they shall repose themselves on lofty beds. Verily we have created the damsels of paradise by a peculiar creation: and we have made them virgins, beloved by their husbands, of equal age with them; for the delight of the companions of the right hand. . . . And the companions of the left hand . . . shall dwell amidst burning winds, and scalding water, under the shade of a black smoke, neither cool nor agreeable. For they enjoyed the pleasures of life before this, while on earth; and have obstinately persisted in a heinous wickedness: and they said, after we shall have died, and become dust and bones, shall we surely be raised to life? Shall our forefathers be raised with us? Say, verily both the first and the last shall surely be gathered together to judgement, at the prefixed time of a known day. Then ye, O men, who have erred, and denied the resurrection as a falsehood, shall surely eat of the fruit of the tree of al Zakkum, and shall fill your bellies therewith: and ye shall drink thereon boiling water; and ye shall drink as a thirsty camel drinketh. This shall be their entertainment on the day of judgement."—*The Koran*.

The Mohamed Ali Dynasty
Rulers of Egypt

Mohamed Ali	1805–
Ibrahim	1848–
Abbas I	1849–
Said	1854–
Ismail	1863–
Tewfik	1879–
Abbas II	1892–
Hussein	1914–
Fuad I	1917–
Farouk	1936–
Fuad II	1952–3

Bibliography

Aga Khan, *Memoirs*. Cassell, London, 1954.

Ahmed, Jamal Mohammed, *The Intellectual Origin s of Egyptian Nationalism*. Oxford University Press, London 1960.

Alexander of Tunis, Field Marshal Earl, *Memoirs*. Edited J. North. Cassell, London, 1962.

Avon, Lord (Eden, Anthony), *Full Circle* 1960 and *Facing the Dictators* 1962. Cassell, London.

Ayrout, Henry, *The Fellaheen*. Schindler, Cairo, 1945.

El-Barawy, *Military Coup in Egypt*. The Renaissance Bookshop, Cairo, 1952.

Bernard-Derosne, J., *Farouk—La Déchéance d'un roi*. Editions Françaises d'Amsterdam, 1953.

Blaxland, Gregory, *Objective Egypt*. Muller, London, 1966.

Blunt, W. S., *Secret History of the English Occupation of Egypt*. Fisher Unwin, 1907.

Bryant, Sir Arthur, *The Turn of the Tide*. Collins, London, 1957.

Cecil, Lord Edward, *The Leisure of an Egyptian Official*. Hodder and Stoughton, London, 1921.

Chandos, Lord, *Memoirs*. The Bodley Head, London, 1962.

Churchill, Sir Winston S., *The Second World War, Vols. III, IV and VI*. Cassell, London.

Ciano, Count, *Diary 1939–43*. Heinemann, 1947.

Cooper, Diana, *Trumpets from the Steep*. Rupert Hart-Davis, London, 1960.

230   *Bibliography*

Coward, Noël, *Middle East Diary*. Heinemann, London, 1944.

Crabités, Pierre, *Ismail: The Maligned Khedive*. Routledge, London, 1933.

Crabités, Pierre, *Ibrahim of Egypt*. Routledge, London, 1935.

Cromer, Lord, *Modern Egypt*. Macmillan, London, 1908.

Douglas, Sholto, *The Years of Command*. Collins, London, 1966.

Galatoli, A. M., *Egypt in Mid Passage*. Urwand and Sons Press, Cairo, 1950.

Glubb, J. B., *A Soldier With the Arabs*. Hodder and Stoughton, London, 1957.

Harris, M., *Egypt Under the Egyptians*. Chapman and Hall, London, 1925.

Heyworth-Dunn, J., *Religious and Political Trends in Modern Egypt*. Washington, 1948.

Hughes, P., *While Shepheard's Watched*. Chatto and Windus, London, 1949.

Husaini, Ishak M., *The Moslem Brethren*. Khayat, Beirut, 1956.

Issawi, C., *Egypt at Mid-Century*. Oxford University Press, London, 1954.

Issawi, C., *Egypt in Revolution*. Royal Institute of International Affairs, Oxford University Press, 1963.

Jarvis, H. W., *Pharaoh to Farouk*. John Murray, London, 1955.

Joesten, J., *Nasser: The Rise to Power*. Odhams, London, 1960.

Kirk, George E., *A Short History of the Middle East*. Methuen, London, 1948.

Kirk, George E., *The Middle East in the War*. Oxford University Press, London, 1952.

Lacouture, J. and S., *Egypt in Transition*. Methuen, London, 1958.

Lane, E. W., *Manners and Customs of the Modern Egyptians*. Everyman.

Leprette, Fernand, *Egypt Land of the Nile*. R. Schindler, Cairo, 1939.

Little, Tom, *Egypt*. Benn, London, 1958.

Lloyd, Lord, *Egypt Since Cromer*. Macmillan, London, 1933.

Lugol, J., *Egypt And World War II*. Societé Orientale de Publicité, Cairo, 1945.

Majdalany, F., *The Battle of el Alamein*. Weidenfeld and Nicolson, London, 1965.

Mansfield, P., *Nasser's Egypt*. Penguin Books, London, 1965.

Marlowe, John, *Anglo Egyptian Relation 1800–1953*. Cresset, London, 1954.

Milner, Lord, *England in Egypt*. Arnold, London, 1899.

Montgomery of Alamein, Field Marshal Viscount, *Memoirs*. Collins, London, 1958.

Moorehead, A., *African Trilogy*. Hamish Hamilton, London, 1944.

Nasser, G. A., *Philosophy of the Revolution*. The National Publication House, London, 1954.

Neguib, M., *Egypt's Destiny*. Gollancz, London, 1955.

Rowlatt, M., *Founders of Modern Egypt*. Asia Publishing House, Bombay, 1962.

Russell, Pásha, *Egyptian Service 1902–1946*. John Murray, London, 1949.

El Sadat, Anwar, *Revolt on the Nile*. Wingate, London, 1957.

Sansom, A. N., *I Spied Spies*. G. Harrap, London.

Schroeder, E., *Muhammad's People*. Wheelwright, Portland Maine, 1955.

Seton-Williams, V., *Britain and the Arab States*. Luzac, London, 1948.

Shah, Ikbal Ali, *Fuad King of Egypt*. Herbert Jenkins, London, 1936.

Shaw, George Bernard, Preface to *John Bull's Other Island*. Constable & Co. Ltd., London, 1927.

Smith, W. Cantwell, *Islam in Modern History*. Princeton, New York, 1957.

Stern, M., *Farouk*. Bantam Books, 1965.

Stevens, G. G., *Egypt Yesterday and Today*. Holt, Rinehart and Winston, New York, 1963.

Stewart, Desmond, *Young Egypt*. Wingate, London, 1958.

Sykes, C., *Cross Roads to Israel*. Collins, London, 1965.

Tugay, Emine Foat, *Three Centuries, Family Chronicles of Turkey and Egypt*. Oxford University Press, London, 1963.

Tully, A., *Central Intelligence Agency The Inside Story*. Arthur Barker, London, 1962.

Vatikiotis, P. J., *The Egyptian Army in Politics*. Indiana University Press, Bloomington, 1961.

Wavell, Field Marshal Viscount, *Allenby Soldier and Statesman.* Harrap, London, 1943.

Wheelock, K., *Nasser's New Egypt.* Atlantic Books, Stevens, London, 1960.

White, A. Silva, *The Expansion of Egypt.* Methuen, London, 1899.

Yusef, Amin, *Independent Egypt.* John Murray, London, 1940.

The Arab World. Life World Library, New York, 1962.

Great Britain in Egypt. Information Paper No. 19, Royal Institute of International Affairs, London, 1952.

The Koran.

The Middle East, A Political & Economic Survey. Royal Institute of International Affairs, Oxford University Press, 1958.

The Palace Collections of Egypt. Sotheby and Company, 1953.

Who's Who in Egypt and the Middle East (Annual). Cairo, 1948.

Other Publications Consulted

Al-Jumhuriyyah, Christian Science Monitor, Current History and Forum, Daily Mail, Daily Mirror, Daily Telegraph, Egyptian Daily Post, Egyptian Gazette, Foreign Affairs, Fortnightly Review, Geographical Magazine, Great Britain and the East, History Today, Illustrated London News, Islamic Review, Life, Literary Digest, Maidenhead Advertiser, Le Monde, Moslem World, National Geographical Magazine, New Liberty, New York Times, News of the World, Newsweek, Observer, Punch, Soldier, Sunday Citizen, Sunday Express, Sunday Pictorial, Sunday Telegraph, Sunday Times, Time, The Times, U.N. World and *'Utarid.*

Index